COVENANT OF THE HEART

COVENANT OF THE HEART

MEDITATIONS OF A CHRISTIAN
HERMETICIST ON THE
MYSTERIES OF TRADITION

Valentin Tomberg

ELEMENT
Rockport, Massachusetts ● Shaftesbury, Dorset
Brisbane, Queensland

Original edition: Tomberg, Valentin: Lazarus, komm heraus.
Hrsg. v. Kriele, Martin
© Verlag Herder Basel, Freiburg 1985

© 1992 English translation Robert Powell and James Morgante

Published in the U.S.A. in 1992 by
Element, Inc.
42 Broadway, Rockport, MA 01966

Published in Great Britain in 1992 by
Element Books Limited
Longmead, Shaftesbury, Dorset

Published in Australia by
Element Books Ltd for
Jacaranda Wiley Ltd
33 Park Road, Milton, Brisbane, 4064

Cover illustration The Old Testament Trinity,
Russian Icon, 16th Century
Photo courtesy The Temple Gallery
Cover design by Max Fairbrother
Text design by Roger Lightfoot
Typeset by Colset, London
Printed in the United States of America by
Edwards Brothers, Inc.

Library of Congress Cataloging-in-Publication Data
Tomberg, Valentin.
[Lazarus, komm heraus.   English]
Covenant of the heart : meditations of a Christian hermeticist on the
mysteries of tradition / Valentin Tomberg.
Translation of: Lazarus, komm heraus.
1. Anthroposophy.   2. Christianity — Miscellanea.   3. Raising of
Lazarus (Miracle)   4. Ten commandments.   5. Spiritual life —
Anthroposophical authors.   I. Title.
BP595.T66   1991   230 — dc20   91-34818

British Library Cataloguing in Publication Data available

ISBN 1-85230-277-1

CONTENTS

PART ONE

THE MIRACLE OF THE RAISING OF LAZARUS IN THE HISTORY OF THE WORLD

INTRODUCTION

This work is neither a theological treatise nor a contribution to the
science of history. For both theology and the science of history —
somewhat in the manner of the games chess and draughts — have their
fixed "rules of the game", which are strictly adhered to in order to
arrive at theologically or historically valid results. Thus, in order to
be considered historically true, an event must not only be attested
to by genuine contemporaneous documentary evidence, but also must
neither contradict the testimony of other documentary sources nor
stand in contradiction to contemporary general life experience. For
this reason, the account of the life of Apollonius of Tyana given
by Philostratus is not considered to be historically true, because at
the judicial proceedings in Rome (under the chairmanship of the
emperor) at which Apollonius was present as a defendant, Apollonius brought the trial to an end by leaving unseen, i.e. by simply disappearing from the court. For although Philostratus' book is certainly
a genuine document from antiquity, it is not contemporaneous (it
was written over two centuries after the death of Apollonius of
Tyana) and, moreover, the report contradicts contemporary general life experience since the disappearance of a defendant during the
course of a trial does not happen nowadays. Consequently Philostratus' account does not belong to historical truth but to the realm
of myth-making, fantasy, error, etc. To put it simply, it belongs to
the sphere of untruth.

It could happen that someone today might hesitatingly venture to
raise the objection that Philostratus' book is avowedly only a literary recasting of the notes of an eyewitness, those of Apollonius'
Assyrian pupil, who accompanied him on his travels — and was
his life-companion for several decades — who was, so to say, his
"Eckermann" (the biographer of Goethe). In this case it might be said
the possibility is not excluded that Apollonius could actually have
made use of suggestion along the lines of that of the Indian fakir, as
experience with hypnosis and suggestion shows. Thus, the Indian
fakir shoots a rope high into the air, making it stand stiff as a pillar,
and then lets the onlooker see how a boy nimbly clambers up it,
whilst a photograph shows only a picture of the peacefully seated
fakir and the just-as-peacefully seated boy. Apollonius was certainly

a pupil in India for a lengthy period of time, so this possibility does exist — and, consequently, Philostratus' account could still be true. I do not know if someone has actually raised this simple objection, but if someone were to do so, the probable reply would be that historical research is in no way parapsychology or psychic research. It would be said that one could certainly leave "the case of the disappearance of Apollonius of Tyana from the emperor's judicial court in Rome" to the Society for Psychical Research, but it lies beyond the scope of historical research. Thus it would be appraised as a matter for parapsychologists, depth-psychologists along the lines of the Jungian school, occultists, etc., but not as something for the research-historian. So, we may conclude that to the best of our knowledge and in good conscience, Philostratus' account could be true in itself, but that it does not count as true from a historical standpoint.

Thus, the science of history acknowledges as true only a segment of past events, in accordance with the application of its "rules of the game". It goes without saying that all the events and occurrences falling in the category of "signs and miracles", which are reported in the Old and New Testaments of the Bible, lie beyond these historically acknowledged segments. This also applies for Christ's resurrection, described by Paul in his *Letter to the Corinthians*:

> . . . that he (Christ) was raised on the third day in accordance with the scriptures, and that he appeared to Cephas, then to the twelve. Then he appeared to more than five hundred brethren at one time, most of whom are still alive, though some have fallen asleep. Then he appeared to James, then to all the apostles. Last of all, as to one untimely born, he appeared also to me. (I *Corinthians* xv, 4–8.)

The resurrection of Christ, despite this careful listing of eye-witnesses, does not belong to the facts of history, because it contradicts general life experience and the knowledge of biological science that is based thereon. The same holds also for the seventh "sign" of the *Gospel of St. John* — the raising of Lazarus. It does not belong to the sphere of history. It is a matter of belief. Thoughts about it have no point of application historically.

However, thoughts about the miracle of the raising of Lazarus do have a point of application for theology. This miracle is a fact in theology, i.e. it is a theological article of faith (*theologice de fide*). Thus it belongs to the truths of faith, since it is reported in a concrete and unequivocal way in the Holy Scripture, i.e. in the *Gospel of St. John*. Since the Holy Scripture is a document of faith and the *Gospel of St. John* belongs to it, and since the account of the Lazarus

belongs to the *Gospel of St. John*, the Lazarus miracle counts as a fact
in theology.

As a fact of belief, a miracle means a revelation of the omnipotence
of God and of the Son of Man working in unity with him. By way
of the miracle, this omnipotence can be wondered at, revered, and
worshipped, and free use can be made of it *in foro interno* (in the
internal forum of consciousness) for other purposes towards the end
of spiritual deepening and edification. But *in foro externo* (in the
external forum, i.e. in the general consensus of opinion) it is not permitted to add anything to it or to take anything away from it. The
miracle of the raising of Lazarus, as it stands in the *Gospel of St. John*,
should remain like a constellation of fixed stars, so to say. That is, it
should not be expanded upon or brought into any other context than
that given in the Gospels; it should remain standing in the heaven of
supra-rational facts of belief. Thus a writing which has as its subject the working effect of the Lazarus miracle in world history does
not signify a contribution to theology, since it considers the raising
of Lazarus not simply as a once-and-for-all event as portrayed in
the *Gospel of St. John*, but beyond this it considers it also in the context of mankind's spiritual history, thus transposing it into another
context than that of the Gospels. Although its subject matter is not
without interest for theology, such a writing is unimportant. For
everything concerning the Lazarus miracle that is of importance for
theology has been said already in the writings of the Church fathers
and teachers and authorized theologians. A deepening of understanding of this miracle, or an expansion thereupon, which considers it
as taking effect in mankind's history, does not belong to theology;
it either belongs to the science of history or to the fringe literature
of depth psychology, journalism, occultism, and similar directions of
untrammelled laymanship.

For the above reasons, this book has no claim either to historical
or to theological validity. Yet there are still further reasons, which
are no less cogent than the above. These arise because this book is
based on a different conception of truth than the conception of truth
upon which theology and the science of history are based. The truth-
postulate underlying this book is that of *material insight* in contrast
to *formal perspective*. Two sayings — one German and the other
Russian — can serve well to explain this truth-postulate: "clothes make
the man" (the German saying) and, "in order to get to know someone,
one must eat a pound of salt with him" (the Russian saying). The
thesis of the first saying is that the outer appearance ("the clothes") are
the key to the being. The thesis of the second saying is the reverse:
one apprehends the being through direct communication, and then

one also grasps the real utterances — or those to be expected — of this being.

However, communication means the way upon which the totality of experience leads to and culminates in direct insight. In other words, the totality of experience does not play the role of a building-stone for a conclusion but rather that of a springboard to spring into the element of Beingness lying beyond experience, i.e. a plunge from the realm of *formal knowledge* into that of *material knowledge*.

Henri Bergson designated such a faculty of knowledge as *intuition*. Thereby he means the kind of material knowledge which is yielded when intelligence, which is capable only of formal knowledge, unites itself with instinct, which is gifted with material certainty of knowledge — in that the former, with its illuminating light, allows the latter to take the reins. Thus, in Bergson's sense of the word, intuition is the faculty of knowledge which results from instinct that is illumined by reason. It is that which brings two opposite poles in man to a unity, i.e. it unites that which is most deeply implanted in him, which works hidden in darkness in the depths of his being, with the reflecting faculty of intelligence, which is most bright in the human being, lying uppermost within him.

Intuition, the highest-ranking and surest kind of knowledge of the nature of being — i.e. material knowledge, or knowledge of the "what" (in contrast to knowledge of the "how" and of the mere interrelationships of things) — is spoken of also by Rudolf Steiner, the founder of the Anthroposophical Movement. For Rudolf Steiner intuition is the aim and the result of the process of a stepwise convergence between the subject and the object of knowledge — it is their blending into a unity. Intuition is the knowledge which results from the unifying of subject and object after having passed through the stages of *objective consciousness, imaginative consciousness*, and *inspired consciousness*. In the first place subject and object stand at a distance from one another; this is the stage of objective consciousness. In imaginative consciousness the object of knowledge approaches nearer to the subject in so far as it makes itself known to the subject in its "speech", i.e. it reaches out into the subject in the form of non-arbitrarily-arising symbolic pictures. In inspired consciousness the object draws still nearer to the subject in that it "speaks itself out", as it were, in the subject, i.e. it no longer makes itself known to him as a symbolic picture, but as a "word" (or "words") full of content and meaning. Intuition then follows the stage of inspired consciousness. Here object and subject become one, i.e. the most direct knowledge of the being of the object takes place through the being of the subject.

Also the aim of Indian yoga — namely *samadhi* (as the third higher stage of consciousness in Indian yoga is designated) — corresponds to intuition, as the condition in which knowledge of subject and object become one. The preceding two stages of higher knowledge — *dharana* and *dhyana* — are stages of the drawing closer of the subject to the object which, *mutatis mutandis* (i.e. with necessary modifications), if not identical with the stages designated by Rudolf Steiner as imaginative and inspired consciousness, at least are analogous to them.

The way to intuition according to the various spiritual streams and authors may well be different, but all are in agreement that intuition is not attained through practical knowledge or intellectual consideration (reflection), but through direct experience of reality. This highest form of knowledge is "an evolving revelation from the inner being of man", as Goethe designated it, and "a direct grasping of the being of things", according to Spinoza.

For those who experience it, this form of knowledge counts as the highest because it is experienced by them as the result of the most profound contemplation and the greatest concentration, in comparison with which that of intellectual consideration and the practical knowledge gained by way of observation appears superficial. However, it does not count in the slightest way as knowledge (let alone as the highest form of knowledge) for the scientific disciplines — which, as such, lay claim to being of general validity. For the scientific approach is not to strive simply for the truth, but rather to strive for that brand of truth which is of general validity, i.e. that which can be comprehended fundamentally by everyone bestowed with healthy understanding and faculties of perception, and which should thus be concurred with. A scientific discipline — whether a spiritual-scientific or a natural-scientific discipline — does not want to, and is not able to, address itself only to those people who are capable of the concentration and inner deepening necessary for intuition. Were it to do so, it would then not be scientific, i.e. generally comprehendible and provable. Rather, it would be "esoteric", i.e. a matter for an elite group of special people. In this sense theology is also "science" since, assuming the authority of Scripture and the Church are acknowledged, it can be comprehended and tested by all believers.

On this account, when confronted with truth which appeals to intuition, the scientific disciplines cannot do anything else other than to echo the words of Pontius Pilate who, after hearing the words addressed to him by Jesus Christ: "Every one who is of the truth hears my voice", could only say: "What is truth?" (*John* xviii, 37–38). For "to be of the truth" means direct knowledge of being. It is intuition of the truth, which is not of general validity, because it is not founded upon the experience and reasoning that is general and accessible to all — namely that of generally valid intelligence — but rather it demands and assumes a basis of "being of the truth and coming from the truth".

This is the deeper reason why this book does not pretend to advance any claim to being of scientific validity; nor has it the right to advance any such claim. It does not pretend to do so because it cannot be recognized by science as belonging to it. It is not allowed to do so because it would be hypocritical if it were to claim general validity, while in reality it is written — and could only be written — for those who have the capacity and disposition to make use of the faculty of intuition as the direct *sense for truth*. Thus, it is addressed to those "who have ears to hear and eyes to see".

I

THE SEVEN MIRACLES OF THE GOSPEL OF ST. JOHN

For human consciousness there are three criteria for assessing whether a being is subhuman, human, superhuman, or divine. These are ability (what is the being able to do?), knowledge (what does it know?), and the faculty of love or moral freedom (to what extent is it able to act charitably or out of moral freedom?). An animal will be assessed as subhuman, since there is much that it is not able to do which the human being is able to, much that it does not know which the human being does know, and it is not so free as the human being is to act of its own accord creatively and morally. For the human being, in contrast, there is the sheer, unbounded capacity for learning, accompanied by ever increasing capability; there is a steadily growing knowledge and capacity for insight; and, similarly, there is a steadily growing moral freedom, which manifests itself as the capacity for self-sacrifice and giving.

A being whose ability, knowledge, and goodness surpass the human level cannot be assessed otherwise than as superhuman — be it in the mildest form of a "genius" or in the more radical form of a "daemon" (to use the ancient designation), or a "god".

Frequent use is made of the above three criteria in the Bible — that is to say both in the Old Testament as well as in the New Testament. Also, Paul speaks of them expressly, in that he writes in the *First Letter to the Corinthians*: "Jews demand signs and Greeks seek wisdom, but we preach Christ crucified, a stumbling block to Jews and folly to the Greeks" (I *Corinthians* i, 22). However, in mentioning the three criteria — "signs", "wisdom", and love — he gives precedence to his apostolic criterion: that of the miracle and the wisdom of love, which embraces the other two and which for him, as an apostle, is actually the absolute criterion. The other two — taken by themselves alone — do not suffice in order to do justice to the mystery of love, the mystery of the Cross. On this account the latter is "a stumbling block to Jews", who "demand signs", and "folly to the Greeks" who "seek wisdom". Thus, the criterion of superhuman love is the decisive one for Paul, since in the case of miracles (the criterion of super-human ability) it is a matter of the power of love, and in the case of superhuman wisdom (the criterion of superhuman know-ledge) it is a matter of the wisdom of love. In other words, miracles are signs of divine love and wisdom is the light of divine love, whilst the Cross on Golgotha is, so to say, "naked" divine love itself. In the last analysis, therefore, it is a matter solely of the Cross, of "Christ crucified, whom we preach", as Paul stresses most strongly.

But the Gospels as a whole are not simply Paulinistic. They grant an allotted significance to all three criteria. Thus we read in the *Gospel of St. Luke* concerning the two disciples of John the Baptist, whom John sent to Jesus with the question: "Are you he who is to come, or shall we look for another?" Jesus answered: "Go and tell John what you have seen and heard: the blind receive their sight, the lame walk, lepers are cleansed, and the deaf hear, the dead are raised up, the poor have the good news (gospel) preached to them; and blessed is he who takes no offence at me" (*Luke vii*, 20–23).

Thus the "Jews" who "demand signs" — and John and his pupils were the best representatives of the Jews, being preparers of the way for Christ in Judaism — were not simply dismissed by Jesus. On the con-trary, they were given an answer which meant that their demands were fully satisfied.

And the demands of the "Greeks"? What answer do the Gospels give to those who refer to the criterion of knowledge, i.e. those who "seek wisdom"?

We read in the *Gospel of St. John*:

Now among those who went up to worship at the feast were some Greeks. So these came to Philip, who was from Bethsaida in Galilee, and said to him, "Sir, we wish to see Jesus." Philip went and told Andrew; Andrew went with Philip and they told Jesus. And Jesus answered them, "The hour has come for the Son of man to be glorified. Truly truly, I say to you, unless a grain of wheat falls into the earth and dies, it remains alone; but if it dies, it bears much fruit. He who loves his life loses it, and he who hates his life in this world will keep it for eternal life. If any one serves me, he must follow me; and where I am there shall my servant be also; if any one serves me, the Father will honour him. Now my soul is troubled. And what shall I say? Father, save me from this hour? No, for this purpose I have come to this hour. Father, glorify thy name." Then a voice came from heaven: "I have glorified it, and I will glorify it again." The crowd standing by heard it and said that it had thundered. Others said, "an angel has spoken to him." Jesus answered: "This voice has come for your sake, not for mine." (*John xii*, 20–30).

The voice from heaven — heaven speaking — was the answer that the Greeks who wanted to see Jesus were given. Heaven was to speak after the Golgotha sacrifice became fulfilled, that is, after the "grain of wheat" of the Son of man had died and began to bring forth "much fruit". And just as the grain of wheat buried in the earth dies and its fruit ripens above the earth, so will the fruit of the earthly death of the Son of man be the speaking of heaven.

Now, however, the "speaking of heaven" is nothing other than the perfect satisfaction of the striving after wisdom, i.e. the striving after sureness and certainty as yielded by the inwardly experienced voice of truth. For wisdom is certainty. It is a knowing which is founded neither upon the grace (and lack of grace) of empirical experience nor upon the probabilities attached to the forming of hypotheses, nor upon the completing of logical inferences. Rather, it is based on the imprinted working of the intrinsic truth of the voice of truth, which through its truthfulness alone is absolutely convincing — in the sense of the parable of the good shepherd and his sheep. The good shepherd "goes before them and the sheep follow him, for they know his voice. A stranger they will not follow, but they will flee from him, for they do not know the voice of strangers" (*John* x, 4–5). Or again, in the spirit of the following from the *Gospel of St. John*: "It is written in the prophets, 'And they shall be taught by God'. Everyone who has heard and learned from the Father comes to me" (*John* vi, 45).

St. Augustine was a "Greek" who became a Christian. (He was in fact a Roman, but he was a Greek, a Hellene, in the sense in which the Gospel understands it: a non-Jew — and later also a non-Christian — counted as a "Hellene".) If one reads his *Confessions* attentively, one will understand how the "voice from heaven" (spoken of in the *Gospel of St. John*) spoke to him. St. Augustine's inwardly experienced certainty went so far that he could say, "God is more myself than I am myself". Yet the experience of the self is the most direct and, consequently, the most certain of experiences which the human being has. Here St. Augustine was able to advance the hypothesis that "the human soul is Christian by nature" (*anima naturaliter christiana*). It is thus that the "voice from heaven" speaks with certainty, impressing its truth upon the human soul.

Is it knowledge (*gnosis*) or faith (*pistis*) which is the source of this certainty?

It is the certainty of inwardly revealed truth, which makes itself known as such, in relation to which all soul forces of the human being — thinking, feeling, and willing — together say "yes". Where does knowledge as experience of the truth finish and where does the act of consent of faith begin?

As is well known, the early Greek church fathers of the Alexandrian school were unable to draw a sharp boundary here. Clement of Alexandria and also Origen and his successors spoke of a "true Christian gnosis" which stood in contrast to the "heretical false gnosis", which latter was a poor alloy of Christianity and the heathen mythologizing of the decadent mysteries. Thus Clement writes, for example:

> As, then, philosophy has been brought into evil repute by pride and self-conceit, so also gnosis by false gnosis called by the same name; of which the apostle writing says: "O Timothy, keep that which is committed to thy trust, avoiding the profane and vain babblings and oppositions of science (gnosis) falsely so called; which some professing, have erred concerning the faith" (I *Tim.* vi, 20–21). Convicted by this utterance, the heretics reject the *Epistles to Timothy*. Well, then, if the Lord is the truth, and wisdom, and power of God, as in truth He is, it is shown that the real Gnostic is he that knows Him and His Father by Him. For his sentiments are the same with him who said: "The lips of the righteous know high things." (Clement of Alexandria, *Miscellanies. Stromata* II, 11; trsl. W. Wilson, Edinburgh, 1869, vol. 2, p. 33)

For Origen faith is the starting point for Christian life. The human being believes before he knows, corresponding to the words of Isaiah, "If you do not believe, you will not understand" (*Isaiah*, vi, 9) — (cf. Origen, *Commentary upon the Gospel of St. Matthew*, xvi, 9). Similarly, the disciples of Jesus went through the initial stage of faith; indeed, Jesus said to them, "You will know the truth" when they already "believed in him" (*John* viii, 31–32).

Does the act of faith precede the act of knowledge or is it that a lightning flash of insight precedes the condition of being convinced (i.e. faith) — as in the following case of Peter's response to Jesus' question: "Jesus said to them: But who do you say that I am? Simon Peter replied: You are the Christ, the Son of the Living God" (*Matthew* xvi, 15–16).

What is an act of faith? Is it that of agreement on the part of the human soul in relation to an insight preceding it, is it this insight itself, or is it both simultaneously, i.e. insight as well as agreement? Which occurs first: the insight (i.e. knowledge) or faith (i.e. the condition of being convinced)?

Origen maintains that faith is primary, that is, faith as the act of readiness of the will (a pragmatic act, as it were) to decide for the good, the better and the best, whilst knowledge, insight and beholding (contemplation) is the subsequent ripe fruit of the preceding act of faith. Also, Clement of Alexandria has the following view:

For the knowledge of insight is, so to speak, a kind of perfection of man as man, harmonious and consistent with itself and with the divine word, being completed, both as to the disposition and the manner of life and of speech, by the science of divine things. For it is by insight that *faith is made perfect*, seeing that the man of faith only becomes perfect in this way. Now faith is a certain inward good: without making search for God, it both confesses His existence and glorifies Him as existent. Hence a man must start with this faith, and having waxed strong in it by the grace of God, must thus attain to insight concerning Him, so far as is possible. We must distinguish, however, between insight and the wisdom which is implanted by teaching. For in so far as anything deserves to be called insight, so far it is certainly wisdom also; but in so far as a thing is wisdom, it is not certainly insight. (Clement of Alexandria, *Miscellanies. Stromata* VII, 10; trsl. F.J.A. Hort and J.B. Mayor, London, 1902, p. 97)

In so far as modern Catholic theology is concerned, we read in the comprehensive classical work by A. Tanquerey, S.S.:

These are three subjective or effective grounds for faith: reason (*intellectus*), which actually calls forth the act of faith; the will (*voluntas*), which effects the consent of reason; active grace (*gratia actualis*), which illumines reason and motivates the will so that the act of faith is supernatural (*supernaturalis*). (A. Tanquerey, *Synopsis Theologiae Dogmaticae specialis ad mentem St. Thomae Aquinatis hodiernis moribus accommodata*, vol. i., p. 113)

In other words, illumination (*illuminatio*) of the intellect through the working of grace is primary, upon which the free consent of the will follows. Thereby the insight and inner revelation of the truth precede the act of consent of the will.

However, is this always so? Can it not happen, does it not sometimes happen, that it is the will which is directly moved by the working of grace — without the mediation of reason. And that it is then the grace illumined will which moves reason to consent? Can it not occur, does it not occur, that the will is so obedient that it directly and immediately reacts consentingly at the slightest sign from above? And do we not find an archetype of this kind of act of faith prefigured in the event that is known as the Annunciation to Mary, where the "unbelievable" was proclaimed to the Blessed Virgin, and where the obedient will of the Blessed Virgin responded to the "unbelievable" with the consent of faith: *Ecce ancilla Domini, mihi fiat secundum verbum tuum* ("Behold, I am the handmaid of the Lord; let it be to me according to your word" — *Luke* i, 38)? And do not the Blessed Virgin's words of consent comprise the formula which brings to expression the trusting and obedient act of faith of the will, which occurs not through insight but through loving trust? Is it not so that obedience, chastity, and poverty can become constitutional in the will, and that thereby the will as such becomes not only an organ for action but also for direct revelation from above?

If, however, the act of faith is called forth as the result of the direct action of revelatory grace upon the will, the objection can then be raised that the will is not free, that then the holiest and highest good of existence — freedom, without which there can be no morality — is done away with. However, the first Vatican Council majestically proclaims:

Si quis dixerit assensum fidei christianae non esse liberum, sed argumentie humanae rationis necessario produci, 'anathema sit'.

(Anathema to whosoever asserts that the acceptance of the Christian faith is not free but is produced necessarily through arguments of the human intellect — Canon 5).

However, what is freedom? For vagabonds, gypsies, and nomads it is the possibility of roaming and moving about without walls and fences; for a resident farmer it is self-government or rule of his own house, household and fields; for the enlightened humanist it is knowing what he does and doing what he knows — autonomy of consciousness and self-responsibility; for the seeker after God it is the fulfillment of his free vows of obedience, chastity, and poverty, that free from his own impulses of will he may fulfil the will of God. The latter's freedom is brought to expression in the prayer: "Not my will, but Thy will be done." If his prayer is granted and divine grace reveals itself directly to the will of the God-loving human being, whose will is longing for obedience, is he then not free? In love everything *is* free. Here there are no duties to be fulfilled or sacrifices to be brought with great difficulty; here there is only the joy of freely giving and receiving.

As may be seen, there are many levels of freedom. But the highest is that of love. Here freedom is at its most perfect level. Thus love is the sole element in human existence that cannot and may not be demanded. One can demand endeavour, veracity, honesty, obedience, the fulfillment of duties, but love may never be demanded. Love is and remains for all time the sanctuary of freedom, inaccessible to all compulsion. For this reason, the highest commandment — "Love the Lord your God with all your heart, and with all your soul, and with all your mind . . . and love your neighbour as yourself" (*Matthew* xxii, 37–39) — is not an imposed command, but a divine-human plea. For love cannot be commanded; it can only be prayed for.

Thus an act of faith can occur as the result of insight or, equally, it can be the cause of insight. It can happen that knowledge precedes the acquiescing will, or it can be that the acquiescence of the intellect is effected by the will set in motion through love. Which, therefore, is primary: belief or insight?

We must renounce answering this question just as we must renounce answering the question: What, in the millennia or millions of years, is primary, the chicken or the egg? Our experience does not teach us anything further than that every egg comes from a chicken and that every chicken comes from an egg. Similarly, our experience does not teach us anything further than this: the more insight one has, the more faith one has, and the more faith one has, the more insight one has.

The Gospels speak similarly — at a single stroke, as it were — concerning belief and knowledge and their effects and possibilities. They make equal use of all three criteria: that of "Jews", that of "Greeks", and that of "Johannine–Pauline" human beings. Even the empirical knowledge of the five senses, which is furthest removed from belief and from supersensible knowledge (gnosis), is not simply dismissed, for Thomas was invited by the Risen One to convince himself of his reality through the use of the sense of touch.

The Gospels speak in three kinds of language: in the language of miracles, in the language of knowledge, and in the language of love. They speak of superhuman faculties, divine knowledge, and divine-human love in such a way that when they are read meditatively they are convincing to an extraordinary degree. Thus it is impossible for a peaceful and concentrated reader (i.e., for a meditative reader) of the Gospels not to begin to love the person of Jesus Christ, and also not to sense him as a working and actual reality. It is also impossible for a reader who steeps himself with peaceful relaxedness in the tone and rhythm of the *Gospel of St. John*, for example, not to experience himself as if raised into another sphere of existence. If he "breathes" himself into it, as it were, he experiences himself as if raised into a sphere of existence of the breathing spiritual cosmos, where one begins to understand the meaning of the Word, the Logos, through whom "all things were made, and nothing that was made was made without him" (*John* i, 3). And it would be extremely difficult — actually impossible — for a meditative reader of the Gospels not to take in the wonderful composition of the Gospels as a whole and, instead, to dismember it and divide it up into "important" and "secondary" parts. He would not be able to allow himself to distinguish "mythological" from "historical" and to sift out the "original teaching" from the "embellishment of the legendary". It would be a matter of course for him that, for example, the miracles of the Gospels belong to them and are equally an organic, permanent part of them as, for example, the Sermon on the Mount or the account of the Passion. For the miracles are not simply the execution of divine power but are also "signs" of divine wisdom and love. They are just as much revelations of the Word-made-flesh as are the human words of the sayings and parables of Jesus and the events of his Passion. The Gospel is proclaimed to us in events, signs, parables, and teachings. Thereby the events are simultaneously signs, parables, and teachings. The signs, however, are also simultaneously events, parables, and teachings. The parables are also events, signs, and teachings; and the teachings are at the same time events, signs, and parables. Everything in the Gospel is event, sign, parable, and teaching, i.e. everything is fact, miracle, symbol, and revelation of the truth.

The miracles of the Gospels are thus also facts — as well as symbols and revelations of truth. And it is the task of this book, on the basis of the Lazarus miracle, to show that this is so.

The *Gospel of St. John* reports only seven miracles — the miracle of the transformation of water into wine at Cana in Galilee; the healing of the nobleman's son; the healing of the thirty-eight-year-old paralyzed man; the feeding of the five thousand; the walking upon the water; the healing of the man born blind; the raising of Lazarus — while many other miracles, recounted in the other Gospels, are not mentioned. One does not have to look far for an explanation of this: there, as the concluding sentence of John's Gospel says, "But there are also many other things which Jesus did; were every one of them to be written, I suppose that the world itself could not contain the books that would be written" (*John* xxi, 25). In the *Gospel of St. John* those miracles are depicted which are, so to say, "representative", i.e. each of them represents a group or category which it summarizes and surpasses. Thus the feeding of the five thousand summarizes, surpasses, and represents the feeding of the four thousand. And the raising of Lazarus also summarizes, surpasses, and represents the raising of the youth of Nain and the raising of Jairus' daughter, since Lazarus had already been dead and buried for more than three days. The *Gospel of St. John* summarizes the miracles of Jesus by selecting those miracles which are most significant according to their worth as "signs" or their meaning in terms of revelation, as well as according to the intensity of their effect. For this reason, these miracles are also to be taken as "typical" miracles, so to say, standing for categories of miracles.

Adhering to the choice of criterion of the *Gospel of St. John*, we have chosen the raising of Lazarus as the subject matter of this work: since the seven miracles of the *Gospel of St. John* are the "typical" miracles or the summarizing *archetype* of all other miracles, and since the seventh miracle of this Gospel — the Lazarus miracle — is the greatest of these seven miracles. Once one has grasped the meaning, significance, and revelatory effect of this miracle in mankind's spiritual history, one will then also understand the meaning, significance, and supra-temporal effect of all the other miracles. For the Lazarus miracle contains, summarizes, and represents all the remaining miracles. It is the miracle which holds the key to all the other miracles.

Also *Genesis* does not give a complete account of the countless details of the archetypal miracle — that of the creation of the world — but limits itself to the seven acts of creation which it designates as *days*, which, just as with the seven miracles of Jesus in the *Gospel of St. John*, portray the most significant acts of the creation. Here, also, there is a selection; one which is presented according to the same criterion as is the case in the *Gospel of St. John*. This concordance is not arbitrary. It is necessarily called for by the nature of the task served both by *Genesis* and the *Gospel of St. John*. For *Genesis* sets itself the task of describing the sevenfold miracle of creation and the event of the Fall, where this creation "fell" into evolution — with toil, suffering, and death as the intrinsic characteristics of the latter. *Genesis* seeks to give the answer to the question: How did it come about that the divine creation became that which we now designate as "natural evolution"?

The task set by the *Gospel of St. John* is to give the answer to the question: How does evolution, i.e. toil, suffering, and death, turn back to the intention of the original divine creation? How does it return to the order which originally prevailed? In other words, how does toil become the way, suffering become knowledge of the truth, and death become life? That is how is the world created through the divine Word to become healed — this world, having fallen away from God, having fallen into sin and having become subject to error, sickness, and death?

Whilst *Genesis* depicts the divine creation and the Fall, the *Gospel of St. John* describes the divine work of salvation: the transformation of this fallen world, its healing, in accordance with its divine archetype. The thesis of the *Gospel of St. John* is the following: that the same divine Word, which created the world in seven acts of creation, become flesh; and that the Word-made-flesh accomplishes the healing of this fallen, distorted world through seven acts of healing, these being the seven miracles of the *Gospel of St. John*. This Gospel shows us how the divine Word ("In the beginning was the Word, and the Word was with God, and the Word was God . . . all things were made through Him and nothing was made that was not made without Him" — *John* i, 1-3) became flesh and accomplished seven creative acts analogous to those of the creation, but now as acts of healing. The Word that was "with God", and which created the world, "became flesh and dwelt among us, full of grace and truth" (*John* i, 14), and now heals the world from within the innermost core of the world itself, i.e. from within the human being. The Son of God through whom the world was created now works in the Son of man as the Redeemer of the world — that is the message of the *Gospel of St. John*. It shows how the seven acts of creation in *Genesis*, the seven "days of creation", are transformed to become seven acts of healing, the seven miracles. But it also shows how the Fall becomes atoned for, the Fall being that which underlies the drama of "natural evolution", which was set in motion by the serpent's promise, "You will be like God" (*Genesis* iii, 5). The atonement for the Fall is shown in the *Gospel of St. John* in the description of the stages of the passion of Jesus Christ: washing of the feet, scourging, crowning with thorns, carrying of the cross, crucifixion, entombment, and the ensuing resurrection. The whole composition of the *Gospel of St. John* is given in the following sentence from the prologue: "And the light shineth in the darkness, and the darkness comprehendeth it not" (*John* i, 5). "The light shineth in the darkness" — the Word-made-flesh reveals itself in the signs and miracles. "And the darkness comprehendeth it not" — the passion, which ends in the triumph of the resurrection. And just as the passion culminates in the resurrection, so do the miraculous deeds of healing culminate in the raising of Lazarus. Both culminate in the overcoming of death — death being the ultimate consequence of the Fall.

Genesis depicts how death arose in the world created by God, the world which was "good" (*tov*). The *Gospel of St. John* portrays how death was overcome in the world which, originally created by God, now is darkened. And it describes this by reporting what Jesus did: the miracles, including the raising of Lazarus; and what happened to him: the passion and the resurrection.

Genesis gives an account of the history of the world's gradual attainment of independence and inwardness, which culminates in the birth of freedom; and, further, it portrays the misuse of freedom and the consequences thereof. In fact, what is the essence of the account of the creation according to *Genesis*? It is essentially nothing other than a description as to how the world in the first instance received its own existence alongside God, then its own movement ("water"), then its own life ("plants"), then its own soul life ("animals") and lastly — in man, as the "image and likeness of God" — its own self consciousness, i.e. freedom? And what is the seventh day of creation — the cosmic sabbath, God's "day of rest"? Is it not the level of freedom attained where God "rests" from his deeds, i.e. where he manifests his freedom in relation to the world, whilst the world, the beings of the world, experience themselves as being left to their own freedom, i.e. to experience their freedom? The seventh day of creation is the *day of freedom*. The blessing of the seventh day is the divine act of creating the highest value of existence, the foundation of all morality: freedom. Here created being attains the highest level of inwardness: freedom. The seventh day of creation is the "day" of the meaning of the world. Here the created world becomes something moral; here the world enters into a free relationship with God and God enters into a free relationship with the world. However, since it is only in love that freedom is perfect, one may therefore also say that the seventh day is the day of the founding and sealing of the relationship of love between the creator and all created beings. Thus love is the foundation, the meaning, and the purpose of the world.

By ending with the blessing and consecrating of the seventh day as the *day of rest*, i.e. the day of interiorisation ("becoming inward"), it is clear what the point of Moses' account of creation is: namely, to depict how the miraculous creation of being, of life, of soul culminates in the miracle of the coming into being of freedom . . . how being is interiorised to become life, how life is interiorised to become experience, and how the experience of freedom is interiorised to become love. The "water" above which the spirit of God (*Ruach Elohim*) hovered on the first day of creation became "wine" on the seventh day; it became endowed with warm inner life. And the relationship between God and the world became transformed from that of Mover and "moved", as it was on the first day of creation, into the relationship of union in the freedom of love. The seventh day, the cosmic sabbath, is in a moral-spiritual sense the festival, the festival day, of the marriage between God and the world.

And the miracle of the transformation of water into wine at the wedding at Cana — the first of the seven miracles of the *Gospel of St. John* — is the "sign" revealing the effect of the power of the seventh day of creation. The blessing and consecrating of the seventh day were "evoked", as it were, through the miracle of the wedding at Cana.

Thus we see that the healing miracle work of the Word-made-flesh, as portrayed in the *Gospel of St. John*, takes place in the reverse sequence to the creative miracle working of the divine Word depicted in *Genesis*. The divine magic of the seventh day becomes the first healing miracle of the Word-made-flesh, that of the wedding at Cana. This reversal is understandable if one considers that creation and healing have to take place in reverse sequence: there, where the creation was completed, lies the starting point for the healing (i.e.

restoring) effect. Accordingly, the prologue of the *Gospel of St. John* also gives the stages of Moses' account of creation (light, life, man) in the reverse sequence: "In him (the Word) was life, and the life was the light of men" (*John* i, 4). The work of salvation takes place in reverse to that of the creation in so far as the last stage of the creation is the first of the work of salvation.

If we consider that each miracle of the *Gospel of St. John* is simultaneously a teaching, a parable, a sign, and an event, then we shall understand the significance and importance of the miracle of the wedding at Cana as the first healing act of the Word-made-flesh. The free union, in love between God and the world, which was celebrated, blessed, and consecrated on the seventh day of creation, became broken off through the Fall. The world was unfaithful toward God. And since this divine-cosmic union is mirrored in the marriage relationship, for which it is the ideal and archetype as well as being the meaning of marriage, the original sickness of the world consists in the breach of the free love-union that existed between God and the world. Analogously, this is mirrored in human life, in the distortion and degeneration of the nature and experience of marriage. The marriage relationship — as it has become — begins with enthusiasm, with the "wine" of the honeymoon period, and ends with the "water" of routine habit. But, when there was no more wine, Jesus transformed water into wine, and the second wine was better than the first (*John* ii, 10). Thereby the miracle of the wedding at Cana was the "sign", the symbol, and the event of the healing of marriage (healing in the service of restoring the marriage relationship to correspond to its divine-cosmic archetype, which is the seventh day of creation).

The sixth day of creation in *Genesis* is an account of the origin of the animal kingdom and of the human being, corresponding to their archetypes (*minah*). Here the archetype of the human being is God himself ("God created man in his own image, in the image of God he created him; male and female he created them" — *Genesis* i, 27). On the other hand, the animals — each "according to its kind" (*leminah*) — were brought forth from the earth and were formed ("made") by God corresponding to their archetypes (*minah*). The account of the sixth day therefore includes the divine-cosmic archetype of heredity, just as the account of the seventh day contains the divine-cosmic archetype of marriage.

It shows that the archetypal nature of heredity is vertical: the archetype (*min*) is above and the form mirroring it is shaped below, on earth. "Heredity" means simply the transmission of similarity from ancestors to their descendants. In this sense, the invisible divinely created archetypes (*minah*) are the "ancestors" of the visible species of animals. And the invisible archetype of man, the divine being itself, is the "ancestor" of the human being. The sickness which arose as a tragic consequence of the Fall was a change of direction in the mirroring process of heredity; it changed from being vertical to become horizontal. This meant that similarity no longer descended from the invisible supra-temporal archetype above, but from the visible ancestors in the temporal succession of generations here below. Instead of becoming the direct "image and likeness" (*tsalam* + *dumuth*, *imago et similitudo*) of their archetype, human beings and other beings of nature became formed in the "image and likeness" of their earthly ancestors, thus only indirectly mirroring their archetype. Thereby heredity, as we know it, became a horizontal stream in the sequence of time, transmitting not only the original mirroring of the archetype, but also everything which entered into the stream of generations with the Fall and which has occurred in this stream since the Fall. It has become a stream which also transmits the "sins" of sickness and death, and through it the "sins of the fathers" have become a reality.

The second miracle of the *Gospel of St. John*, the healing of the nobleman's son, where the healing of the son took place through the faith of the father, was fulfilled, like the first, at Cana in Galilee. It comprises the transformation of the relationship father — son (i.e. heredity) from being a stream transmitting sickness to a stream transmitting healing. The second miracle of the John Gospel is the event, sign, and teaching, which has to do with the divine-archetypal heredity of the sixth day of creation. It has to do with the distortion of this "vertical" heredity through the Fall, in that the original relationship to the "image and likeness of God", as it was on the sixth day of creation, was restored by the father bringing his son into a direct relationship to the divine archetype — through his faith in Jesus Christ, the new Adam. He himself, as the earthly father and "model" for the son, retired into the background, as it were. He brought his son into connection with the new Adam, who, in place of himself, entered into the hereditary relationship "father-son". Thus the healing of the nobleman's son took place. And just as the miracle of the wedding at Cana is the healing and consecration of marriage (i.e. the essence of the sacrament of marriage as the renewal of the blessing and consecrating of the seventh day of creation), so the miracle of the healing of the nobleman's son is the "sign" of the essence of the sacrament of baptism as the restoration of fatherhood and sonhood, which have their archetype in the sixth day of creation.

The objection could be raised that this conception concerning the relationship between the miracles of the *Gospel of St. John* and Moses' account in *Genesis* of the creation is not really "biblical" but

"Platonic". However, neither Moses nor John was a Platonist, who conceived of the world of manifestation as mirroring a world of archetypes or "ideas". In this connection there is only the following to say: How can one think of the creation of animals, for example, "each according to its kind", if here "kind" is not conceived of as "archetype"? What if one did not think of it in this way, that the "kind" as a spiritual archetype precedes the concrete form — not necessarily in time, but as a necessary fact of knowledge (*in ordine cognoscendi*)? Then one would have to assume that first of all the animals were created and that later their kinds (species) appeared as if "by themselves" from the individual animals. In other words, one would have to assume that the creation "just happened" and that it was a success, in that the various species came *post factum* into manifestation from amongst the colourful multiplicity!

One must either give up thinking and bring it to a halt, or one must think platonically if one does not want to — or is unable to — accept things without further thought.

In addition, we may add that we are in good company when we think platonically. The Jewish philosopher Philo of Alexandria, although he does not see pure platonism in Moses' account of the creation, sees in it the true source from which Plato drew his inspiration. Not that *Genesis* is platonic, which, in any case it cannot be, since it is older than platonism historically, but rather platonism derives essentially from Moses. This is the assertion of Philo, who could do nothing other than to see in essence an identity between these two spiritual directions.

The same view was shared also by Clement of Alexandria, Origen, and St. Augustine. They also saw no other possibility than either to stop short at *Genesis* without further thought, or to form thoughts about it — and to think about *Genesis* other than "platonically" is hardly possible. The same applies to the *Gospel of St. John* — the Gospel of the Logos who is the Light of man.

To think "platonically" is nothing other than to think vertically — in the direction "above below". And how is it possible to manage without this kind of thinking if one has a book in front of one that begins with the sentence: "In the beginning God created heaven and earth" (*Genesis* i, 1)? Or a book which begins with the sentence: "In the beginning was the Word, and the Word was with God, and the Word was God" (*John* i, 1)?

Genesis and the *Gospel of St. John* demand a thinking that runs in categories from above, below, i.e. *platonic thinking*. In actual fact, however, it is not platonic — if one takes platonism historically — it is older. It should actually be called *hermetic*, since the basis of this mode of thought is to be found concisely formulated in the writing of Hermes Trismegistus known as the "Emerald Table" (*Tabula Smaragdina*): "True it is without falsehood, certain and more true, that which is above is like to that which is below, and that which is below is like to that which is above . . ." (*Verum, sine mendacio, certum verissimum: Quod est inferius, est sicut quod est superius, et quod est superius est sicut quod est inferius*).

"As above, so below; and as below, so also above" — this is the basis of analogy, which presupposes the unity of the world and the interrelationship of all beings and things, in the sense of the first sentence of *Genesis*: "In the beginning God created the above (heaven) and the below (earth)". Whether "platonic" or "hermetic" is not important to us; let us continue with this mode of thought in our study of the seven miracles of the *Gospel of St. John*, viewed as the transformation of the seven days of creation (in *Genesis*) into seven healing miracles.

The fifth day of creation in *Genesis* is the account of the waters bringing forth ensouled movement: in the horizontal "swarms of living creatures" (*scheretz nefesch chajah, reptile animae viventiae,* — *Genesis* i, 20); and in the vertical direction "birds that fly above the earth across the firmament of the heavens" (*ve 'voph je 'vophaph 'al ha 'aretz, et volatile super terram sub firmamento coeli,* — *Genesis* i, 20). This means to say: "fish" and "birds" (*reptile et volatile*). The result of the fifth day of creation is ensouled movement in the world. The result of the third miracle in the *Gospel of St. John* is the healing of the man who was paralysed for thirty-eight years, i.e. the restoration of ensouled faculty of movement to the paralysed man, who lay there waiting for healing through the water brought into movement by an angel. "Now there is in Jerusalem by the sheep gate, a pool, in Hebrew called Bethesda, which has five porticoes. In there lay a multitude of invalids, blind, lame, paralysed, waiting for the movement of the water; for an angel went down at certain times into the pool, and moved the water; whoever stepped in first after the water had been moved was healed of whatever disease he had" (*John* v, 2–4). Here the *Gospel of St. John* describes the place, with details of the circumstances, where the miracle of the healing of the paralysed man was accomplished. However, the healing itself was not brought about by the paralysed man entering into the water, but alone through the words of Jesus: "Rise, take up your pallet, and walk" (*John* v, 8). These words "rise, take up your pallet and walk" contain the working effect of the fifth day of creation, namely the creation of ensouled movement in the vertical ("rise", *surge*) and in the horizontal ("take up your pallet, and, *tolle . . . et ambula*). These words restored ensouled movement to the paralysed man in that the same force which operated on the fifth day of creation, and which created ensouled movement, gave back to him the faculty of movement. The faculty of movement is essentially cosmic, not only according to its effect, where every movement, even the slightest, exerts an effect ultimately upon the whole world, but also according to the causes stimulating it. For the human being stands within a stream of cosmic energies — his thoughts in the streams of the thought world, his feelings in the streams of the world's psychic forces, and his impulses of will are immersed in the streams of world-will-energy and are "plugged in" to them. And just as someone, for example, who holds his breath and takes in no more air will suffocate, so will someone who cuts himself off from the streams of cosmic energies become paralysed. It is the "cutting oneself off" which is a "sin" against God, against mankind, and against nature. For this reason Jesus later said to the healed paralysed man, when he saw him in the temple, "See, you are well! Sin no more, that nothing worse befall you" (*John* v, 14).

The third miracle of the John Gospel accomplished the re-"plugging in" of this human being into the ensouled movement of the world, who, through sin, had become cut off from it and thereby paralysed. (The fifth day of creation in *Genesis* points to the mystery of the ensouled movement of the world). In this respect, the third miracle is the archetype of the healing effect of the sacrament of the forgiveness of sins, i.e. the sacrament of penance.

Following the account of the healing of the paralysed man, Jesus speaks the words: "My Father is working still, and I am working" (*John* v, 17). With these words he clearly expresses the fact that the creative reality of the Father (in the days of creation) is the archetype of the healing reality of the Son (in the miracles), and that the miracles of the *Gospel of St. John* have their origin and archetype in the days of creation described in *Genesis*. In the same context, this is still more clearly expressed in the following: "The Father loves the Son, and shows him all that he himself is doing; and greater works than these will he show him, that you may marvel" (*John* v, 20). That is, the supra-temporal works of creation of the Father are shown to the Son by the Father, and are fulfilled by the Son (the Word-made-flesh) in the form of signs and miracles. And, moreover, still greater signs and miracles than that of the healing of the paralysed man (including the raising of Lazarus) are still to come, so "that you may marvel". For "the Son can do nothing of his own accord, but only what he sees the Father doing; for whatever he does, that the Son does likewise" (*John* v, 19).

Thus the fifth day is that of the coming into being of ensouled movement, which was originally in harmony, in accord with the whole. The third miracle of St. John's Gospel is the healing deed of restoration of this harmony in the case of the paralysed man, who through sin had fallen into disaccord with the harmony of ensouled movement in the world. This harmony of the individual movements of the multiplicity of beings, each of which moves on his own accord, we can comprehend best by way of comparison with a conducted orchestra. For in an orchestra each member plays his own instrument and has his own music score, and yet the result is not dissonance, but harmony. This happens, it is true, due to indications of time and tempo given by the conductor who — equally with the piece of music itself — leads the playing of the orchestra, standing before it.

In this sense the fourth day of creation "stands before" the "play" of the many kinds of spontaneous movement of the fifth day and "leads" it. For the fourth day of creation is that of the coming into being of those principles of the world orchestra which direct "time and tempo" — the creation of the "sun, moon, and stars": "And God made two great lights (*luminaria*): the greater light to rule the day and the lesser light to rule the night; he made stars also; and God set them in the firmament of the heavens to separate the day from the night and let them be for signs and for seasons and for days and years" (*Genesis* i, 14, 16–17). What are these other than organs of direction, i.e. conductors of time and tempo for the world-orchestra, in accordance with the music-score of the stars?

The fourth day of creation is the genesis of that all embracing world rhythm, in which all beings partake and which unifies them into a world-embracing community (*communio*). Consider, by way of analogy, human consciousness. It does not become chaotic through the strife of wishes, desires, whims, moods, notions, and countless impulses from without and within — from fantasy and from memory. Rather, it orders itself around a central point — the self — which represents the center of gravity of the soul life, i.e. the permanency of the identity of the personality. Moreover, aided by the light of reason it works in such a way as to bring order even into the "night" of the subconscious, leading the whole soul life (conscious and unconscious, i.e. "day" and "night") in the direction of the ideals. (Ideals can be likened to "stars", enabling orientation and pointing the way.) Analogously, in the macrocosm there is an active midpoint — a center, a "sun" — which radiates forth light, warmth, and life, representing the community-building principle of the awake world of "day", while its reflected light ("moon") is the community building principle of the unconscious, sleeping world of "night". This "sun" leads and supports the whole — the "day world" and also the "night world" — in harmony with the world of stars. The sun (or rather the inner nature of the sun) in the great world corresponds to the creative, leading, and ordering role of the self in the "small world" of the human soul. The moon in its inner nature corresponds to the rational capacity for reflection, which casts an evaluating light on the irrational urges of the soul life. The inner nature of the stars in the great world correspond to the ideals which give direction to human soul life.

The fourth day of creation is the account of the origin of the universal community, of the unity embracing all beings of the world. It is therefore the divine-cosmic archetype of the sacrament upon the altar, that of holy communion.

And the fourth miracle in the *Gospel of St. John* — the feeding of the five thousand in the wilderness — is the corresponding healing work of the Word-made-flesh. This work consisted in the reinstatement of the original community of beings from the fourth day of creation, and the corresponding ordering given on this day of creation by the sun, moon, and stars. For as the Sun — raying out light, warmth, and life — "nourishes" all beings and unites them in a "community of nourishment", so Jesus Christ functioned at the feeding of the five thousand as the "nourishment giving center" for the five thousand. He carried out during the short time of the "feeding" what the sun effects in the course of the year, when it brings about a "multiplication of bread" through the sprouting, growth, and ripening of corn. For there takes place yearly on earth a "multiplication of bread" effected through the power of the sun, so that the small amount of corn that is sown multiplies tenfold. And as the moon, reflecting the light of the sun, tones down the light in passing it on — so did the disciples, who were with him on the mountain, as they received from Jesus the bread which he had blessed and passed it on to the people gathered there. They distributed it, that is: they toned down the creative stream of augmentation by handing it out in portions.

The *Gospel of St. John* describes this in the following words: "And Jesus took the loaves, and when he had given thanks he distributed to the disciples, and the disciples to them that were set down" (*John* vi, 11).

The disciples received and passed on the blest (eucharistic) bread, just as the moon receives and passes on the light of the sun in a dimmed, toned-down form. When one is talking of the effect of light, "dimmed and toned-down" means "not too dazzling", and when one is talking in terms of potency, it means "bearable". This mediating effect of the moon, which transforms the boundless, streaming strength of the sun such that it becomes more individually acceptable, can also be understood in relation to the experience of the sacrament of holy communion received at the altar. It is extremely rare for members of the church taking communion to be profoundly shattered or find themselves in a state of ecstacy when receiving the holy communion. Actually this should always happen, because the sacrament of communion is an inner meeting and unification with Jesus Christ, similar to the meeting which Paul experienced on the way to Damascus, which so shattered him that he was blind for three days. What takes place, however, is a mild inner light that arises in the people as a mood and works into a cheerful calmness. This mild light, rather than an inner shock, is the result of the merciful intervention and tempering effect of the moon-principle.

Also, at the feeding of the five thousand, it was the disciples who took up the mighty, enlightening, warming, life-giving force of the cosmic Word-made-flesh and passed it on as "reflection", i.e. they toned it down to the level of "refreshment and nourishment". Thus the five thousand people did not pass into a condition of ecstacy, but were simply refreshed and strengthened, i.e. they were "fed".

This fact is at the same time a key. (Here we are careful to say "a key" and not "the key".) It is a key to an understanding of the basic hierarchic principle in the world, not only from the fourth day of creation when the sun, moon, and stars were instituted as the hierarchical order of the world, but also with respect to the hierarchical order among mankind. For each lower rank of hierarchy is a "moon" in relationship to the "sun" of the rank above it. The angels transmit the tumultuous, strong impulses of the archangels in a bearable form, suited to human individuals, i.e. in the form of the soft light of moral clarity. The archangels adopt the radical, valid-to-all-mankind commandments and prohibitions of the principalities (archai) to suit the special characters and capacities of the various peoples, thereby protecting them from becoming over-pressured. And something similar is effected by the principalities in relation to the powers (exusiai), the powers toward the virtues (dynamis), the virtues toward the dominions (kryriotetes), the dominions toward the thrones, the thrones toward the cherubim, the cherubim toward the seraphim, and the seraphim toward the eternal Trinity of God. This process is mirrored, too — as Dionysus the Areopagite already showed — in the hierarchy of the Church, where the priest as confessor plays the role of "angel", as it were, to the individual human being, while the bishop, in likeness to the archangel, is responsible for the welfare of a whole diocese.

Those people who deny the hierarchic principle — such as those protestant Christians who take the standpoint "between me and my God no intermediary is necessary or allowable" — neither know what they are saying, nor what they want. On the one hand they are conscious that they are sinners, i.e. living in darkness — and acknowledge it — but they do not want to recognize the reflected light of the moon-principle, which was established for the purpose of ruling the "night" and the "darkness". On the other hand, they demand that the sun itself shall shine into their darkness, but in such a manner that they may not be blinded by it. Other people, again, those who like to call themselves "humanists", take the view that the reflected toned down light of the moon-principle suffices for them — for their living and dying. They stick to their conscience and are content to "do their best", forgetting that there is not only relative but also absolute truth — that the sun does exist!

After this digression, let us return to our consideration of the miracle of the feeding of the five thousand in the wilderness. We have seen that through this miracle, Jesus Christ accomplished the "sun effect" of multiplying the bread, while the circle of disciples carried out its transformation in distributing it and making it suitable ("stepping it down"). Here Christ worked as the sun and the disciples as the moon. Through this cooperation, the aim in view — the feeding of the hungry — was achieved. ("When Jesus then lifted up his eyes and saw a great company come unto him, he said unto Philip: Whence shall we buy bread that these may eat?" — *John* vi, 5).

Now, in the course of this miracle there happened something else which went beyond the boundaries of the goal aimed at: twelve baskets of fragments remained over, which were gathered after the "feeding". There followed upon the original multiplying of the bread by Jesus Christ, which was distributed by the disciples, a second multiplying which happened after the distribution. A third element entered in, pointing to the effects of a third principle besides those of the sun and moon — a third kind of power working. For, aside from Christ and the circle of disciples, the people (the five thousand) also participated in the miracle. In addition to the sun and moon-principles, the "star-principle" was also at work in the "sign" of the feeding of the five thousand.

The miracle was still more wonderful than merely feeding the five thousand with five loaves and two fishes! It comprised also an active, miracle-working participation of all the five thousand people who took part in the miracle. They all — and each of them separately — also became "bread-multipliers" within their individual boundaries, i.e. they became in themselves individual sources of light. For a while they became "stars"! And this "becoming stars" represented the climax of the miracle.

By this we are saying that the five thousand not only received the miraculously increased nourishment, but also the multiplying-power ("I am the bread of life") into themselves. Or rather, they experienced it springing up within them. They became — within their individual boundaries — like Christ, i.e. "bread-multipliers", becoming creative founts of life-giving light. The Christ, who before the distribution of loaves was on the mountain external to them, was now actively present within them. There took place the miracle of the sacrament of holy communion as the climax to the miracle of the "feeding". The five thousand became effective sources of light. They rayed forth, each within his own individual limitations.

Now "to ray forth within your own individual limitations" means nothing else than to become an individual — but limited — sun. And this is the star-principle. It is different from the sun-principle in that the latter works unboundedly, universally ("The sun shines upon good and evil alike") while the star-principle is an individually concentrated and limited sunlike quality. It differs from the moon-principle, however, in that it does not reflect light but rays it forth out of itself. "Stars", in this sense, are "sun-seeds", sprouting sun-corn.

There thus arises a wonderful picture out of a deeper consideration of the miracle of the feeding of the five thousand: in the centre, high up on the mountain, Jesus Christ, as the shining and life-giving sun; then the circle of disciples as the silver moon; and round about the mountain a swarm of thousands of stars — the people.

The people, the five thousand, experienced more than the stilling of their hunger; they experience the reality of the hierarchal principle, as it was founded on the fourth day of creation. That is the reason why, after the feeding, they wanted to make Jesus Christ king (*John* vi, 15). For, during the "sign" they experienced the kingly effects of the cosmic ruling center-point, but interpreted this experience according to the concepts of their ordinary day-consciousness in such a way that they said: "Truly, this is the prophet that should come into the world" (*John* vi, 14), and they thought that he should become king in an earthly sense. This interpretation brought the divine-cosmic nature of the event down onto the level of human-earthly nature. Therefore Jesus "withdrew again into the mountains by himself" (*John* vi, 15).

Alone, "by himself", is the key to the next, the fifth miracle of the *Gospel of St. John* — as it is the key to understanding the third day of creation in *Genesis*. How may this be understood? Summarizing thus far: the seventh day of creation is the "day" of a free covenant of love between the world and God, and the first miracle is the renewal of this covenant in humanity; the sixth day of creation is the "day" of the coming into being of true heredity, and the second miracle is that of the reinstatement of true heredity in the human race; the fifth day of creation is the "day" of the genesis of spontaneous movement, and the third miracle is the regeneration of spontaneous movement in the human being who has fallen out of the wholeness of the world; lastly, the fourth day of creation is that of hierarchical world order, of universal community, and the fourth miracle is that of the reinstatement of hierarchical community in mankind. Continuing further, the third day of creation is the "day" of procreation, of the mystery of seed and of growth, while the fifth miracle of St. John's Gospel is the "sign" of individual generative power as it came into being on the third day of creation.

The account by Moses of the third day of creation in fact reaches its climax in the words: "And God said: Let the earth bring forth grass, plants yielding seed, and fruit trees each bearing fruit after its kind, whose seed is in itself upon the earth; and it was so. And the earth brought forth grass, and plants yielding seed each according to its kind, and trees bearing fruit, whose seed was in itself after its kind" (*Genesis* i, 11).

The third day of creation is the generation of the seed principle, of the principle of potential formative force becoming actualised and bringing to visible realisation its own inner, invisible shape. The third day of creation is the coming into being of the seed-principle in the world — that is, not only of the plant-world manifest to us as plants and trees, but also such "trees" growing in paradise as "the tree of knowledge of good and evil" and the "tree of life". Also included here is all that which grew out of the "seed of Abraham", and that in the New Testament which as the Kingdom of God was sown as "seed" and shall in the future become a mighty tree. The words of Jesus, too, which fell on hard or on good ground and bear fruit accordingly — all these belong in the realm of the seed-principle that came into being on the third day of creation. Yes, Jesus Christ even designated himself as a "seed", who must die in order to bear much fruit — comparing the essence of Christianity and its history with the seed and its development: its germination, sprouting, and growth. In each of the above cases there is a reference to the power of inwardness which later comes to manifestation in an external form.

The language of the Bible is neither merely realistic, nor merely symbolic. It is *real-symbolic*, i.e. instead of employing abstract concepts it makes use of real facts, each corresponding to a principle embodying a basic and essential truth. Therefore the trees of which "each bore fruit after its kind, whose seed was in itself" were not just ash trees and oak trees, but also the tree of knowledge and the tree of life. And the fruit of the tree of knowledge bears the seed of death;

the tree of life, on the other hand, bears the seed of an uninterrupted metamorphosis of growth.

So it would be entirely correct in the sense of the Bible and of biblical language if, for instance, we were to designate the basic formula of the *Tabula Smaragdina* ("as above, so below; and as below, so also above") as a seed out of which a many branched tree of though-life has sprung, embracing Pythagoreanism and the Cabbala, Platonism, Neoplatonism, Alexandrine theology, the theology of Dionysus the Areopagite, Hermetic philosophy, Alchemy, Rosicrucianism, and a great deal more as well. Here the power of growth and the fruitfulness of a thought-seed reveals itself with the greatest clarity. Is the designation *thought-seed* merely a comparison? No, it is the result of insight into the reality of one and the same seed-principle, revealing itself both in the growth of an oak tree out of an acorn, and in the growth of a many branched tree of metaphysical thought arising from the basic formula of analogy.

Thus the biblical words: seed, trees, the sea, and the dry land, as also heaven and earth, mean much more than the concrete things designated by these words. The "seas" which in Genesis' account of the third day of creation are described as "the gathering together of the waters under the heavens unto one place" signify the state of concentration ("gathering") of force-substance, whereby it retains its mobility in the sense of being able to be moved. On the other hand, the "dry land" means a state of still greater concentration ("gathering unto one place"), where the force-substance is so condensed — contracted — that a coagulation into solidity is reached. The account of the third day of creation begins with a description of the appearance ("becoming visible") of the dry land as a kind of process of crystallisation: "And God said: Let the waters (plural in the original Hebrew) under the heavens be gathered together in one place, and let the dry land appear (become visible)". The creative impulse of the Word that is indicated here is that of concentration (condensation directed towards a central point in space) taking place on two levels, the level of "sea" and the level of "dry land". Alternatively, if we compare it with the process of crystallisation, these levels can be thought of as that of solution and that of solidification, forming crystals. The solid state is the liquid condensed.

Now, the process of concentration is not simply one of quantitative compression and crystallisation. It is also a qualitative process of distillation — like making an extract. "And God said," the narration of *Genesis* continues, "Let the earth bring forth grass, the plants yielding seed . . ." The account of the third day of creation consists of two parts, both of which begin with the words: "And God said". The first part (*Genesis* i, 9–10) speaks of the process of concentration (condensation) causing the "dry land" to appear out of the "sea". The second part tells of the arising of seed "each after its kind". The seed is the qualitative concentration of the entire "kind", just as the "dry land' is the quantitative concentration of the "sea". The second part of the narrative concerning the third day of creation is the more inward repetition (recapitulation) of the first part. The coming into being of the "earth" out of the "sea" is recapitulated as the genesis of the "seed" out of the "earth". It is repeated in a more inward manner, for the "seed" is not merely a quantitative condensation of force-substance, but also a qualitative selection "after its kind" from the forces and substances for an extract containing an inner "sea" of latent mobility and an inner "earth" of substantiality.

The account by Moses of the creation (*Genesis*) is a description of the miracle of creation in seven stages. The miracle of the third day of creation does not consist in existent substances and existent forces being so combined that out of them "seeds" were formed, but rather in the fact that by means of the power of the Word ("and God said") active centers were established which caused the qualitative selection of substances and forces into which they were embedded. The miracle of the third day of creation is the genesis of monads, in the sense of Leibniz' monad-teaching. There came into being entities (monads) which are sovereign over the world of energies (the "sea") and also sovereign over condensed substance (the "earth"), because they bear their own solidity in themselves and can condense themselves, as well as bearing within them their own mobility, their own energy or "sea". They are independent of both the "sea" and "earth" principles, because they bear in themselves these principles. They are in the world — the world of "sea" and of "earth" — but not of the world.

We now find ourselves — at least in thought — in the midst of the fifth miracle of the *Gospel of St. John*: the miracle of the the walking on the water. For this miracle — as an event and as a "sign" — is the revelation of the independence of the Son of man with regard to the sea and the land. Jesus Christ walking on the sea needs no support, for he supports himself, and he does not climb into the disciples' ship in order to be carried by it. Rather, it is he who brings the ship to the other shore, for he is not the one borne but the bearer, not the one moved but the mover. This is not only shown as a "sign", but is clearly expressed by the words of the "seed-force" spoken by Jesus in doing the miracle: "It is I: be not afraid." These words (which in the light of the third day of creation actually can be understood as "I am the seed of the Kingdom of Heaven") belong as much to the fifth miracle of St. John's Gospel as the words "I am the bread of life" to the fourth miracle, the words "I am the door" to the third miracle, the words "I am the way, the truth and the life" to the second miracle and the words "I am the vine" to the first miracle. The words "I am the light of the world" belong to the sixth miracle, and the words "I am the resurrection and the life" to the seventh — the Lazarus miracle — of the *Gospel of St. John*. For if it be true that "all things were made by the Word, and nothing that was made was made without him (*John* i, 3), i.e. the seven days of creation are the work of the "Word that was with God", then the seven miracles of St. John's Gospel are the work of the "Word-made-flesh". In this sense each of the seven "I am" sayings is an aspect of the divine Word, the Logos, and each refers to a stage of his work — both of creation and of regeneration (healing).

Thus we have stated that the Word revealed by the fifth miracle of the *Gospel of St. John* — the walking on the water — is the creative Word of the third day of creation. It is the Word which lies at the basis of the seed-principle. The word (divine saying) "It is I: be not afraid", spoken in the course of the miracle of walking on the water (and which we interpreted above as "I am the seed"), is also found in St. John's Gospel in the form: "I am the good shepherd". This latter speaks with greater clarity of the fact that Jesus Christ was not the one borne but the bearer, not the one led but the leader, not the one supported but the support — as shown by the miracle of the walking on the water. Just as the seed determines the future ways and stages of growth, so the Good Shepherd decides the ways of development of the true being of mankind and leads them along these ways.

The third day of creation, the "day" of the seed "each according to its kind" (i.e. of independent nature), is the divine-cosmic background of the sacrament of confirmation, which belongs to the fifth miracle of the *Gospel of St. John* — the walking on the water. This sacrament has as its archetype and source the spiritual event of the miracle of the walking on the water. At every confirmation this miracle — to a certain extent — is repeated: the wonder of pure faith, unsupported by anything but inner certainty, which stands above the threatening sea of relativeness and doubt, and goes its own way.

The second day of creation according to Moses' account is the genesis of the firmament, dividing the waters which were under the firmament from the waters which were above the firmament. "And God called the firmament heaven (*schamaim, coelum*)". It is the "day" of the coming into being of "vision", of knowledge, of true gnosis. For the "firmament" or "heaven" which divides the waters above from those below is the "light" of the first day of *Genesis* — which now not only divides the waters above from those below, but is also the connecting link between them. The "heaven" of the second day is the crystalline clarity which divides and connects the waters above and below. The waters below mirror the heavens, and likewise the waters above mirror them. This double reflection is the principle of vision, of knowledge itself, for knowledge is the transformation of the seen into insight, of that which is perceived into truth. It is the realization of the connection between things and ideas, between the real and the ideal.

Now, the reflection of the heavens in the waters below is the realm of things ("the real"), while ideas ("the ideal") are represented by the reflection of the heavens in the waters above. And knowledge, or understanding, is the process of relating the real to the ideal corresponding to it. To understand ("stand under") means to make a movement which brings into relation the reflection above, the ideal, with the reflection below, the real. This is why the *Tabula Smaragdina* of Hermes Trismegistus (quoted earlier) makes the statement "as above, so below; and as below, so also above" — indicating the prerequisite for knowledge. The principle of analogy is founded on the insight that the active, creatively functioning light (of "heaven") is reflected both above as ideas and also below as realities.

And what is the light which forms the firmament of heaven, and which is reflected both in the waters above the firmament and also in the waters below the firmament? It is the Logos, the Word, by which all things were made. The Word bore witness to himself through the lips of Jesus Christ at the sixth miracle of St. John's Gospel — the healing of the man born blind — "As long as I am in the world, I am the light of the world" (*John* ix, 5). The Logos, however, is not only the intelligence of the world, that is, the connection of the ideal with the real, but also the perception of the ideal and the real. For it is he who mirrors himself by way of ideas and by way of the facts of existence. All seeing, hearing, touching, etc., presupposes an intermediate connecting link, an organ, between the percept (the object of perception) and the perceiver (the subject of perception). With all perceiving there has to be the possibility of a projection of the object into the subject, and simultaneously a projection of the subject out into the object. The eye is not merely the receiver of light permeated impressions, it also rays forth light itself. The eye's glance can be shining and active too. The glance "speaks" at the same time as it perceives. The eyes — and the senses altogether — represent the concrete reflection of the cosmic principle of cognition, i.e. of the second day of creation.

It is the Logos who makes seeing possible, i.e. the connecting of the seen with the seer — analogous to the "heaven" of the second day, which connects the reflection in the waters above the firmament with the reflection in the waters below the firmament. Vision is reflection:

it is analogous to cognition. For this reason the sixth miracle of the *Gospel of St. John* is the healing of the man born blind — the healing effect of the creative power of the Word which was active on the second day of creation. The healing of the man born blind took place in the following sequence: After Jesus had spoken the words: "As long as I am in the world, I am the light of the world", he anointed the eyes of the blind man with clay (that Jesus had made from his spittle with the earth), and then said to the blind man: "Go, wash in the pool of Siloam (which means "sent"). So he went and washed and came back seeing" (*John* ix, 5–7).

The healing took place, after these words had been spoken, with the aid of two "waters": (1) the spittle, closest to the Word, accompanying and mirroring it, which was mixed with earth; and (2) the water from the pool of Siloam, which flowed forth from the earth. The miracle of the healing, however, did not end merely with the opening of the eyes of the man born blind, but with his recognition of the incarnated Son of God and his faith in Him. This miracle culminated in a "seeing faith". The Gospel says it clearly: "When Jesus had found him, he said unto him: Do you believe in the Son of God? He answered: Who is he, Lord, that I may believe in him? And Jesus said unto him: You have seen him, and it is he who speaks to you. And he said: Lord, I believe. And he worshipped him" (*John* ix, 35–38).

The miracle of the healing of the man born blind is a pure act of God. It does not presuppose a willingness to repent, nor any act of faith on the part of the man born blind. For neither had the man born blind sinned in his life before birth in the spiritual world or in a previous life on earth, nor had the sin of his parents caused his blindness. The cause lay in the future (*causa finalis*). He was born blind "that the works of God might be made manifest in him (*ut manifestentur opera Dei in illo*)" (*John* ix, 3).

In other words, at the basis of this man's destiny lay the decision to renounce the sight which is blind to the revelations of the Divine, and to wait for the miracle of the reinstatement of the true, original faculty of beholding which sees all things visible as "works of God revealed". Therefore, Jesus, in the account of St. John's Gospel, summarised these events in the words: "For judgement I came into this world, that those who do not see may see, and that those who see may become blind" (*John* ix, 39). For the true and original vision which preceded the Fall (at which "their eyes were opened") was a vertical vision. That is, it was a beholding with the "upper eye" and with the "lower eye" — with the "upper eye" of the reflection of the Logos in the waters above the firmament, and with the "lower eye" of the reflection of the Logos in the waters beneath the firmament.

However, when through the Fall vision became horizontal, i.e. the "lower eye" became the sole organ of seeing, then "Adam and Eve saw that they were naked". This means that vision became devoid of ideas, a perception of the "bare facts", i.e. of facts alone, without the corresponding ideas in the waters above the firmament. It became basically cynical. And it was this vision, limited to the bare facts, which the man born blind had renounced at the time of his pre-birth choice of destiny, in order that the true, original vision — the vision of the real combined with the ideal, as prefigured on the second day of creation — might be reinstated in him.

The man born blind was a soul who wanted either to see truly, or to see nothing at all. He chose a radical challenge of destiny: that of the miraculous healing of fallen vision. And the miracle happened. Jesus spoke the word, gave the "waters above" the direction toward the earth (mixed the spittle with earth), salved his eyes with this clay and sent him to wash in the "lower waters" (springing forth from the earth at the pool of Siloam, which also mirrored the Word and was therefore named "sent") — and he became a seer. And he saw the Word-made-flesh and worshipped him as the Son of God.

The sixth miracle of the *Gospel of St. John* is the archetype of the sacrament of ordination, the sacrament of the regeneration of original and true vision. This vision occurs when the "upper eye" is opened for the reflection of the Word in the waters above the firmament and the "lower eye" sees the things of the outer world in the light of the "upper eye". The priest is, as it were, "twice baptised": in the "upper waters" and in the "lower waters" of the second day of creation. He connects "above" and "below" in the "seeing together" of the ideal and the real.

The first day of creation is the genesis of the world in its seed-condition, i.e. with all its latent possibilities. In this sense the "days" which follow it are those of unfolding and actualizing in detail that which had been created as a foundation on the first day. Expressed *in ordine cognoscendi*, it can be said that the account of the following days represents a kind of explanatory commentary on the first day of creation. The miracle of the first day embraces and contains in itself the whole miracle of creation in essence, i.e. it includes within it the remaining six days of *Genesis*.

For the content of the account of the first day of creation is the beginning (*reschith, principium*) of the beginnings, i.e. the theme and principle of creation. It is not a question of that which is first in time, but of the deepest and highest foundations of existence — of the primal foundation (in the sense of the archetypal ground) underlying the world. How else could we understand the saying: "In the beginning God created heaven and earth", when we know that heaven was not made until the second day ("and God called the firmament heaven") and the earth did not appear out of the sea as "dry land" until the third day of creation ("and God called the dry land earth . . .")? The "heaven" and the "earth" of the first day are not the heaven and the earth of the following days, but rather their essential archetypes or "points of departure". The text of *Genesis* concerning the first day of creation must be read in the deeper language of spiritual morality. We must comprehend it not as an allegory, but as a concrete moral-spiritual happening.

We cannot make anything of the first sentence of *Genesis* if we do not read it meditatively. It proclaims nothing; it reveals nothing, apart from a scanty idea that in the beginning God created an above and a below. We have to take the time to deepen the words of this sentence to depths of concrete spirituality. "In the beginning (*bereshith, in principio*) — i.e. as the primal ground of the world process — God allowed two tendencies, two impulses, to proceed in opposite directions: in the direction "above" and in the direction "below". In the beginning was the vertical, which was made up of the exalted and the humble: On the one hand, out of the striving for active cooperation with God, a striving to be a "likeness" (*dimuth*) of God, and on the other hand out of the striving to give oneself up to God, to mirror Him, to be an "image" (*tsalam*) of God. The striving or the yearning for the exalted, for cooperation with the Divine, is designated in the account of the first day of creation as "heaven" (*schamaim*), while the striving or the yearning for humble devotion, for pure mirroring of the Divine, is referred to as "earth" (*aretz*). Both directions of striving are unbounded: therefore *Genesis* speaks of "heavens" (*ha-schamaim*) on the one hand, and of the "waters" (*ha-maim*) and the "deep" on the other hand. That which in the first sentence is called "earth", is designated in the second sentence as "waters" and "deep" (bottomless depths). The heights (heaven) and the depths (earth) — as soul-spiritual directions — is the first polarity, the *primal phenomenon* of the world. It is this polarity which gave birth to the primal breathing (*ruach elohim*) of the world: "And the Spirit ("breath") of God (*ruach elohim*) moved upon the face of the waters."

In the beginning was the breathing — the upward and downward moving breath of the exalted and the humble, of the striving to be active together with God, and the striving to mirror him.

But the mirroring essence, the "water" of the "earth", although moving in breathing, did not reflect. "And the earth was without form and void (*tohu va-bohu*), and darkness was upon the face of the

deep." The earth was formless and void of content, which meant
that it did not reflect. It was mantled in darkness. "Darkness"
means absence of reflection. And reflection means consciousness.
For consciousness is the capacity for reflection. To become conscious of something means to have it inwardly present as a reflection.
Consciousness is light, i.e. the reflective activity above ("heaven")
mirrored in the reflecting medium ("water"). It presupposes two principles: an active one that is reflected, and a passive one that reflects.
Thus the brain — and the body altogether — is the reflecting principle
in man, and his "inner life" is the reflection both of the outer world
and also of the soul's inner world.

The world was sunk in sleep; it breathed, but was unconscious.
The darkness over the deep is absence of reflection, i.e. unconsciousness. The creative primal words: "Let there be light", are the awakening words for the sleeping world. It signifies the same as "wake up",
i.e. the deed of waking or the awakening of consciousness. The
sleeping world wrapped in darkness was woken to consciousness
by the words "Let there be light", i.e. the "waters" began to reflect
and the "earth" was no longer formless and void (*tohu va-bohu*).
The spirits of the hierarchies were awakened out of the sleep of
their "rest in God" — and so there was light, the consciousness of the
world.

The "darkness", however, which preceded the light of which
the second sentence of *Genesis* speaks, is not absence of light, but
unreflectable light — that is, the absolute light of the Godhead.

An inkling of the essence of that "darkness" of the first day of
creation which preceded the reflectable light, can be had from the
writings of St. John of the Cross, when he speaks of the "night of
the spirit" as the blinding, absolute light of the Godhead. The same
is true of the "negative theology" of Dionysus the Areopagite, where,
concerning God, only that can be spoken of (i.e. brought to consciousness) which He is not. Also, in the so-called *Corpus Hermeti-
cum* (the collection of writings and fragments attributed to Hermes
Trismegistus) can be found the teaching about "perfect night", the
gift which precedes the highest gnosis. The Cabbala, too, transmits
a teaching about the lightless, highest spiritual experience, which
it calls the "burden", the "burden of silence" (*dumah*). This is the
highest of the six stages of prophetic revelation: appearance, vision,
revelation, countenance, word, and burden (*Zohar* II, 130b). This
"burden", which is lightless, wordless, and motionless, wholly corresponds to the "spiritual night" of St. John of the Cross. It is the absolute
light that is too great to be reflectable, i.e. that "darkness" in which
the world was mantled at the beginning of the first day of creation.

This darkness was the absolute light of the Godhead which "moved upon the face of the waters".

Then sounded the divine words: "Let there be light", and the absolute light was supplemented by the relative light of the spiritual hierarchies, woken out of the darkness of "resting in God"; there appeared the seraphim, cherubim, thrones, dominions, mights, powers, principalities, archangels, and angels. Consciousness, that is, reflectable light, appeared or came forth out of the darkness of the absolute divine light. The world became a stage for consciousness, a stage for the revelation of the toned-down divine light embracing the spiritual hierarchies, who were called forth by the Word, the Logos, from their "rest in the Absolute", to come forth into the relative light.

And this call of the divine Word, the Logos, which awakened the hierarchies on the first day of creation, resounded powerfully again in the call of the Word-made-flesh: "Lazarus, come forth", at the raising of Lazarus in the seventh miracle of the *Gospel of St. John*. The Lazarus miracle is that of the calling forth of light out of darkness. It signifies the awakening of consciousness for all that which is relative — relative for the soul immersed in "rest in the Absolute", in the sleep of death. This miracle at the same time encompasses the six preceding miracles, for Lazarus was not only a soul and spirit who was called back; he was also a corpse — that is, blind, deaf, and without movement. Thus each miracle was repeated in his case: the miracle of the healing of the man born blind; the miracle of the reinstatement of an independent bearing (the walking on the water); the miracle of nourishment, i.e. the regeneration of the used up and devastated organic substances of the body (the miracle of the feeding of the five thousand); the miracle of the reinstatement of movement (the healing of the paralysed man); the miracle of the healing of sickness (which in this case had led to death) through the regeneration of "vertical heredity" issuing from the new Adam (the healing of the nobleman's son); and, lastly, the miracle of the changing of water into wine, by which the liquids in the body were transformed into circulating warm blood.

Just as the first day of creation in essence contains and encompasses the entire account of the creation, so does the seventh miracle of St. John's Gospel contain and encompass the other six miracles. It is the archetype of the sacrament of extreme unction, the sacrament for the dying, which is directed toward future resurrection — thereby in essence containing and encompassing the other six sacraments.

Because the following chapter is devoted exclusively to the Lazarus miracle, we will close here our brief consideration of the relationship between the miracles of the *Gospel of St. John* and the days of creation in *Genesis*. This is intended to serve the purpose of providing a cosmic-spiritual background as the foundation for further considerations. For, in fact, up to now we have been concerned with a preparatory exercise to stimulate the endeavour of deepening thought. This more profound level of thought will be required of the earnest reader in the considerations which follow.

II

THE MIRACLE OF
THE RAISING OF LAZARUS

1. FORGETTING, SLEEP, AND DEATH

We are accustomed to saying that sleep is the younger brother of death. It would be just as correct, however, to say that forgetting is the younger brother of sleep. For, death is the general human experience whereby one of our fellow men disappears from the realm of sense-perception and plunges into the darkness of the unseen. Similarly, sleep is the experience of consciousness disappearing from the region of perception and deeds, while the unconscious bodily form permeated with its own life remains in the realm of sense-perception. Analogously, forgetting is the subjective experience of the disappearance of certain contents of the mind from the realm of consciousness and their diving down into the darkness of the unconscious, while the continuity of the "conscious being" as a whole remains intact. Forgetting is a partial sleep of the conscious mind, while sleep is a complete forgetting of consciousness. And remembrance is a partial awakening of the conscious mind, while awakening from sleep is a remembrance of consciousness itself, as a whole. Moreover, dying is a forgetting or sleep which embraces the whole human being, including life-functions and bodily form. Death is the process of "forgetting" which extends as far as the body. It is the third stage of forgetting. Forgetting, sleep, and death belong to the same family; they are brothers, that is—stages of basically one and the same process. Sleep, in this sense, is the younger brother of death; and forgetting, in the same sense, is the younger brother of sleep.

Now, forgetting is not a final and irreversible event; for things which have become forgotten can be recalled to memory. Indeed a continuous to-and-fro of forgetting and remembering occurs in the inner life of the human being. Actually, all the contents of consciousness—all ideas, thoughts, and fancies which fill the mind— slip down again and again into the darkness of the unconscious; on occasion they then re-emerge from there into the conscious mind, i.e.

they are remembered. Indeed, forgetting is a prerequisite for any concentration of attention on a particular matter. For instance, if I have to do a simple task involving calculation, I have to eliminate from my mind (that is, forget) everything I know about theology, philosophy, psychology, history, and art. All this and many more things of my personal life-experience then fall away into the darkness of unconsciousness during the time in which I devote myself to my task of reckoning. Only afterward do they become accessible to my conscious mind again. Not that I would have had them all simultaneously present in consciousness. They remain waiting in the dark region of the unconscious, but, as it were, within "arm's reach". I know that I can call them back at any time into consciousness from the darkness of the unconscious.

However, when the to-and-fro of forgetting and remembering is disturbed, i.e. when one cannot forget, or is unable to call something back into memory, then it it a matter of an abnormal state. In this case either an idea becomes "fixed" — then it becomes, as it were, like Ahasuerus, the eternal Jew who cannot die — or else it cannot be brought back from the realm of unconsciousness into the mind. Then a partial amnesia is present, where, as with Orpheus, one cannot bring Eurydice back out of Hades, so to say. These two conditions — the fixed idea and the partial amnesia — are analogous to sleeplessness and to sleeping sickness. For sleeplessness is analogous to being unable to forget, and not being able to keep awake is analogous to not being able to remember.

Whatever may be the cause and manner of the disturbance in the to-and-fro across the threshold which divides consciousness from the unconscious, psychological research into the subconscious has been able to establish beyond any doubt that in reality there is no such thing as forgetting. Thus, those ideas which have vanished altogether from the realm of waking consciousness — i.e. which have been "forgotten" — do indeed enter into that region which for ordinary consciousness appears "unconscious"; but there they live on. Things which have long been forgotten can (for example, by way of hypnosis) be conjured up again.

It is similar with the apparent extinction of consciousness in sleep. Who has not had the experience which comes to expression in the adage: "Morning time has a golden chime"? — that is, of experiencing one state of mind on going to sleep and a changed state on waking up? In this case one cannot help admitting that during the time of sleep a process of consciousness has taken place, whose results and fruits one finds on awakening. It is not that one remembers these processes or the work of consciousness done during deep sleep. (They are not reflected because the brain, which acts as a mirror, was out of operation.) Nevertheless, one confronts the fact of a changed state of mind resulting from a process of consciousness that took place in the dark, during sleep. If someone goes to sleep depressed, plagued by doubts and indecision, and then awakens with clear insight and a firm decision, how can this person doubt that something important took place with (and within) his consciousness, which was apparently "extinguished" during sleep?

Not only theosophists, anthroposophists, and occultists of all shades (eastern and western) maintain that there is continuity of consciousness during deep sleep. It is fairly widespread as a matter of human experience. If this is heeded, it teaches that consciousness during the sleep-state does indeed cease being reflected by the brain, but that during this time it lives on and even proves capable of "learning". It is a fact that there is neither a "forgetting", in the sense of a complete disappearance of memory-content, nor does there exist a "sleep", in the sense of a temporary extinction of consciousness as a whole.

Now we will turn to the "older brother" of sleep and of forgetting — death. Can it be basically different in the case of death, than in the case of sleep and forgetting? All religion, whether it be Christian, Judaic, or Islamic — also Hinduism, Buddhism, and even the ancient "heathen" religions and the religion of "primitive peoples" — teaches and taught at all times and everywhere, that the dissolution of the physical body (the human being's mirroring apparatus) does not in itself bring with it the disappearance or extinction of consciousness. It is the same as far as thinkers were concerned. The greatest of them always had the same conviction, with the exception of those who have elevated the empirical scientific method to a world-conception under the name of "materialism", thereby sacrificing all thought concerning the essential problems of existence. What was at first a methodological renunciation turned later into disavowal. Self-chosen empiricism, as a method of research, led to the renunciation of metaphysical research; this resulted in agnosticism. And agnosticism transformed itself in time into a denial of metaphysical reality altogether; this resulted in materialism as a confession of faith.

However, all representatives of human spiritual life who have taken the problem of death seriously, and who themselves are worthy of being taken seriously, have recognized the continued existence of consciousness after death, as well as its continued existence in the state of sleep, and furthermore the continued existence of forgotten memories. For forgetting, sleep, and death are stages of manifestation of one and the same process.

This fact is emphasized in the St. John's Gospel account of the miracle of the raising of Lazarus. Here, after the sisters Martha and Mary had sent the message to Jesus about the sickness of their brother Lazarus, something remarkable took place: "When he (Jesus) heard that he was ill, he stayed two days longer in the place where he was" (*John* xi, 6). After the two days had passed, Jesus tells his disciples: "Our friend Lazarus has fallen asleep, but I go, that I may awake him out of sleep" (xi, 11). Not until later does he say to the disciples: "Lazarus is dead" (xi, 14).

The abiding "in the place where he was", as a reaction to the news of the sickness of Lazarus, whom he loved, was a deed of conscious forgetting, of consciously allowing a state of forgetting of the sickness and of the sick person to prevail, while he waited for two days before going to Bethany to heal him. The information was given to the disciples that the forgotten friend, Lazarus, was asleep. Not until later were they told that Lazarus had died.

The story of the Lazarus miracle gives the impression that the "door of forgetting" had been opened, so that Lazarus might sleep and so that his sleep might lead over into death. This impression is strengthened and becomes a certainty when one considers what, in this connection, the words of Jesus mean: "This sickness is not unto death, but for the glory of God, that the Son of God might be glorified thereby" (xi, 4), which he spoke right at the beginning when he received the news of the sickness of Lazarus, and also the words: "And for your sake I am glad that I was not there, so that you may believe; nevertheless let us go unto him" (xi, 15), which follow immediately after the news that Lazarus had died. The former words ("this sickness is not unto death") reveal a divine dispensation over and above forgetting, sleep, and death, using them as tools for something greater than the mere healing of sickness. The latter words ("I am glad that I was not there") are related to more than an outer physical or bodily presence; they refer to an absence in a full and real sense, just as the subsequent "but I go" is to be taken in a full and real sense. Jesus did not go to the nobleman's son to heal him, but he was there in the sense that he healed him from a distance through the intermediary of the father's faith. This means that in the case of the nobleman's son it was not his spatial presence or nearness which effected the miracle of healing, but his spiritual presence. Why, in the case of Lazarus, did it have to go into the realm of forgetting, as the door to sleep and death?

That a work of highest significance was to be accomplished, enhanced through the stages of forgetting, sleep, and death – i.e. that it was the will of the Master that this should happen to Lazarus – was comprehended by Thomas, called the Twin, in that he said to the other disciples: "Let us also go, that we may die with him" (xi, 16). In other words: Let us share the fate of Lazarus, since it is the will of the Master — the will which can only intend the highest good.

This utterance on the part of Thomas is at the same time a key to an understanding of the sickness of Lazarus from which he died. For Thomas does not say "Let us commit suicide", but "let us also go, that we may die *with him*" — i.e. let us put ourselves into the inner situation of Lazarus, *identify ourselves with his path of destiny*, so that we also may die. This proposal or call to the disciples would have been senseless, if it had simply been the case of an ordinary sickness — if it had been, say, pneumonia following a chill, or else some contagious disease. For then, only suicide would have made sense. But what Thomas means in the *way*, the path of destiny of Lazarus which led to death and so obviously accords with the will of the Master.

Lazarus died as a result of the way which he had taken, so that when Thomas says: "Let us go also, that we may die", he means the same way which led to death. He means too: Let us take the same path as Lazarus.

The path of Lazarus, his "sickness", which ended with death, was an excess of spirituality. If human life is a pendulum-swing between the moment and eternity, then Lazarus had — in spirit, soul, and body — chosen eternity completely and radically. His breathing became ever more "vertical" — that is, it took place increasingly in the direction above-below and became ever more shallow in the direction outer-inner, until it stood still, i.e. until he died. The force of attraction of the eternal Divine Trinity was so strong for Lazarus that he had no interest in the life of the moment, including breathing and nourishment; also his bodily functions became "paralysed", so to say, in the breath of eternity. Viewed from outside, the sickness of Lazarus consisted of a fading away. Seen from within, however, it was a yearning which embraced and took hold of the whole human being (spirit, soul, and body) — a yearning for the absolute values of eternity, accompanied by the loss or forfeiting of all relationship to the relative values of transiency.

Only when we comprehend the sickness and death of Lazarus in this manner can we appreciate and understand, not only what Thomas meant when he said to the other disciples "Let us also go, that we may die with him", but also what was really signified by the call of the Master: "Lazarus, come forth," which effected the miracle of his raising. It is the call of remembrance for the suffering earth, and for mankind languishing in toil, suffering, and death. One can acquire a sense for this call, which came forth out of eternity for the sake of the toil, pain, and transience of the moment, when one considers that in the Holy Mass (before the over-hasty changes in the liturgy instituted after the Second Vatican Council), when the Creed was read or sung, it was only at the words *et homo factus est* ("and he became man") that the people kneeled. It is a matter here of reverence for the exalted humility of love on the part of the Son, who is of like essence with the Father, and "by whom all things were made", who through the Holy Spirit became incarnate from the Virgin Mary and was made man. Here one kneels (*hic genuflectitur*) because there is no greater love than that of the sacrifice of eternity for the limitations of existence in the transient moment.

And it was this love, this greatness, which sounded in the call: "Lazarus, come forth!" It brought the miracle to pass, not only of the raising from the dead, but also the still greater miracle of the sacrifice of eternity for the sake of the passing moment. *Hic genuflectitur.*

2. REMEMBRANCE, AWAKENING, AND RESURRECTION

Forgetting, sleep, and death are stages of basically the same process. Now, in contradistinction to them stand remembrance, awakening, and resurrection. Just as forgetting, sleep, and death are stages of an apparent disappearance into the darkness of a realm held to be unconscious by normal day-consciousness, disappearing beyond waking experience, so do remembrance, awakening, and resurrection signify basically the one single process of reappearance, the return of what had been submerged in the darkness of the unconscious. Let us look into this more closely, beginning with the process of remembrance.

To remember means to call back into the inner arena of waking consciousness an idea which had previously descended into the darkness of forgetting. This means that it is fetched out of the dark realm of the unconscious into the conscious mind, i.e. across the threshold which separates the conscious from the unconscious. Actually, in every process of remembering we have a kind of "raising from the dead", a conjuring up of a departed one or one in the depths of sleep. It is an act which repeats on a small scale what took place on a large scale on the first day of creation. There "darkness reigned upon the face of the waters" and then the primal creative Word resounded: "Let there be light!" Similarly, the dead Lazarus was called out of the dark sepulchre into the daylight of human life by the cry of Jesus: "Lazarus, come forth!"

The analogy becomes especially convincing when the remembering activity of memory fully reveals its true nature. For memory, like thinking, reveals itself at first incompletely — at the beginning of life's path, in childhood—and does not reach maturity (i.e. the stage of revealing its true nature) until a more advanced age. Just as we judge the quality of thinking (for instance of Kant) by the thought achievements of his advanced years—and not by those of his childhood or early youth—so too it is the memory-life of older years, and not that of youth, which is the measure for knowing the nature of memory. The "how" of remembering reveals itself more in accordance with its true nature in later years, just as the nature of thinking, in its depth and purity, manifests itself more in maturity than in youth. For both thinking and memory are at first, at an early age, volatile. Thoughts and memories pop into consciousness as if automatically, quite by themselves. They both happen as if of themselves, without being directed or activated by conscious will. In a manner of speaking, thoughts and memories "haunt" the minds of young people. They arise mainly on the basis of laws of association, but more mechanically rather than as consciously-working lines of relation (attraction) or non-relation (repulsion) of ideas and thoughts among themselves. The association of ideas is a "will-of-the-wisp" process which can indeed be of significance, symptomatically, e.g. for depth psychology, in as much as it shows the subconscious predispositions and tendencies of people; but it is—unless it be directed and controlled—not a path of attainment that leads anywhere. Neither does it have any general validity; it is and remains completely subjective. Thus, for example, a person who sees some milk can allow to arise in his mind the picture of a cat sipping milk out of a saucer, while another person may have before him instead the image of a cow being milked, and a third could have in his mind, say, the picture of a baby sucking milk from a bottle. This mosaic of pictures and images, which arise quite by themselves and string themselves together, renders useful service in outer practical life. It makes much material available to consciousness at any given moment, presenting a choice of what is needed. It is not convenient to be so well served that when one thinks of a particular person, his name, his address, and his telephone number arise spontaneously in the mind.

This mechanical memory is especially active in early years. Yes, what we ordinarily mean by a "good memory" is the smooth functioning of this mechanical form of memory.

Now, as age advances, this type of memory gradually recedes and is replaced in growing measure by another sort of memory—logical memory. One remembers more by way of reasoned thought-combinations, than by way of the automatically functioning association of ideas. One hardly forgets what one has understood and incorporated into a system built up around a concept. And should one forget something of it, then it is easy to recall it again by means of thoughtful consideration. Here the process of remembrance is ruled, directed, and controlled by thinking. It is the meaningful significance of the role which a given fact plays in the structured thought life which makes it unforgettable or memorable. However, the "logical memory" is, in comparison with the wealth of "mechanical memory", poorer — especially in people who have not developed any intensive thinking-life, i.e. in the majority of people. For if one only remembers things which one has carefully considered, or which on consideration have shown themselves to be significant, then countless other things, which one either has not considered or which on consideration have not had any thought-provoking or symptomatic significance, vanish from memory. So the life of memory grows deeper, indeed, in "logical memory", but more circumscribed than in "mechanical memory" — the latter in any case being more superficial. For this reason we often speak — with a sigh — of the "weakening of memory" in old age, in comparison with the "good memory" of early youth. But we forget the fact that the strength of memory in early youth consists mainly in its receptivity, in its quick, but not at all prolonged retention. So it was that the present writer, when he was seven years old, spent a summer vacation of some two months in a foreign country and learned to speak its language fluently. However, when he returned ten years later to that same country, he understood not a word of that tongue. We learn easily in youth, but we forget just as easily. For the ebb and flow of the automatically functioning memory takes place quite by itself, and does not require much effort of thought or moral endeavour on the part of the human being himself.

In old age a further refinement of the memory process takes place. The predominantly "logical memory" of middle age is gradually replaced in older years by "moral memory". The force which calls back into the light of consciousness those things which are submerged in the darkness of oblivion is then neither the automatic "gadding about" of the free play of associations, nor the logical demands of thinking, but the moral faculty of love. Thereby the capacity of the life of memory contracts quantitatively still further, especially in the case of people who have not developed an intensive moral life. For just as the "logical memory" can be experienced as a contraction of the memory faculty in people who have developed no intensive thought-life up to middle age, so too can the stage of "moral memory" in later years be experienced as a contraction or shrivelling of the memory faculty in those people who, upon reaching old age, have not developed an intensive moral life and who have no intense "inwardness of the heart". Then "weakness of memory in old age" is spoken of. But what actually happens is that the people in question have neglected in their development to keep step with that gradual process of "turning inward" which the successive stages of life demand. For the biologically based energy which operates in the automatic memory of early youth loses intensity in middle age, and the gap caused by this should be filled by the energy of thought. Then with the further passage of the years it happens that people's thought-life — if it was intensive — concentrates itself on the more significant things, ultimately on that which is most significant, and interest in a thousand-and-one problems of second- or third-rate importance gradually fades. Thus the thought-life becomes deeper and more intense, not in breadth of horizon, but in depth and height. Thereby a chasm is made in the memory activity in the dimension of breadth, to the extent of this activity in the dimension of depth. This, in turn, should be filled out by a more human (that is, a more inwardly refined) energy, in the same way as the retraction of the automatic biological energy of "mechanical memory" demands the substitution of the more inward energy of thinking.

The intellect, as the driving force of the middle stage of refinement of the life of memory, is replaced at this third stage by the heart. The moral memory of old age is where the process of memory (that is, the calling up of memories out of the darkness of the unconscious into the life of consciousness) no longer takes place through associative or logical combinations but rather through moral connections. There the voice which calls up memories from the depths of darkness is the voice of the heart. All those things which we love are not forgotten. It is the stage of memory through love. And the more threads of warmth of the heart stretching in all directions of existence to beings and things in the world, the more comprehensive, clear, and profound is moral memory.

Now, it is really the case — as a matter of experience — with these three stages of memory, that although they come to the fore mainly in three consecutive stages of life, they are at the same time present during the whole of life — in three layers, as it were. Even a very young person has the moral memory belonging to old age, as well as the logical memory of middle age. On the other hand an elderly person also possesses to a certain extent the associative, automatic memory and even more so the logical memory. The three forms of memory described here, then, are layers of the memory-life, of which the topmost level is the so-called "mechanical memory", the next deeper level the "logical memory", and the deepest the "moral memory". And it is the deepest level, the essential being of memory, which plays the predominant role in advanced age, while the middle level — logical memory — predominates in middle age, as the first and most on-the-surface level does in youth.

The real essence of memory, however, reveals itself most completely in moral memory, because it is the most inward, the most profound, and the least superficial. Here memory's inner operative power and seed-potential show themselves undisguised. There is nothing mechanical here, nothing impenetrable to consciousness takes place, nothing schematic (i.e. no abstract shadowy symbolism lacking dimension). Here there is the inner moral magic of the recalling out of the darkness of forgetting into life in the light of consciousness, in the sense of call: "Lazarus, come forth!" It is the magic of love which reveals itself here.

Now, if sleep is the "older brother" of forgetting, then awakening is the "older brother" of remembering. The sleeping person is someone who has forgotten himself — his whole being and consciousness — from top to toe. And the awakening from sleep is like a process of recalling himself to memory. His total consciousness emerges out of the depths of sleep's darkness, just like an idea emerges at the moment of remembrance out of the darkness of forgetting into the light of consciousness.

The analogy of remembrance with awakening is not limited to the mere fact of this emergence from the darkness of forgetting and of sleep, it extends further and deeper. For just as we can distinguish in the process of memory layers of the automatic, the logical, and the moral — so also there are layers in the process of awakening. One can actually awaken further and more wisely than is the case in the automatically operating awakening which takes place when we have slept our fill. When awakening happens of itself — either when one has slept one's fill or else when one is awakened by impressions impinging on one's senses from the external world — one actually only awakens to a certain degree. It is a fairly superficial awakening which then takes place. Deeper levels of the human being — of his consciousness — sleep on. Yes, it is an indisputable fact of experience that in the case of many — of most — people, a full awakening is never reached. Certain deep levels of consciousness sleep continuously within them. So, for instance, it is a fact that most people live their whole lives through as if they were never going to die. They are awake, indeed, to the reality of the outer sense-world with its requirements, tasks, joys, sufferings, worries, and temptations, but they are asleep to the reality of death. They all "know", it is true, that they are mortal; but this "knowledge" exists as a mere shadowy dream. It is an ineffective, deferred, and repressed knowledge which differs enormously from the knowledge that tomorrow I shall move into the new house which I bought for myself. With regard to the latter knowledge I am awake, while in regard to the former I am asleep or dozing. And yet death is the only absolutely sure fact in the destiny of every human being. This everyone "knows" and yet does not know, because he does not allow its weight and meaning to reach the full intensity of day-consciousness.

What is true for this example of the fact of death, is true also for many other things which, by outwardly awake people, are "dozed" through. For, the superficial, self-propelled awakening from sleep is not a full awakening; certain parts of human consciousness sleep on. Something must be added to the automatic functioning of awakening so that it may become more complete. This something is basically the strength and effectiveness of that pondering which we will call "meditation".

The human being can, by concentrated pondering, by meditation, actually awaken more fully than he does by the so called "natural" or automatic awakening from sleep in the morning. Meditation is a means for arousing the slumbering deeper layers of consciousness which otherwise remain sunk in sleep even after the outer "natural" awakening. Through meditation we begin to awaken for the range and significance of the things of outer and inner experience. It is the putting into practice — consciously permitting it to effect one — of the power of truth.

It is the working of the power of truth which causes a wider awakening of consciousness than the waking which happens automatically every morning. It is that which makes it possible for us to reach the second stage of awakening. It is the stage of awakening to the truth of experience.

A further stage of awakening can be reached by means of the following: the thought-permeated meditation which initially is directed toward knowledge grows deeper and more inward through becoming gradually transformed from a process of cognition into a process of conscience. It grows more and more moral, i.e the meditation turns from being a matter of the head to become a matter of the heart. It turns within and is deepened by leaving the realm of concentrated bright thought-light and entering one of clear and warm conscience-light. The deep and clear meditative thinking becomes transformed into an *exercitium spirituale*, a spiritual exercise, which in time can bring the whole being of man to an awakening: the whole thinking, feeling, and willing human being. The awakening of the total human being — down to the deepest layers of his will — is just what the *exercitia spiritualia* of St. Ignatius of Loyola intend and effect. The human being who has passed through them is in a special position in that he can allow himself, without batting an eyelid, to open himself to any experience and to take up any path of investigation or study without fear or danger for his spiritual-moral convictions. All experiences and all true research can only enrich and deepen him — never can they damage his religious conviction and ideals. He is open for everything, but not to be influenced by anything or for anything — not liable to suggestion, incorruptible. For he is awakened and fully conscious of the significance and range of the works of redemption. This is something which can only be compared with the transformation which happened to the apostles after the event of Whitsun. For the event of Whitsun brought with it an awakening which actually made the disciples into apostles — unshakeably secure, and ready for every effort and for every sacrifice.

This awakening is thus a vast process, certainly containing the automatic waking from nightly sleep, but reaching far beyond it. Its nature reveals itself most fully in the wakening voice of conscience, whose magic awakens the deepest levels of the human being, his actual core, sunk in the darkness of sleep, awakening it to the realm of activity in the present. It calls it forth out of the darkness of the unconscious into the light of consciousness. And the power which effects this is rooted fundamentally in the divine creative Word: "Let there be light!" — and consequently also in the divine-human redemptive Word: "Lazarus, come forth!"

Now, if it is a fact that what is forgotten can be brought back to mind, and that what is sleeping can be awakened, how is it with regard to what has died? If there be a return from the realm of forgetting and from the realm of sleep, shall there be no return from the realm of death? Is there no possibility of a reappearance, analogous to that of remembrance and awakening, for those who have died?

Faith in the resurrection from the dead is the affirmative answer to this question. Just as Jesus Christ, first-born of the resurrection, rose again — so will all the dead arise in good time. It will be the lot of all those who have died to emerge again from the realms of forgetting, sleep, and death, i.e. to appear "remembered", "woken" and revived, gifted with form, countenance, glance, voice, and the power of word and deed — just as was the resurrected Jesus Christ. The concept, idea, and ideal of resurrection is different from the concept, idea, and ideal of eternal life, as a resting in God, where the soul returns to the "Father's house" and remains there for all eternity. Resurrection is not merely the end of the old, but actually means the beginning of a new world-creation — with "a new heaven and a new earth". It is not the soul's rest in eternity, not the eternal rest of Nirvana, but an active cooperation with God in a renewed world, healed of the consequences of the Fall into sin. The "new Jerusalem" is a new world-order related to the old one in the same way as the resurrected man is related to mortal man. The resurrection may be conceived of as the reappearance and active participation of the total human being—as spirit, soul, and body—in the domain of the "world-in-progress". As an idea, the resurrection is the realisation that God is divinely generous, that he does not take away again what he has once given and granted, but that his gifts—existence, consciousness, freedom, and creative activity—are valid for all eternity. Therefore existence will never be taken from anyone—all are immortal. Consciousness will never cease—the continuity of consciousness is eternal. Freedom will be maintained for all eternity—with all the endless possibilities for its use and misuse, reaching to highest heaven and to deepest hell. Always, in all eternity, there will exist for each and every being a creative work and a field for creative work.

The resurrection—as an ideal—is the "alchemical ideal" of the Great Work: the transformation of all ignoble things into the most noble, the changing of evil into good, of constraint into freedom, of the ideal into the active, of sleeping into waking, of death into life. It is not the ideal of releasing the individual soul from the world of constraint, sickness, and death, but the ideal of freeing the world from constraint, from sickness, and from death.

A Utopian ideal? It may seem so to many, but if having an ideal is a matter of importance, then this is the only one worth having. For it is divinely lofty, and there lives in the consciousness of humanity nothing more noble, more capable of arousing enthusiasm for all that is good, true, and beautiful, than this ideal. It is the heart of Christianity itself, and lies at the basis of all other religions as light, as warmth, and as life.

Such is the concept, the idea, and the ideal of resurrection. Seen in the light of this concept, this idea and this ideal, the raising of Lazarus is not the resurrection of Lazarus. For it is not Lazarus but Jesus Christ who is the first begotten of the resurrection. What happened with Lazarus was his awakening from death, i.e. the miracle of the calling back of his soul-spirit being into his healed body. It was the highest miracle of the healing of spirit, soul, and body which was performed on Lazarus—of healing, but not of resurrection. Lazarus died later on, at his appointed time. He was healed and re-awakened, but he remained mortal like all other human beings.

Aside from Lazarus, other individuals who had died (for instance, the daughter of Jairus and the Youth of Nain) were awakened by Christ. The apostles, also, raised some from the dead after the event of Whitsun. In all these cases it was not a question of resurrection, but of re-awakening (*John* xi, 11).

When it is a matter of the reappearance in earthly circumstances of persons who had passed through the gate of death, the Gospels use four different words, namely, "arise", "appear", "awaken", "resurrect". Thus Herod was told by some that Jesus was John who had arisen, by others that Elias had appeared, and by others again, that one of the ancient prophets had resurrected (*Luke*, ix, 8).

And that these opinions of people were basically no illusion was substantiated by Jesus Christ himself when he said of John the Baptist: "And if you are willing to accept it, he is Elijah who is to come", (*Matthew* xi, 14). *Re-awakened* is an individual who, after he has died, is called back into the same — now healed — body, so that he takes up again in the same destiny-situation the life which was interrupted by death, and carries it on until the hour of his truly destined death. This was the case with Lazarus. *Arisen* is one who has died long ago and now manifests again by being re-born — by coming back into a new body. *Re-appearance* means either a perceptible manifestation from the supersensible, or else the working with and through an embodied human being, of a spirit being who is not incorporated. This being then works — inspiring and enlightening — with and through the embodied person with whom it stands in a deep inner connection. *Resurrection*, lastly, means the confluence of all three above mentioned forms of reappearance in a fourth condition, in which spirit, soul, and body are equally deathless, i.e. when the body is so spiritualized and ensouled that it no longer shares the mortality of nature but partakes of the immortality of spirit and soul. The first-begotten of the resurrection, the Risen One, was on the one hand as free from earthly constraints as one who had died; on the other hand, he was just as capable of operating and working in the earthly realm as an embodied human being. Thus he could appear in a house whose doors were locked and, after having thus appeared, could not only allow himself to be seen, heard, and touched, but could also partake of a meal with the people gathered there. The body of the Resurrected One does not "consist" of matter, but rather it is the faculty — belonging to the soul and to the spirit — of materializing and making use of matter formatively and functionally. He is not the result of a composite of materials, but rather the power which gathers, forms, and moves them. He is master over matter.

One can have an inkling of a concept of the nature of the resurrection-body when one considers that matter is nothing other than concentrated energy, and if one proceeds further to the insight that energy is nothing but concentrated consciousness (i.e. will), just as matter is concentrated, consolidated energy. Then one reaches the insight that "will" lies at the basis of all matter, and that feeling and thinking underlie all will; and that as energy can be changed into matter and matter into energy, so also will is changeable into energy and matter, and conversely, matter and energy are changeable into will. Now, imagine that a body ("and his grave was empty") were totally changed into will, and you have an inkling as to what on the one hand happened with the body of Jesus, and on the other hand of what the body of the Risen One was made. In it, matter was redeemed, i.e. the will, previously bound in the matter of the body, became free. And this freed will was capable at any time of taking the path to materialization and back again into dematerialization or dissolution. Thus the Risen One appears and disappears as he wills. He controls the processes of formation and dissolution. He is master of life and death. For every time when he materializes and takes on sense-perceptible form he repeats in a moment the whole process of incarnation and growth, and every time he dissolves again the created form, he rapidly repeats the whole process of dissolution which happens in and after death. Thus he is master of embodiment and disembodiment — of coming into existence and going out of it again — of life and death.

That this actually is so can be ascertained from the fact that the Risen One did not appear in the likeness of Jesus, as those nearest to him had known him immediately before the Crucifixion and earlier; that is, not as the resuscitated or re-awakened Jesus who had been crucified, nor the Jesus who had been baptised in the Jordan — but Jesus in a new form. For this reason those people who had known him recognised him only by some intimate sign. Thus, Mary Magdalena, who at first took him for a gardener, recognised him only by the manner in which he pronounced her name "Mary". Thomas recognised him when the Risen One showed him the marks of his wounds. The two disciples from Emmaus knew him in the breaking of bread. It was always through a sign that the Risen One let himself be known. For the form and appearance of the Risen One differed from Jesus of Nazareth through the fact of being timeless and ageless. His countenance was simply the expression of his being — of his spirit and his soul — and could only be recognised by those who through the sheath of his bodily self had known something of his true being, his soul, and his spirit. And the signs by which the Risen One let himself be known were such as to give — to those persons who were to recognize him — a pointer and an indication toward their personal earlier experience and knowledge of the soul-spiritual being of Jesus. They were reminded of their earlier experience and knowledge of the being of Jesus Christ.

The state of the risen Jesus Christ is the goal and the hope of the path of destiny of mankind. It is the most perfect ideal of which one could ever think or dream. For it unites the most far reaching hopes of the noblest ideals of this world with the highest and deepest ideals of the world beyond. In it are wedded life and death (this world and the next) with that which is the glory (*gloria, doxa*) of the breath of eternal life, where embodiment and disembodiment are an in-and-out breathing.

Now it is so, that just as the flower blossoms suddenly, although it has been prepared for a long time in the bud and in the whole organism of the plant — and is the result of a long many-staged process of preparation — so also the resurrection, although it may happen of a sudden (*sono tubae*) is all the same the result of a long, many-staged process of preparation. In the depths of man's spirit-soul-bodily being the resurrection matures through thousands of years of the life of mankind. Preceding its full revelation are stages which are oriented toward and related to it. So, for instance, certain departed human beings keep the faculty and possibility of participating actively in earthly events. They do not "vanish" wholly into the beyond, as is the case with most departed ones, but somehow keep their "earthly citizenship" with the right to participate actively in earthly events. We mean here the canonized and non-canonized saints. (The canonized saints, i.e. those who have been officially declared so by the Church, are only the representative types of corresponding groups of saints who have not themselves been canonized; there exist more saints than those who have been officially recognised.) It is not a question here of undertaking a theological investigation of the being and significance of the saints or of the veneration accorded to them, or of their role in the work of salvation, but only of considering the facts experienced by that part of mankind which fosters a relationship with them. The extraordinary thing about this relationship is first of all the fact that no one who turns to a saint asking for help would dream of imagining him being steeped "in the blessedness of rest in God". No one turns to a saint on the basis of a self-evident presupposition that he is not blind and deaf to earthly events, but that he has earthly events at heart and is ready, willing, and capable of intervening effectively and helpfully in earthly things when asked to do so. The basic presupposition and conviction underlying intercourse with saints — or the cult of saints, if you will — is that the saints have more life than other departed souls, i.e. that they can do and effect much in earthly realms that other departed ones cannot do . . . yes, that they can even do more than incarnated earthly men with their medicine, their psychotherapy, and their organisations for social welfare and their money. Countless numbers of people have to thank St. Nicholas of Bari, for instance, for wonderful assistance. The same is true of the two other great wonder workers — St. Patrick and St. Gregory the Thaumaturgist — to mention only a few highly effective saints known and recognized far and wide. But it is not possible to determine how large the host of saints is in reality, for not only do new ones join them, but also old ones who have fallen into oblivion or remained anonymous have been rediscovered.

Be that as it may, what is common to all saints is that through the millennia they have kept alive the belief that they, as active beings, are not wholly "departed", have not so much died, are not so "dead" as ordinary people, but that despite death and even thanks to death they can take part in earthly events. The theological argument that it is only their intercession with God which shows itself to be effective, not however their personal intervention in earthly things, makes no difference in the face of the two thousand years' experience of their appearance in dreams and in waking states, the advice and comfort given by them in highly individual forms, and the healings carried out by them — in which certain individual saints have even in a way "specialized" themselves (for example: St. Blasius for throat and mucous membrane diseases). It is self-evident that ultimately all good things come from God. An ordinary doctor or pastor cannot bring about any good unless support of divine origin is given to him. But to reduce the significance of saints to intercession only does not correspond with the experience of generations of people who have lived and still live in communication with saints, and in veneration of them. Experience teaches that the saints accomplish deeds, that they are capable not only of intercession, but also of action. They work just like living people, in spite of the fact that they have died.

On the other hand, from the scientific standpoint it can be argued with a torrent of words and hollow thoughts about the "psychology of the primitives". This term labels those primitive peoples who attach themselves to a belief in spirits and project outward their own psychic tendencies, and thus may come to hallucinations and delusions. This psychic attitude of the primitives can, as a layer, live on within civilized people, etc. Now all this is of course well known, all too well known. In contradiction to it stands the phenomenon of the veneration of saints which has lived for two thousand years and does not allow itself to be confused by this scientific talk. A village priest (I am recounting a fact) was on his way at a late hour to offer the sacrament to one who was dying. He lost his way, and prayed in despair for help, so that he might not arrive too late. There appeared to him St. Nicholas, who led him to the right place at the right time, then vanished. How can this priest accept the "scientific explanation" of a "psychological projection" of a hallucinatory nature, when the whole point was not the vision, but his reaching the dying man in good time? And he did indeed arrive there at the right time.

Regarding the arguments which are brought from Christian protestant circles against the veneration of saints and communication with them, we must say that the surgical amputation of this essential part of the organism of the spiritual life of Christian mankind is a thoroughly regrettable mutilation, signifying a crippling and diminution of that organism. It is also a sheer misunderstanding to view the veneration of saints as a kind of diversion from an immediate relationship to God. For just as love of one's neighbour is no diversion from the love of God, so love of the saints — who are indeed our neighbours — is no diversion from it. The veneration of saints, and intercourse with them, is actually based on nothing else but faith in love as being stronger than death, and consequently that love of your neighbour is stronger than death. This is what we believe when we appeal to the neighbourly love of a departed person, whose neighbourly love (and love of God) we know to be great. For the saints are not gods, but human individuals with a great love that is stronger than death and is therefore capable of working over to here from the beyond. If one believes, however, that brotherly love stands in competition with divine love, or that divine love alone is stronger than death, then one should give up not only the veneration of saints but also, for example, the recourse to medical aid, since this too could be conceived of as being a diversion from a direct relationship to God. For the doctor also stands between the sick person needing help and the healing love of God. If we recognize, however, the justification of a helpful brotherly love on the part of our incarnated fellow men — for example, doctors — so too we should allow the helpful neighbourly love of our disembodied fellow men, the saints, to be justified.

But here it is not a matter of clearing out of the way all the arguments and scruples raised against the veneration of saints, neither do we intend to convert anyone to it — but rather to view the veneration of saints and the communication with them in a new light, which points to the fact of the special position the saints have in comparison with other departed people. This special position consists, namely, in the possession by saints of qualities and capacities which in part they have in common with the Risen Jesus Christ. Their effectiveness in the realm of earthly events speaks of the fact that they stand closer to the state of the Risen One than do others who have died. A stage of maturing towards resurrection — a preparatory process towards resurrection — shows itself in the saints. They are able to act not only in heaven but also on earth. This means, however, that they live on after death, not only as spirits and souls, but also bodily. Admittedly their "resurrection body" has not reached the complete maturity of that of Jesus Christ — in the sense of total concretization. They can function, indeed, yet they work more as "spirits" than as bodily beings; however, they do represent a certain stage on the path to resurrection. They "appear" in the sense of an appearance such as is spoken of in *Luke* ix, 8 in reference to Elias.

The saints represent a stage on the path to resurrection, in so far as they possess a spiritualized and ensouled body, giving them the possibility to manifest, to "appear". However, preceding this there is a stage of "arising" — or return of consciousness — when the soul-spiritual being of the dead person does not make use of his own spiritualized and ensouled body (as is the case with the saints) but plunges down again into the stream of heredity, i.e. incarnates again, by taking on a new body. To a great extent this body stems from the stream of heredity. It is only partially fashioned by the human being himself, in so far as he takes part in forming it by way of the forces of heredity, according to his powers and the level of his development. This body, formed in this way out of the stream of heredity, is not a totally new creation. It is only "new" to the extent that it is a "family-body", "folk-body", or "race-body". In so far as it is individual, it is also the "own body" of the soul-spiritual being who incarnates in it. Having an individualized body thus represents an initial stage on the path of resurrection. The more strongly an individual imprints himself upon his bodily nature, the further advanced he is on the path to resurrection. And the more his body is merely an expression of his family, folk, and race, the further away he is from the ideal of resurrection.

Decisive for the individualization of the body is the structural and functional individualization of those parts of the body which are related to the soul and spirit — that is, the brain and the nervous system, of which the soul and spirit most immediately make use. The individualization of the bodily parts turned toward the outer world — the limbs, the senses, and the physical form — is not so important to begin with. Thus it can happen that a man's outer form appears as an exact copy of the family, folk, and race type, while the inner configuration of his brain and entire nervous system is individual through and through. For instance, Goethe said: "From my father I have my stature and my earnest way of life — from my dear mother, my joyous nature and delight in inventing fables." Nevertheless, the inner configuration of his brain and nervous system was all the same so fashioned that he was capable of developing his mother's "delight in inventing fables" to the heights of creating the *Faust* tragedy, and was able to raise up his "father's stature" to the "Olympian classical heights" of a synthesis of art, science, and religion.

It was the individuality, not the results of heredity, which came to expression in this achievement. Also, he was not referring to heredity when he said: "I hear in myself seeds of sickness since three thousand years," or when in a poem dedicated to Frau Von Stein he wrote: "Once you were my sister or my wife." What was meant was the experience of destiny in repeated lives on earth. The belief in reincarnation is not confined to the world of Buddhism and Hinduism; it extends far beyond their frontiers. But how does the age old and widespread conviction that there are repeated lives on earth relate to the ideal of the resurrection? Does it stand in an irreconcilable contradiction to the ideal of resurrection and to the path which leads to it? Or does it represent an aspect of that ideal and a stage on the path of its realization? Does it have a place within the organism of the resurrection's work of salvation, or does it not fit in at all?

First we must point out and emphasize that reincarnation, or the repetition of lives on earth is not an ideal; it does not even qualify as a way of salvation. It is valid merely as a fact which by some is regarded as regrettable; by others, in contrast, it is judged to be necessary. Therefore, although we can place the ideal of resurrection over and against the ideal of *Nirvana* (the release from the wheel of rebirths), we cannot compare faith in reincarnation with the ideal of resurrection. One can do this just as little as one can. For instance, compare the process of repeatedly going to sleep and waking up with the ideal of a righteous and wisdom-filled life. For if justice and wisdom are the end products of someone's life, then they are neither the fruits of a life without sleep, nor of a lifelong sleep, nor of the alternation of sleeping and waking states — but of the use which was made of the opportunities offered by life to foster justice and wisdom. Neither days nor nights are of themselves a path to the ideal, still less an ideal in themselves; it is solely the use which is made of them — and this alone — which counts. Equally, a life of say seventy years is not in itself a path to the ideal — and still less an ideal in itself — just as ten earthly lives each of seventy years are in themselves no path to the ideal, and still less do they represent an ideal.

It is simply the extent of the opportunity for experience which makes a difference. For, just as an eighty-year-old person has had more opportunity to acquire experience and to work upon himself than a twenty-year-old, so has an individual who has lived ten times on earth had comparatively more opportunities than a person allotted only one short life. But the path, i.e. the use made of life's experiences, is something other than the opportunities offered. This is the same for a single life as for many. Whether the path be taken in one life or in many, it is the same path which goes through the stages: Washing of the Feet, Scourging, Crowning with thorns, Carrying the cross, Crucifixion and Entombment, and leading to Resurrection. Whether the purification, enlightenment, and communion with God which are achieved on this path happen in one or in many lives — this changes nothing with regard to the path, nor is anything changed concerning the goal and ideal of this path.

Consequently, neither the opinion that only one life is allotted to man, nor the view that man can live repeatedly on earth, belongs to the truths of salvation, i.e. to dogma or to the unshakable truths of faith (*de fide*). For neither of them has any decisive influence on the cardinal truth concerning resurrection or the path leading to resurrection. Therefore the first viewpoint cannot be maintained as a dogma, but only as a prevailing opinion; and the second view, correspondingly, cannot be considered an erroneous teaching or heresy. ·

The view that the soul of man is newly created by God at awakening from sleep each morning cannot be declared a dogma, i.e. a truth essential to salvation; and the view that it is the same soul which awakens every morning from sleep (and that the soul does not awaken only on one day, but on many) cannot be declared heretical. Analogously, neither can the view that life on earth occurs only once be declared a dogma, nor can the view that earthly lives are repeated be declared a heresy. Neither viewpoint belongs to the body of essential truths of salvation. Rather, they belong to the sphere of the secondary truths of knowledge and experience which are freely open to acceptance or rejection, and to which also the results of scientific, historic, psychological, and philological research belong. As the Ptolemaic conception of the planetary system is not a truth essential to salvation, everyone today is free to conceive of the solar system in a Ptolemaic or Copernican fashion, although for one-and-a-half millennia the Ptolemaic conception was the ruling philosophical and theological opinion. It is also open to us to regard the story of creation in *Genesis* either as a "six days' work" or as a process of evolution lasting millions of years — whereby other possible interpretations also remain open.

The view that repeated earthly lives are possible belongs to the realm of freely acceptable or rejectable opinions. In particular, Jesus Christ himself basically indicated this view by saying to his disciples regarding John: "And if ye will receive it, he is Elijah who was to come" (*Matthew* xi, 13). "If ye will receive it": nothing can more clearly and surely express the fact that the reappearance of Elijah in John — and with it the entire complex of reincarnation — does not belong to the essential truths of salvation, but to the sphere of freely acceptable or rejectable opinions. Correspondingly, the antithesis of reincarnation — that there exists only one single life on earth — also belongs to the realm of opinions freely open for acceptance or rejection.

Now, the teaching of reincarnation, as taught by Theosophy, was pronounced in the twenties of this century by the Congregatio Sancti Officii (now Congregatio Propagandae Doctrinae Fidei) to be foreign to and inconsistent with the Catholic Christian Faith. This pronouncement has a twofold significance: firstly, that reincarnation does not belong to the traditional teaching of the Church; and secondly, that the problems which the teaching of reincarnation claim to solve are solved in a different way by the traditional teachings of the Church.

Concerning the first point, both the Catholic who is convinced of repeated earthly lives, and also the Catholic who is far removed from such a conviction, will without doubt admit that neither the sacred Scriptures, nor the apostles, nor the Church fathers, nor the authoritative teachers of the Church have taught reincarnation, and consequently it does not belong to the body of traditional teachings of the Church — just as little, for example, as does the modern theory of evolution or the teachings of modern depth-psychology or modern atomic physics.

It is not quite so straightforward with regard to the second point, i.e. the assertion that the destiny of the human soul in birth, life, and death has a traditional explanation sanctioned by consensus, to which the teaching of reincarnation stands in contradiction. For tradition contains not one, but three different answers to the question: Where does the soul of the newborn child come from? The first answer, that of "creationism", says: it is newly created each time by God. The second answer, that of "tradutionism", says: the soul of the child issues at conception from the soul of the father. The third answer, that of "pre-existentialism", says: the soul descends at birth out of existence in the spiritual world into earthly existence; an incarnation takes place.

The Church fathers who had made the Platonic way of thinking their own — namely, Clement of Alexandria and Origen — as also the Priscillians and Sotians, represented pre-existentialism (i.e. the view that the soul comes to earth from heaven and returns there again) — and this view they had in common with Plato, Empedocles, Pythagoras, and Hermes Trismegistus. Tradutionism, which seemed to explain hereditary sin satisfactorily, was taught by the Church Fathers Tertullian, Rufinus, and Fulgentius — in more recent times, however, by a few Protestants and one or two Catholics (for example, Klee and Hermes). Lastly, creationism is recognised today as the view which is taught by the Church. Already in the thirteenth century the situation was such that tradutionism and pre-existentialism were regarded as having been rejected by the Church, and creationism established as the orthodox teaching. St. Thomas Aquinas said (*de Potenf.* q.3, a.9), after having described the teachings of tradutionism, pre-existentialism, and creationism, that "*Quae quidem opiniones, quamvis aliquo tempore sustinerentur, et quae earum verior in dubium verteretur . . . ; tamen primae duae postmodum judicio Ecclesiae sunt damnatae et tertis approbata*". (Which opinions, although for a certain time they were held, so long as it was doubtful as to which of them was more true; later the first two of them were condemned by the judgement of the Church and the third was adjudged to be good.)

Thus the authoritative theological background of the judgement of the Holy Office concerning reincarnation is perfectly clear: if pre-existentialism, which is a precondition for repeated earthly lives, was once rejected by the Church, then the same is valid for reincarnation, which can be comprehended only as a logical consequence of the pre-existence of the soul. So the Holy Office has pronounced a well-founded authoritative theological judgement; it has remained strictly within the framework of its duties and its competence and has acted accordingly. And its decision is, in the sphere of disciplinary theology, impeccable.

But what is the significance of this decision of the Holy Office? What can it mean for a Catholic who is convinced of reincarnation as a fact? (And there are many such Catholics.) Firstly, it can mean that he has the duty to reconsider his conviction once again with all the means at his disposal and as thoroughly as possible. Secondly, if it so be that after this reconsideration the decision of the Holy Office with its whole authoritative theological background has been able neither to wipe out the remembrance which came to him of a previous earthly life, nor to weaken for his knowledge and conscience the moral and logical reasons which speak in favor of repeated earthly lives, then the decision of the Holy Office can only signify the duty to preserve his conviction "*in foro interno*" and to be silent about it in public — "*in foro externo*" — which is what most practicing Catholics who are convinced of reincarnation do. This is the only thing still within their power to manifest in deed their loyalty to the Church.

If the theme of reincarnation has been spoken of here, it is not in

order to persuade anyone of its truth, but only in order to consider
it in relation to the ideal of resurrection. Here it is the author's desire
that those people who cannot do other than accept repeated earthly
lives as true, should not believe themselves to be at variance with the
cardinal truth of salvation, the resurrection; and that they see that
their conviction in no way contradicts the redemptive truth of resurrection, but on the contrary, receives therefrom its significance and
fulfillment. For reincarnation does not only mean repeated opportunities to gather experience and to overcome the trials of earthly life,
but it signifies also the repetition of the earthly constraints of suffering, sickness, and death. So it is not only an increased period of grace,
but also a lengthened period of shouldering the burden of the cross.

Resurrection, on the other hand, is also a reappearance in the
body, but without the earthly constraints of suffering, sickness, and
death, i.e. without the earthly necessities of destiny against which
man struggles in each of his incarnations. Thus resurrection appears
to be the crown and victorious fulfillment of the battle against constraint, suffering, and death which mankind fights ceaselessly both in
the course of the generations and through repeated earthly lives. It is
the great hope of final victory over constraint, sickness, and death,
i.e. it is the meaning and goal of repeated earthly lives. It is solely the
hope for resurrection which makes it worthwhile to live many times
on earth.

The relationship of resurrection to reincarnation — i.e. the whole to
the part — becomes especially clear when one takes a closer look at the
miracle of the raising of Lazarus from this point of view.

Lazarus had died and been buried. Then it happened that the Son
of God — He who became man — came and called him back to life on
earth with the words: "Lazarus, come forth!" This call, expressing the
united will of the Son and of the Father, signifies the divine prayer,
admonition, and command to return to life on earth in order to take
up again and carry on earthly experience and the earthly task. This
was the eternal will of God, which performed the miracle of the raising of Lazarus. This miracle, however, is not just a onetime event, but
also a revelation of the divine will. It reveals the content of the divine
will in the sense, namely, that God wills it that man may fulfill his
earthly experience and task, even when they have been interrupted by
death. Now the earthly task of man (and of humanity) is not fulfilled
until he (and mankind as a whole) have trodden the Way of Christ
("I am the Way") up to the resurrection. The raising of Lazarus — and
also the raising of the youth of Nain and of Jairus' daughter — reveal
the will of God, that man and humanity shall have the opportunity
to tread the whole path of earthly experience in fulfillment of the

earthly task. Thus, reincarnation is consistent with this divine will. It is consistent, too, with the ideal of resurrection as the completion of the path of mankind.

For a Christian who is wholly oriented toward the ideal of resurrection and who at the same time is convinced of repeated earthly lives, reincarnation signifies the possibility granted by divine goodness and mercy for every human being to tread the whole path of earthly experience in fulfillment of the earthly task until its completion, i.e. until resurrection. Reincarnation means to him a step-by-step preparation for resurrection as an overcoming of death — just as repeated awakening is a gradual preparation for the overcoming of death's "younger brother" (sleep), and just as repeated remembrance is a gradual preparation for the overcoming of the "younger brother" of sleep (forgetting). For just as the ideal state of eternal remembrance (unforgetting) is preceded by a rhythmic alternation of forgetting and remembrance — and as the ideal state of full awakening of consciousness is preceded by a rhythmic alternation of sleeping and waking — so for the Christian who is convinced of reincarnation, the ideal state of deathlessness (resurrection) is preceded by the rhythmic alternation of death and birth.

These three rhythms are already essentially contained in the Breath of God (*ruach elohim*) on the first day of creation. The Spirit breathes into the world a forgetting and remembrance, a sleeping and waking, a birth and death. And there ripen and blossom in the world eternal remembrance, eternal wakefulness, and eternal life, i.e. the world sabbath of the seventh day of creation.

If we wish to sum up our considerations concerning remembrance, awakening, and resurrection, it would be best not to do so in the form of more or less abstract sentences, but by means of concrete spirit-beings, who represent the profoundest essentials of these three conditions.

Plato teaches that the essence of knowledge is a recognition here and now of that which once in heaven was experienced and known — in other words, knowledge is remembrance. The force of conviction and inner certainty of metaphysical knowledge lies in the fact that something already known, but fallen into forgetfulness, is remembered again. And all arguments, drawing of comparisons, logical consequences, and other methods of cognition which are made use of in the here and now, are only ways and means of calling back memories out of the depths of the human soul-spiritual being into earthly day-consciousness. Altogether they represent, as it were, the "work of a midwife" at the birth of memory. Knowledge is not made, it comes to birth. And the man who remembers not only the experiences of his earthly existence, but beyond it and those that preceded it, is wise. For wisdom is the capacity for remembering the pre-earthly existence.

So, since ancient times the wise were always revered by mankind as great men of memory. The Rishis in ancient India, whose memory reached back to the primal beginnings of world evolution, laid the foundation for all Indian wisdom for thousands of years. Thus one of them proclaimed in the tenth book of the Rig-Veda:

> At first there was neither Being nor non-Being.
>   no kingdom of air, no sky beyond it.
> Who straddled what, and where? Who gave shelter?
>   Was water there, unfathomed depth of water?
> There was no death then, nor immortality,
>   no sign of stirring, no curtain of day or night.
> Only one thing, Breath, breathed, breathing without breath,
>   nothing else, nothing whatsoever.

(*Rig-Veda* x, 129; translated by P. Lal, "The Song of Creation" in *The Golden Womb of the Sun*, Calcutta, 1965).

Regarding the same primal beginning, we read in *Genesis*:

> And the world (earth) was without form and void, and darkness was upon the face of the deep; and the breath of God moved upon the face of the waters.

For an Indian, Moses too is a Rishi—a spirit in whom cosmic memories arose. What is *Genesis*? It is certain that the story of Creation, of the Fall into sin, of Cain and Abel, of the Flood, and so on are not philosophical speculations. *Genesis* is no system of teaching, but an account of what "was". And this account can only be true if it is remembrance. The theological argument that it is a revelation inspired by the Holy Spirit does not in any sense take away from the view that *Genesis* is a memory of primeval ages. Why should it not be the Holy Spirit who awakens in the human spirit memories of the cosmic past? For in the New Testament, too, it is the Comforter, the Spirit of Truth, who "will teach you all things and bring all things to remembrance, whatsoever I have said unto you" (*John* xiv, 26).

Also, Hermes Trismegistus, Pythagoras, and Plato were venerated as Wise Men, i.e. as spirits possessed of great memory.

Alongside the ideal representatives of wisdom, a large part of mankind looks with reverence toward the ideal representative of the fully awakened one, the Buddha. The Buddhas (of which there are more than one) differ from the Wise Men, as remembrance differs from awakening. A Buddha is more than one who remembers; he is one who is fully awakened. He is completely awake to the reality of the fate of mankind and the world, i.e. to the fact of the Fall into sin and its consequences.

For example, all human beings know about the facts of birth, sickness, old age, and death — and yet live as if they knew nothing of them. But Gautama Buddha became completely awake to these facts, awake to their range and significance right down to their ultimate consequences. Thus he taught — so that others might also become conscious of them — the eightfold path of meditation, together with a way of life consistent with it and able to promote it. And just as the Buddhas of the past were fully awake to the reality of the Fall into sin, and to the sorrows of mankind and of the world which is sunken in error, suffering, and death, so the Buddhist section of humanity awaits a new Buddha — the Maitreya Buddha — who will be fully awake to the good and to that which brings healing to the world and mankind.

Just as the Wise Men are valued and venerated as overcomers of forgetting, and the Buddhas are honored as overcomers of sleep, so Christian mankind looks up to Jesus Christ with faith, hope, and love as the overcomer of death.

The Wise Man, the fully Awakened One, and the Risen One are the stars signposting the path of mankind in their striving toward the overcoming of forgetting, sleep, and death.

3. HOW IT HAPPENED

"Now a certain man was sick, named Lazarus, of Bethany, the town of Mary and her sister Martha." Thus St. John's Gospel begins the story of the miracle of the raising of Lazarus.

The name Lazarus is the Hellenized form of the Hebrew name Eleazar, "God has helped". The name Lazarus appears only twice in the New Testament; once in *Luke* xvi, 19–31, in the parable of the poor man and his fate after death (it is the only time that in one of Jesus' parables someone is named), and then in *John* xi in the account of the raising of Lazarus. After his re-awakening Lazarus is mentioned as participating at the festive meal in the house of Simon the leper, which was prepared for Jesus in Bethany (*John* xii, 1–2 and *Matthew* xxvi, 6), where many came not only because of Jesus but also in order to see Lazarus who was woken from the dead (*John* xii, 9). Furthermore, it is reported in St. John's Gospel that the high priests decided, because of the great sign of the raising of Lazarus, that Jesus should die (xi, 46–53); and they wanted to kill Lazarus also (xii, 10). About the further destiny of Lazarus the Gospel is silent, while both tradition and also the visions of Anne Catherine Emmerich agree in reporting that with his sisters Martha and Mary he fled from the first persecutions of Christians in Palestine to Gaul (Marseilles).

St. Epiphanius says that according to tradition, Lazarus was thirty years old when he was raised from the dead. Afterward he lived another thirty years. Regarding his death there are two conflicting traditions — the Greek version according to which Lazarus died in Cyprus, and the general folk tradition in Provence that after he had (with his sisters, Joseph of Arimathea, and other disciples of Christ) proclaimed the Gospel in that land, he died a martyr's death at an advanced age in Marseilles. It should be added that Anne Catherine Emmerich, whose visions give a very detailed report on the life and deeds of Lazarus both before and after his raising, mentions him as the "first bishop of Marseilles", but says nothing about his death.

Lazarus, whom even the modest accounts of Anne Catherine Emmerich describe as a "very mysterious personality", belonged neither to the circle of the twelve disciples who accompanied Jesus, nor to the wider circle of seventy disciples; but occupied a special position in relation to the Master and the apostles. This special position was similar to that of Nicodemus, Joseph of Arimathea, and Nathanael, in that although in spiritual intimacy with the Master, they stood at a distance from his followers. Yet they did not stand apart as onlookers, but as friends. Therefore, Jesus said to his disciples: "Lazarus, our friend, is sleeping" (John xi, 11).

The message which the sisters Martha and Mary sent to the Master to tell him about the sickness of Lazarus was: "Lord, see! He whom thou lovest lies sick." The Greek verb *phileo*, which has the same root as the word *philos* (= friend), means "to like, to love, to show love for, to be pleased, to show pleasure, to be well disposed towards". The Gospel itself says concerning the relationship of Jesus to Lazarus and his sisters: "Now Jesus loved Martha and her sister and Lazarus" (John xi, 5). The word *agapao* means "to love, to revere, to honor" and also "to forgive someone". Thus *agapao* signifies a deeper and more intensive feeling than that which the word *phileo* indicates. The latter implies a friendly disposition, whereas the former signifies over and above this a loving appreciation.

Lazarus and his two sisters in Bethany were therefore people who were on especially friendly terms with Jesus. They belonged to the circle of "friends" or "helpers" that existed alongside the circle of apostles and that of disciples. The people who belonged to this special circle were of the kind who participated in a helping and supportive way in the work of Jesus Christ as Teacher, Healer, and

Redeemer — whether it be as "preparers of the way" (for example, John the Baptist), or as "foster-guardians" (for instance, Joseph the foster-father), or else as "connecting links" with the various spiritual streams of the time, above all with the traditional schools of Palestine (e.g. Nathanael, Nicodemus, and Joseph of Arimathea). It is characteristic of them all that they were in a sense "knowers", i.e. they were consciously expecting the coming of the Messiah and they consciously recognized the One who had come. In the case of John the Baptist this is obvious. But also the conversation between Jesus and Martha just before Jesus entered Bethany (*John* xi, 21–27) shows that Martha had recognized Him who had come. For she said: "Yes, Lord, I have believed that thou art Christ, the Son of God, who is to come into the world". Martha does not say that she has now recognised and believes that Jesus is Christ, but says that she "has believed" him to be so. The confession of Peter, which came to him like a lightning revelation, had been carried as a conviction by Martha over a longer period: "I have believed", she said.

Another sister Mary, "who had anointed the Lord with oil and dried his feet with her hair", received him in Bethany with the words: "Lord, if you had been here, my brother would not have died" — in which words the certainty and security of insight speaks, going far beyond a mere supposition.

The two sisters belonged to the circle of "friends" or "helpers" not only because they were persons who understood, but because they had placed themselves at the service of the Lord. Martha (her name means "lady" in the sense of the "lady of the house") took on the task of offering hospitality in the name of earthly humanity to him who had come from heaven — that hospitality which had been refused to him in Bethlehem at the time of his birth. She took care of the reception and accommodation of the Lord and of his often numerous disciples — not only at her house in Bethany, but also in various other places which Jesus visited with his disciples on his wanderings. She organized in advance the journeys of the Master and his companions, by making ready guesthouses and inns for the wanderers and taking on herself the cost of their lodgings. This made it possible for Jesus to move through the land teaching and healing without becoming a burden to anyone — and also without being dependent on the good or bad will of the people at each place. Thanks to the caring help of Martha, he could devote himself entirely to his work and be free from everyday worries.

The service rendered to him by Mary was of quite another kind and on a different level. If Martha took care of what was necessary in an outer sense, it was Mary who did what in an outer sense was "unnecessary", but in an inner sense was immeasurably valuable — she surrounded him with soul-warmth. The precious aromatic ointment with which she anointed him, and the drying of his feet with her hair were, of course, entirely unnecessary — which Judas also pointed out — but they were things which offered human warmth to him who had come to die on the Cross. This warmth, which he had already been deprived of at the hour of his birth in Bethlehem, made it humanly easier for him to accept his task — death on the Cross — and strengthened him in his mission. Therefore Jesus answered Judas when he complained of purposeless waste: "Let her alone; against the day of my burying hath she kept this" (*John* xii, 7).

And according to Matthew's Gospel Jesus said: "She did it for my burial. Verily I say unto you: Wherever this Gospel shall be preached in the whole world, what she has done will be told in memory of her" (*Matthew* xxvi, 12–13).

Now, if Martha was a friend and helper to Jesus in the sphere of his outer activities, and Mary contributed soul-warmth for the cold time of his Passion, in what did the service of Lazarus consist? How did Lazarus distinguish himself as a friend and helper?

Lazarus was the spiritual friend of Jesus, just as Mary was a friend in the soul-sphere and Martha in the sphere of outer events and daily life. And the service he rendered Jesus was of a spiritual kind. This is to say that he took part in the most essential core of Christ's work — his death and resurrection. The participation of Lazarus in the work and the way of Jesus Christ went beyond mere believing acceptance and understanding; it went so far as to actually go through an experience which was not, of course, identical, but analogous to the experience of death, entombment, and resurrection that Jesus Christ underwent. For when the future apostles stood perplexed before the enigma of Christ's words: "A little while, and you will see me no more; again a little while, and you will see me . . . because I go to the Father" (*John* xvi, 17) — there was one who knew from his own experience the going and the returning, and therefore was in a position to understand the mystery of the Way, the Truth, and the Life which was revealed through Jesus Christ. In Lazarus earthly humanity possessed a kind of "organ" for the mystery of Christianity, so that it could be understood — and not remain forever an unknown and unknowable miracle. "The light shineth in the darkness", in the darkness also of the mysteries of faith. This light does not reveal itself in rationalization (in making plausible the mysteries of faith to reason), but in ever deeper insight into the moral weaving of world events, in the working of the cosmic Word of which St. John's Gospel speaks in the prologue. To allow the logic of the Logos to hold sway in human reason was the intention, for instance, of Hegel. Yet Hegel was striving exclusively after truth — that is, after the one aspect of the indivisible unity of the Way, the Truth, and the Life. As he was concerned with thinking alone — i.e. solely with the truth aspect — and detached it from the trinity of the Way, the Truth, and the Life, he was not successful in mirroring intact in human consciousness the true logic of the Logos, which embraces thinking, the heart, and the will. What he experienced was merely partial, a mere torso of the logic of the Logos.

Another and far more successful attempt to allow the logic of the Logos to reflect itself in human consciousness is signified by the spiritual lifework of Rudolf Steiner, the founder of Anthroposophy. Here it is not simply a matter of creating an all-embracing, absolute thought-system (as with Hegel). Rather, it is a question of the method — of the path of spiritual and soul-development of the whole human being — so that he might grow and become capable of reflecting the logic of the Logos in his consciousness in a pure and complete way. Thus not the truth alone, but the way *and* the truth were the concerns of Rudolf Steiner.

Alas it happened, however, for reasons which we need not go into here, that Rudolf Steiner gave his work the form of a science, so-called "spiritual science". Thereby the third aspect of the indivisible threefoldness of the Way, the Truth, and the Life — namely Life — was not given enough attention. For the scientific form into which the logic of the Logos had to be cast, and by which it was limited, left little room for pure mysticism and spiritual magic, that is, for Life. So there is in Anthroposophy a magnificent achievement of thought and will — which is, however, unmystical and unmagical, i.e. in want of Life. Rudolf Steiner himself was conscious of this essential lack. Therefore it was with a certain amount of hope that he indicated the necessary appearance of a successor (the Bodhisattva) who would remedy this lack and would bring the trinity of the Way, the Truth, and the Life to full fruition.

Be that as it may, it is a fact inherent in the spiritual history of mankind — and not only in the nineteenth and twentieth centuries — that there has always existed (and still exists) a striving to go, to know, and to live the Way, the Truth, and the Life in the sense of the invocation of the Master of all Masters: "Seek and ye shall find; ask and it shall be given unto you; knock and it shall be opened unto you". This invitation is valid also for the mysteries of faith. These also are waiting for "seekers", "askers", and "knockers" in order to be found, to be given, and to be opened unto knowledge.

The search for the Grail, now become legend — together with Rosicrucianism, which is surrounded by a forest of symbolism — both testify that there has always existed a striving for a conscious participation in the logic of the Logos, a quest for a Christian initiation. And it was Lazarus, the special friend of Jesus Christ, who was called to be the first Christian initiate, thereby laying the foundations and forming the starting point for the entire history of Christian initiation.

Therefore the sickness of Lazarus, about which the sisters sent messages to the Master, was no ordinary sickness "leading to death", but a sickness "to the glory of God". In other words, the sickness of Lazarus was not to bear witness to the transience of nature, as every natural sickness does, but to the reality of the divine Word-made-flesh, who is Lord over life and death, i.e. who is the resurrection. The sickness of Lazarus was not merely a going away, but a departure in order to return; it was a dying in order to be reborn. Now it is just this act of dying — to the world in order to live and to work in the world out of forces and motives of action — which is not of this world. This is exactly what has always been regarded as the essence of initiation. An initiate was always looked up to as one "twice-born". However, what was experienced in the pre-Christian mysteries as a cultic process of consciousness was, in the sickness, death, and raising of Lazarus, a real and complete event embracing spirit, soul, and body — an event which was simultaneously human destiny and divine grace. It was human destiny insofar as it signified the victory of death over life, and it was divine grace insofar as it was the beginning of a new life, one stronger than death. Now, the start (*initium*) of the world on the first day of creation, as well as the commencement of the life of the man Lazarus after he had died (i.e. the re-commencement), was the experience of beginning (*initium*) or initiation. The event of the death and raising of Lazarus was an initiation carried out by Jesus Christ as initiator. It consisted of three parts: the sickness of Lazarus which was "not unto death, but to the glory of God"; the death of Lazarus and his sojourn for four days beyond the threshold of death; and his return to earthly life, his re-awakening. We have already spoken above concerning the sickness of Lazarus as a phenomenon. Here it is a matter of understanding its essence more deeply.

The law of gravitation formulated in physics by Isaac Newton also has its soul-spiritual counterpart in the inner life of man, which is placed in equilibrium between the heavenly and earthly gravitational fields. Both forces of attraction reach into the inner life of man, where they function as urges or yearnings. Goethe points to this fact by letting Faust say to Wagner:

You know of only one o'erwhelming urge.
O never learn to now the other!
Two souls, alas, within me sink and surge,
Each would be riven from its brother.
One seeks to grasp in gross desire and lust,
With clamorous organs all this world of greeds;
The other strives up strongly from the dust,
Aloft to high ancestral meads.

The depth of psychoanalysis of Sigmund Freud led to the discovery of the first urge, that of "gross desire and lust", which grips the world "with clamorous organs", and the depth psychoanalysis and psychotherapeutic experience of Carl Gustav Jung complemented it by discovering the second urge which "strives up strongly from the dust, aloft to high ancestral meads". Freud named the fundamental urge which he discovered and investigated "libido", while Jung described the power of attraction of the "high ancestors" as "archetypes".

Gautama Buddha, the historical founder of Buddhism, in his depth-analysis of human existence, described the basic urge which fetters men to the world of appearances — and which thus keeps human beings alive — as the "urge for life" (*tanha*); this he set over and against the urge for liberation. When the latter — through meditation, self-discipline, and renunciation — one day attains predominance, it becomes a stream flowing, as it were, of itself and leading to liberation in the state of *nirvana*. Someone who has attained self-control is called *strotapatti* ("he who has entered the stream"). For him there is no going back; the stream bears him irresistibly in one direction. For he has entered a realm in which the heavenly forces of attraction predominate and earthly gravitation works in him ever more weakly.

The reality of the existence of "the heavenly forces of attraction" reveals itself not only in Buddhism and Hinduism, but also in Christianity. The anchorites of the Egyptian desert (e.g. St. Anthony and St. Paul the Hermit) were not men who were fleeing the world, but rather they lived for heaven. They were not opposed to the world, but were so much for heaven that they sought for a way of life — and found it — which was suited to their state of being gripped by the field of gravitation of heaven. So we are faced with the remarkable phenomenon that while some men founded and built cities, others on the contrary left them and retired into the loneliness of the desert. Neither the former nor the latter acted according to a planned program; they could do nothing else, because they were placed in contrary "fields of gravitation".

Now what happened to Lazarus was a radical conversion from the earthly to the heavenly gravitational field. His sickness lay in the fact that the long process of conversion over decades, which the desert fathers experienced, was in his case shortened to a few weeks and days. The process of conversion was thus correspondingly intense. The intensity was so great that the body could not keep pace with it; he was overwhelmed by the measure of spirituality to which he had to convert. He succumbed. So it happened that Lazarus died. Now, the direction of the stream caused by the heavenly gravitational pull is opposite to that of earthly attraction. For if the stream which lives in men as the urge to grasp this world "in gross desire and lust" is directed toward the future, that is, in the direction of children and grandchildren — then the stream which lives in men "striving strongly from the dust aloft to the high ancestral meads" is directed toward the past, that is, both to the heights and to the ancestors.

This is shown, too, in the gradual conversion which happens almost naturally in the course of advancing age in human life; from an interest in the future to a preoccupation with the past. Older people turn gradually more and more to appreciate and contemplate the past, while the present and future gradually lose colour and significance, as if becoming ever more abstract. Thereby a certain transformation of the past takes place too. It no longer appears merely as a factual memory, but is insofar transformed as to appear in a certain measure idealized and transfigured so that what was haphazard, superficial, and insignificant is greatly outshone by the essential, deeper, and more meaningful aspects of life's destiny and of human kindness and wisdom. In other words, the past is seen more in a heavenly light than in the light of earthly facts. It appears transfigured. And woe unto him who disturbs an aged person engaged in devotedly re-evaluating the past in the light of heavenly illumination, by trying to wake him up to the "reality of the bare facts"! For just as one who despoils a child's light-filled world deserves to have a millstone hung about his neck and to be cast down deep into the sea — equally is the fate deserved by he who dares to explain to an old person the nonsense of his light-filled world. In both cases it is a matter of preserving and admitting the validity of the same light; the child still has his eyes full of heavenly light, while the old person already has them full of the same light. It goes without saying that here we mean neither the symptoms of old-age sclerosis, nor those of handicapped development of the young (such as Mongolism), for both of these are abnormal diseases, and neither can pass as being "natural" symptoms of either youth or age.

The "death-stream", which flows in contrary direction to the future-aimed life-stream, begins to become already noticeable in the second half of a normal human life. It sets in at first admittedly in a delicate and intimate manner, but its intensity increases with time. It is therefore not difficult to understand that the direction taken in old age (which becomes ever more definite the nearer the course of life gets to the point of death) remains dominant after death also. The human soul freed from the body, which in old age has turned from the future toward the past, appears in the spiritual world just as much permeated with a dynamic impulse toward the distant past, as the soul of a newborn child appears on earth permeated by a future-oriented impulse. As the child, after the event of birth, enters the future-oriented life-stream of earthly life full of expectation, so does the soul-spiritual being of man after death enter the past-oriented life-stream full of yearning for its origin. It is just as much attracted toward this origin as the earthly human being is drawn toward his goal. Knowledge of this can be found in the Bible where it is expressly said that the souls of the departed make their way to the patriarchs, and in the parable of "poor Lazarus" recounted by Jesus Christ himself, "poor Lazarus" finds himself at a place, or in a state, which is described as "Abraham's bosom" (*Luke* xvi, 19–31). The state of existence "in Abraham's bosom" is there described as a blissful fulfillment of the deepest yearnings of the soul — that is, of the urge to rise to the "high ancestral meads" as Goethe called it. "Abraham's bosom" was for the Israelites the "origin", corresponding to the "high ancestral meads". It meant for them the state of soul in which — through Abraham and together with him — is attained the same relationship with God as that in which Abraham stood. Through "Father Abraham" the soul attained to the experience of the Father of all beings and all worlds. Abraham was something like a moon, which reflected the light of the divine Fatherhood. And living in this reflected light was the essence of the bliss of resting in "Abraham's bosom". "Abraham's bosom" was for the soul "the place of coolness, of light, and of peace" (*locus refrigerii, lucis, et pacis*).

So it was not Adam and his paradisiacal state toward which the soul of the Israelite people yearned — for it was Adam who signified the origin of the turning away from God and the history of mankind's Fall into sin. It was Abraham, the obedient, who was the origin — and thus the true ancestor — of the history of the work of redemption that would attain its fulfillment in the coming of the Messiah. For the Israelite soul it was not Adam, the disobedient, but Abraham the obedient who was the real origin of the true life which revealed itself, not in the world, but solely in the mission of Israel. It is not earth, water, air, and fire, nor sun, moon, and stars which teach and reveal for the Israelite the true life — but Moses and the prophets, stemming back to Abraham. He was the first, the actual representative of the true

creation as it was before the Fall. That is why all the yearning of the
Israelite souls turned toward Abraham, and so the path they took
after death led to Abraham, to "Abraham's bosom".

This attitude toward Abraham explains, too, how the anger of
the Jewish hearers was aroused so that they picked up stones to
stone Jesus, when he spoke the words which signified a turning point
in mankind's destiny, in the life and death of humanity: "Before
Abraham was, I am" (John viii, 58).

These words signify a turning point in the destiny of mankind —
both on earth and also after death — in that no longer Abraham, but
now the "new Adam," the "I am", is established as the beginning and
the end, as Alpha and Omega (or Aleph and Tau). Thereby Abraham was no longer valid as the ideal for incarnated human beings,
but rather the Son of man. And it is no longer Abraham to whose
"bosom" disembodied human beings return, but the "I am before
Abraham was". Thus the way of the departed soul leads, since Christ
became man, further back into the past than the point signified by
Abraham. It leads to the timeless origin in eternity, in the bosom of
the heavenly Father, with whom the Son is one. After the incarnation
of Christ, and as a result thereof, the destiny of human souls after
death underwent a profound change. Their yearning and their path
to the "high ancestral meads" no longer led back to Abraham (or in
the case of non-Israelite souls to some corresponding ancestor in the
past) as the origin, where "origin" meant a condition in which the
nearest possible archetypal relationship to God the Father could be
found and renewed. Their new path was directed, not to the reflection
of divine Fatherhood, but to the divine Father himself through the
Son who is one with the Father. Thus the path of those who die in
Christ leads not into "Abraham's bosom" but into the "bosom of the
eternal Father", where the Son is eternally begotten.

And as the story of the "beggar Lazarus" who was conducted by
angels into "Abraham's bosom" signified for pre-Christian mankind
the culminating point of the path of destiny after death — so the
account of the seventh miracle in St. John's Gospel concerning the
sickness, death, and raising of the other Lazarus, the spiritual friend
of Jesus Christ, is the culminating point of the path of destiny after
death for Christian humanity. For the path taken by Lazarus after his
death in Bethany was determined by the power of attraction — or the
yearning after — the timeless origin, where the divine Word is born
eternally out of the Father, i.e. the bosom of the Father. The primal
beginning in eternity, however, is the eternal first day of creation,
when the divine Word — which Moses expresses in the words: "Let
there be light" — sounds forth eternally. There, to the heights and

depths of the first day of creation, to that primeval darkness and to the eternal lighting up of the primal light, Lazarus was led already by the path which he had undertaken on earth by way of his "illness". He became submerged in the primeval original darkness of the first day of creation, and experienced the eternal transformation of darkness into light, the eternal coming into existence of consciousness as the internal transmutation of darkness into the light of understanding, of insight, of affirmation — this transmutation taking place by way of "internalization", becoming more and more inward. The transmutation through internalization of the primal mystery — for primeval darkness is the primal mystery — into primal cognition (primeval light being primal insight into the primal mystery) was what Lazarus experienced. And this experience of the first beginning in the eternity of the first day of creation, of the eternal *initium*, was the initiation of Lazarus. For initiation is the experience and firsthand knowledge of the transformation of primeval darkness into light. It means being witness to the birth of consciousness in eternity, the birth of the world. Only haltingly can we speak (and all that we have said here is but a stammering) of what further took place. Lazarus experienced the miracle of transmutation through internalization of the primal mystery of primeval darkness into the primal insight of primeval light. He experienced the universal Word such that at that moment the "Let there be light" of the world-creative Word condensed itself into the words "Lazarus, come forth" of the Son of Man. These words bore within them, with primal directive power, all the consequences of what had been experienced and known in the bosom of the Father on the eternal first day of creation. Thus, Lazarus obeyed this Word and departed out of the eternity of the first day of creation for the sake of the earthly "world of time" to which the eternal creative Word of God — now clothed for him in a beloved human voice — commanded him to return. So it happened that Lazarus returned.

This it was which took place above and beyond the threshold of death. What happened below this side of the threshold of death?

To put it briefly: there took place a "prelude" to the resurrection, i.e. a partial process of resurrection taking place and sheltered within the existent body. For the soul of Lazarus did not return into the old body, which in the meantime had become a corpse, with a nervous system that had become unusable. He returned into a renewed body, whose inner organization — necessary for reflecting the life of the soul and spirit — had been created anew. That, which in the body's inner organization had been partly or wholly destroyed, became newly fashioned or newly formed into organic matter through a "densification" of the will. It was a prelude to the resurrection insofar as there occurred a partial manifestation of fundamentally the same process as took place in the case of the Risen One, when he appeared, spoke, ate, touched, and was touched. Only in the Risen One the whole body was transformed into the will and life, while in Lazarus this transformation was limited to the soul and spirit-related inner organization of the body. The new — the renewed — body of Lazarus was therefore a union of the old inherited body with the new resurrection body functioning in him. The latter, which manifested itself primarily by way of a renewed nervous system and re-enlivened blood, signified at the same time the healing of the sickness of Lazarus — of the inability of his body to cope with the intensity of the spirituality which overwhelmed him. For now the inner organization of his renewed body was the condensed mirror of this spirituality itself. The schism between spirituality and its bodily reflection was thus removed. Lazarus was not only awakened; he was also healed.

The Gospel gives a clear indication that both a revivification and a resurrection took place at the raising of Lazarus. It can be seen in the conversation between Jesus Christ and Martha, which took place before the arrival of Jesus at the burial place of Lazarus. Martha said: "Lord, if you had been here, my brother would not have died. And even now I know that whatever you ask from God, God will give you." Jesus said to her, "Your brother will rise again." Martha said to him, "I know that he will rise again in the resurrection at the last day." Jesus said to her, "I am the resurrection and the life; he who believes in me, though he die, yet shall he live. And whoever lives and believes in me shall never die. Do you believe this?" (*John* xi, 21–26).

Then the miracle was fulfilled which was the reflection in the world of time of the eternal first day of creation, and which revealed the mystery of Love as breath, tears, and word. Again we can only speak of it haltingly, for what happened is too great to be described in a smooth and flowing manner. For such things to be expressed, a suitable style has not yet been found.

Be that as it may, the attempt must be made to regard the miracle of the raising of Lazarus itself on a level that is worthy of it.

The raising of Lazarus was the result of the cooperation of the purest and deepest humanity with the most all-embracing, highest divinity. It took place between the eternal breath of the first day of creation (when the divine breath — *ruach elohim* — moved over the face of the waters) and the breath of a humbly sorrowing (i.e. weeping) humanity. "When Jesus saw Mary weeping, and the Jews who came with her also weeping, he was deeply moved in spirit and was troubled, and said: 'Where have you laid him?' They said to him,

'Lord, come and see.' And Jesus wept. So the Jews said, 'See how he loved him!' . . . Then Jesus, deeply moved again, came to the tomb. It was a cave, and a stone lay upon it" (*John* xi, 33–38).

Tears have a spiritual-magical power and significance. Goethe indicates this by letting Faust say: "My tears are flowing, the earth takes me back again!"

There exists indeed a whole rainbow of tears — tears of gratitude, of admiration, of compassion, of suffering, of joy, and of sorrow . . . but always their characteristic is (whether they express an over-measure of deprivation or an over-measure of grace) that they are the bearers of a humility capable of mirroring the light. The eye of pride is always dry. He who weeps also kneels. And he who kneels weeps inwardly. And to kneel signifies an inner approach to the earth, a partaking in the earth's humility, in the presence of heaven's sublimity. "My tears are flowing, the earth takes me back again."

That tears have a purifying, rejuvenating, and light-bearing power and capability — this was known by the Masters of spiritual life; the hermits, monks, and members of spiritual orders in the past. The "gift of tears" was highly esteemed by them, and often they prayed for this gift. For it meant to them the breath of the moving spirit and the mobility of the soul as an image or reflection of the first day of creation, when light was born in the darkness of moving waters through the moving divine breath. And just as moving waters precede the appearance of the rainbow in the primeval light, so does weeping precede the rainbow of illuminating light in the soul.

Jesus wept. Then the rainbow of the Holy Spirit arose over the crowd of weepers. And some of them said, "Could not this man, who opened the eyes of the blind, have caused that this man should not have died?" However, others said, "See, how he loved him!" Then Jesus, deeply moved again, came to the tomb. The crowd followed him. There stood the rainbow of the Holy Spirit over the dark cleft of the grave, on which a stone was laid. At his word the stone was taken away.

Thereupon the Son-made-flesh lifted up his eyes to the heavenly Father and thanked him, that he had heard him. Then he cried with a loud voice, which condensed the rainbow of Spirit into lightning, bearing within it the rolling thunder of the Father:

"Lazarus, come forth!"

And he that was dead came forth, his hands and feet bound with bandages, and his face wrapped with a cloth. Jesus said to them: "Unbind him, and let him go!"

Thus it happened that the soul of Lazarus, called out of the bosom of the Father by the Word of the Son, turned back through the portal of the rainbow of the Holy Spirit into the realm of earthly life. In Christ he had died, out of the Father he had been born, and through the Holy Spirit he was brought to new life. The three lines of the Rosicrucian verse — *Ex Deo nascimur; In Jesu morimur; Per Spiritum Sanctum reviviscimus* — take their power and their substance from the Mystery of the Raising of Lazarus.

4. WHAT HAPPENED

Just as the days of creation are not "days" that pass, but timeless events in the background of the world of appearances, so the seven "typical" miracles of St. John's Gospel are also timeless, in the sense that they are constantly working in the spiritual history of mankind, working behind the scenes. They are not events which took place only once at some time in the past, but are consistently repeated as happenings belonging to the very structure of mankind's spiritual history, i.e. they comprise an intrinsic part of this structure, functioning as its breath or heartbeat, as it were. To them apply the words of Jesus, "Heaven and earth will pass away, but my words will not pass away," if instead of "words" we say "deeds". Thus we would say, "Heaven and earth will pass away, but my deeds will not pass away", whereby "not pass away" has the meaning that they will never become merely of the past ("past history"), but will be eternally present and effective.

The sacraments rest on this foundation. The sacrament of the altar, for instance, rests on the fact that the words spoken at the transubstantiation — "This is my body; this is my blood" — have a timeless significance and effectiveness. They are not the "past" in the sense that they belong to a past time, but they are today and for all future time equally effective as when He Himself spoke them.

The sacraments rest on the timelessness of the words and deeds of the Son who became man. The same is true also for his deeds — the miracles — which he did and consequently always continues to do. They are just as timeless as are the sacraments and the days of creation. The call "Lazarus, come forth!" sounds out unceasingly in the world of the living and in the world of forgetting. And out of the dark cave of forgetting emerge newly awakened memories of lost wisdom, of things imbued with great love and great truth which had fallen into oblivion. Renaissances of all sorts happen in the spiritual-cultural history of mankind, caused by the call, "Lazarus, come forth!" In consequence of such a call, many awaken to insight into — and a re-evaluation of — many things. And the dead are continually — either through birth, or by "arising" in other living people — "woken" to activity on earth in consequence of this call. Is not every papal coronation actually the expression of the conviction that the timeless call: "Peter, come forth!" will not fail, and cannot fail? For, the throne of Peter — the papal office and its responsibility — does not depend on each single pope making the effort to represent Peter, but on the fact that the pope does in reality represent him. This means to say, the holy apostle really is present in every pope, and really obeys the call, "Peter, come forth" in the case of each pope.

The miracle of the raising of Lazarus works irrespective of time and place, where that which is forgotten is remembered, where that which sleeps is awakened, and where that which is dead is brought to life. The following considerations attempt to show that this really is so.

III

THE LAZARUS MIRACLE
IN THE SPIRITUAL-CULTURAL
HISTORY OF MANKIND

1. WHAT IS SPIRITUAL-CULTURAL HISTORY?

More than fifteen centuries have passed since the appearance of St. Augustine's great work *The City of God (Civitas Dei)*. This work represents the first comprehensive survey of world history, as far as it could be known at that time, reaching beyond the political, social, and economic aspects. This history of the world embraces not only the conflicts and struggles between various human interests, but also — and especially — the workings of a providence which transcends them. For Augustine, the history of the world was not only the history of mankind's coming to terms with nature, nor merely the coming to terms of groups of people with each other, but primarily the history of mankind's relationship with the superhuman, i.e. with God. In other words, it was the first work of philosophical history in the West which was intended at the same time to be a further pursuance of the biblical method of approach. Augustine learned from the Bible to distinguish the essential from the inessential, and to perceive the relationships of essential significance between events in the course of the destiny of mankind. Making use of this method that he had learned from the Bible, he also applied it to a consideration of post-biblical times. Thus arose in the occident the first work that had something to say about the meaning of world history.

The Augustinian/biblical method of comprehensively viewing the collaboration in world history of the effects of nature, the deeds and decisions of human beings, and the operation of divine providence, bears within it a tremendous potential for further development. However, very little use has been made of it since the age of Enlightenment (that is, since the dawn of our scientific age). Thus, historical research having entirely neglected it, it has fallen into oblivion. The comprehensive viewing of God, man, and nature was just as much replaced by specialization, as the comprehensive viewing of man as body, soul, and spirit was replaced by physiology, psychology, logic, ethics, and aesthetics. There arose political history, social history, cultural history, and now there is also coming into existence a psychological history. Today, for instance, if one is suffering from fits of dizziness, one can consult the dietician about diet, the medical doctor about blood pressure, the eye specialist about the eyes, the dentist about the condition of the teeth (which can cause an infection of the whole organism), the nerve specialist for possible disturbances of the nervous system, and lastly even the psychiatrist for possible psychic causes for the fits of dizziness. So, too, if one is interested, for example, in the age of Charlemagne, one has to ask a cultural historian what the "Carolingian renaissance" was, the political historian what political significance the founding of the Holy Roman-German Empire had, the social-economic historian what social-economic effects feudalism had, and the Church historian what significance that age had for the papacy and the Catholic Church. Lastly, one would have to ask the psychologizing historian about the meaning of, say, the two "father figures" — emperor and pope — to whom at that time the whole world needed to look up; and about the significance, then, of the psychological phenomenon of childish obedience toward two "fathers", two authoritarian "father figures". It is obvious that neither the single answer of the questioned specialist, nor a compounding of all their answers, can really answer the question: What was it that took place in the destiny of mankind during the age of Charlemagne? To have a perception at all of this "what" (not only of the "how"), we must not look simply for progress in economics, politics, and culture, or for psychological tendencies, but rather for the goal of mankind and for the path leading to it.

There are thinkers and seers who have regarded world history thus. Controversial though they may be, much can be learned from them. To these thinkers and seers belongs Fabre d'Olivet, author of the work *L'histoire philosophique du genre humain* ("Philosophical History of the Human Race"), from the beginning of the last century. Fabre d'Olivet considered the history of mankind to be a movement resulting from the cooperation of three determining factors: fate, freedom, and providence.

Our century has bestowed on us three thinkers and seers who were able to describe world history as a path toward a goal: they are Rudolf Steiner, Pierre Teilhard de Chardin, and Arnold Toynbee. The picture of the world history given to us by Rudolf Steiner is that of a world directed by providence through the spiritual hierarchies which lead mankind from stage to stage of consciousness, firstly preparing them for the reception of the Christ-impulse, and afterward reserving and fostering the ripening, growth, and final victory of the Christ-impulse in mankind, until man shall have reached the stage which the apostle Paul describes in the words: "Not I, but Christ in me."

Pierre Teilhard de Chardin, however, does not base his views on transcendental-spiritual premises, as Rudolf Steiner does, but starts with a consideration of the phenomena of matter, movement, force, growth, the structure of form, and the arising and development of consciousness — in biological evolution, and in world history viewed as a continuation of biological evolution. He sees in all these phenomena a line — a path — of ongoing interiorization. The path starts from the latent stage of mere existence to movement, then proceeds from outer to inner motion (in the atom, in the molecule, in the organism). From there the path moves more from inner movement to its further interiorization in reflection, leading to consciousness of self, and lastly from that to a conscious cooperation with the whole evolutionary process. Eventually the path leads to the attainment of the ultimate summit of this process of interiorization, the omega-point, or God.

Arnold Toynbee bases his views neither on transcendental-spiritual nor on immanent-biological premises, but on the essential nature of the human soul — that is to say, on immanent psychological laws which in the course of world history are elevated to become a metaphysical (i.e. divine-spiritual) operation in world history.

When we speak here of the spiritual-cultural history of mankind, we mean, in actual fact, the biblical mode of cognition in the form which has now become possible after the above-mentioned contributions have prepared the path. Today, therefore, a world of concepts stands available to spiritual-cultural history which at the time of St. Augustine was very much lacking. For instance, at the time of Augustine the complex of concepts belonging to the central idea of evolution was lacking; also lacking at his time were the many concepts for which today we must thank oriental wisdom and our getting to grips with it. All this now exists as a thought-language available to an Augustinian/biblical mode of cognition. Thus the spiritual-cultural history of mankind, as meant here, is an Augustinian/biblical way of looking at history, which has been further developed within the thought-language of the twentieth century.

2. THE "DAY" AND "NIGHT" ASPECTS OF HISTORY

The biblical way of looking at history means more than merely regarding — in the light of the work of redemption — the grounds of historical events (having become crystallized as facts) as they appear in the realm of day-consciousness (= normal waking consciousness). It means, in addition, a viewing of the crystallization into facts of preceding movements, events, or deeds prior to their becoming facts. This process is wrapped in darkness as far as factual day-consciousness is concerned, which is only aware of actualized facts and not of their process of becoming. The history of that which has become actualized is related to the history of the process of becoming as day is to night.

Just as the full reality of human life consists of days and nights — of the bright day-consciousness and the dark sway of the unconscious (or subconsciousness, or superconsciousness) — so the full reality of humanity's biography, the history of mankind, consists of a day aspect and a night aspect. The day aspect comprises the account of the actuality of that which has become, and the night aspect embraces the activity of its becoming. That the biblical way of looking at history concerns itself not only with the day aspect but also with the night aspect — applying both to that which is in becoming and that which has become — is convincing when one considers the Bible itself from this point of view.

So, for instance, the whole story of Abraham (*Genesis* xi–xxv) is a description of events and deeds which are not the effects of causes which belong to the realm of day-consciousness, but of causes which belong to the realm of night-consciousness, of the supersensible. A superconsciousness aimed toward the future directed the deeds and events in Abraham's life, which was entirely future orientated. If one wishes to speak of causality, then it is a question in describing the course of Abraham's life, of understanding that here we do not have causes operating out of the sphere of things past, but rather of goals; that is, of causes which lie in the future and belong to the sphere of becoming. It is a matter of finalistic causality, whereby the impulsating and determining *causae finales*, or goals, did not arise out of Abraham's day-consciousness, but out of the revelations of the super-consciousness directly influencing his day-consciousness. It was not his own goals which directed Abraham to journey to a far distant land, but tasks laid upon him out of the night of superconsciousness. "And the Lord said to Abram: Go from your country and from your kindred and from your father's house, to a land that I will show you" (*Genesis* xiii, 1). There is no mention here of any enemies in the country of Abraham, or of poverty or homelessness forcing him to emigrate or even to flee. On the contrary, there are mentioned a circle of friends and relatives, and his father's house. All of this he is asked — out of the superconscious sphere — to leave, and to journey into a land quite unknown to his day-consciousness. "So Abram departed, as the Lord has spoken unto him; and Lot went with him," the Bible story goes on. Thus we are told that Abraham's day-consciousness received with trust and obedience the commands from the night of superconsciousness, and that he was not emigrating because he was seeking new friends or a better economic situation but solely because the voice which he trusted more than himself told him to act thus.

From the biblical story we see that Abraham was a man who was determined in his decisions and actions more by the night aspect of his consciousness than by its day aspect.

On the other hand, if one wanted to explain his exodus from his homeland and his journey to Canaan solely from the day aspect of his consciousness — to suit the view of the historian — one would have to speak about a sheikh who set out with a few hundred people and large herds of cattle, going from his homeland westward on the search for new and freer pastures. This "pure" historical interpretation would perhaps represent that it played a role in his motives that he wished to be less disturbed in the practice of his private monotheistic religion than he was in his homeland, where polytheism was the official religion. And this would be all that would count as historical fact — all else would be mere mythological decoration!

Yet this flat way of looking at things (limiting them to the one dimension of day-consciousness only) is valid neither for the story of Abraham nor for that of the other patriarchs, nor for Moses, the judges, kings, or prophets. The Bible portrays them in two dimensions: in that of surface actuality — the day aspect — and that of depth, or the night aspect of reality. Joseph's dream and his interpretation of pharaoh's dream belong just as definitely to the chain of causality which brought Jacob and his sons down to Egypt, as the dearth in Canaan and the selling of Joseph into slavery by his brothers. And the experience of Moses in the revelation of the burning bush was at least as determining a factor for the exodus out of Egypt later on, as were the oppression and exploitation of the Israelites in that country.

The view of history which one can learn from the Bible — where the factors of causality of the day, together with the intervening effects of the finalism of the night, make up the cross of totality of historical events — is nothing else than a striving to bring to realization what Paul writes in his letter to the Ephesians: "So that you may be able to comprehend with all the saints what is the breadth and length and depth and height" (*Ephesians* iii, 18). This means to say that history is not to be understood as something which plays itself out on one level, but must be comprehended also in its dimension of height and depth.

Two arguments can be raised against this: the one from the scientific aspect and the other from the religious. The first argument would say: it is unscientific to mix historic facts with unverifiable metaphysical elements — for the former are objective, whilst the latter are subjective.

To that we must answer as follows: obviously the biblical way of considering the working together of "day" and "night" in historical events is not scientific, if only that is considered "scientific" which is generally valid, that is, demonstrable and verifiable for everyone. Also it is obviously subjective, if we regard as "subjective" any insight which one person has and another has not. It is not a matter of "scientificness," as regards the biblical way of looking at things, but of truth, i.e. of as full as possible a comprehension of the whole of what is happening in the history of mankind — both in its sense-perceptible day aspect and also in its supersensible night aspect.

The second argument, which could be raised from the religious point of view, would say: the Bible is a revelation; it is a divinely inspired scripture. It is not man's prerogative to dare to extract from it a method for human cognition. Its method should remain the prerogative of its divine author to whom it belongs; it should not be reduced to the level of human concerns. To this it can only be said that precisely because the Bible is without doubt divinely inspired, one should learn from it and through it as much as possible and as completely as possible. And not only should one learn what it says but also how and why it says it; that is to say, one should also learn its structure and method. Who will presume to set a limit to what can be learnt from the Bible, and thereby indirectly from its divine author? As human beings we have to think and know. Shouldn't we learn from the Bible how to think and know, thus doing so from a divinely inspired thinking and knowing? And if it be presumptuous to regard the Bible as a teacher for human thinking and knowledge, would an "emancipated" human thinking and knowing which followed no pattern of divine origin and simply ignored the Bible be less presumptuous? In short, if we take from the Bible the Ten Commandments and the Beatitudes of the Sermon on the Mount as guiding stars for our actions and endeavours, why should we not also take as guiding stars for our thinking and cognition the whole manner and method of treatment of spiritual-cultural happenings presented in the Bible?

This much can be said to meet arguments against the use of the biblical method of viewing the cooperation of the day and night aspects of historical events in the realm of post-biblical history.

Post-biblical history (as "day" and "night" history) is, seen from its day-aspect, the history of the coming to terms by mankind with the three temptations in the wilderness: the temptation of power, the temptation of plunging down into the instinctivity of the subconscious ("to cast oneself down from the pinnacle of the temple"), and the temptation of materialism ("to change stones into bread"). Seen from the night aspect, it is the working of the nightly rainbow of seven miracles of which St. John's Gospel tells.

Now it is necessary to substantiate the first part of the above statement, namely, that the whole picture of post-biblical history — when regarded as a continuation of biblical history — is nothing else than a constant coming to terms with the three temptations in the wilderness (*Matthew* iv, 1–11; *Luke* iv, 1–13; *Mark* i, 12–13). Here we shall seek to transform this statement from a mere assertation into a meaningful and substantial result of historical experience. To this end we first have to make clear what should be understood by "coming to terms with temptation".

The coming to terms with a temptation does not signify a smooth and immediate rejection of the temptation, nor does it signify immediately becoming a complete prey to it. Rather it is a step-by-step procedure comparable with digestion, in which an alchemistic process takes place of the separation of valuable true elements from damaging untrue ones, whereby the former are absorbed and the latter eliminated. It is the process of transformation of a "yes" into a "no". This entails purification, whereby growing insight and sobriety disentangle and separate the tempting mixture of true and untrue, worthy and worthless, which is characteristic of every temptation and is the cause of its tempting effect. The final step is to eliminate the added poisonous and deceptive (lying) elements. To come to terms with a temptation means to live consciously in a state of dissension, and to live long enough in it for the inner conflict to be overcome. The internal conflict entailed in the state of coming to terms with the temptation can be of an intellectual kind — then we have to do with the condition of doubt; on the other hand, it can be of a soul nature — then we have to do with being exposed to enticement; lastly, it can operate in the sphere of the will itself — then we have to do with seduction. Seduction relates to the will, enticement to feeling, and doubt to thinking. But the temptation which puts the whole human being — in his thinking, feeling, and will — in a state of schism encompasses all three: doubt, enticement, and seduction.

Of this kind, too, were the three temptations of the God-Man in the wilderness of which the Gospels tell. They represent the summation and essence of all temptations to which mankind is exposed in the course of history. For, in the history of mankind it is a matter of constantly coming to terms with temptations manifesting in a thousand different forms. Thus, to explain quality by means of quantity, the living by means of the dead or mechanical, and to fashion qualitative "living" things out of quantitative mechanical ones is, in other words, to turn "stones into bread". Then there is the temptation to replace by force and compulsion the growth of insight and the ripening (in inviolate freedom) of conscience and reason — this signifies the temptation to force the conscience and reason of men to obedience by the aid of power and dominion ("the kingdoms of the world and all their glory").

Lastly, with the temptation to let oneself be guided by instincts working in the darkness of the subconscious instead of by high moral ideals — this is the temptation to "cast oneself down from the pinnacle of the temple".

The temptation "to cast oneself down from the pinnacle of the temple" is present whenever individuals or peoples give themselves up to the guidance of subconscious urges instead of being led by the light of consciousness, i.e. when they put themselves into one of the many kinds of states of intoxication out of which they draw the determining impulses for their thoughts and deeds. This state of intoxication can manifest as the "revolutionary fervour of the masses" or as "religious fanaticism" or else simply as the effects of the whirling dance of the shaman or dervish — in each case it is a "fall from the pinnacle of the temple" (the "pinnacle of the temple" representing consciousness and conscience), and a succumbing to the electrifying directives of the subconscious freed and separated from conscience. This state of intoxication expresses itself not only in lynchings, in pogroms, and in barricade-happy street demonstrations of mobs and frivolous students, but also in the more peaceful forms of various superstitions which even today are tremendously widespread. For the essence of superstition is a renunciation of clarity of consciousness in favour of the darkness of the subconscious freed from conscience, i.e. it is equally a state of intoxication in which the conscious mind has "cast itself down from the pinnacle of the temple". Actually superstition is present everywhere — whether in magic or in science — where the "what" is renounced in favour of the "how", that is to say, where a manipulation of forces and things is practised without any insight into their true nature.

In the same way as with the temptation to "cast oneself down from the pinnacle of the temple", the temptation to "turn stones into bread" manifests itself in many forms and on many levels. When, for instance, Friedrich Engels set up the axiom that quantity becomes quality through increasement, then this axiom signifies nothing else but an adherence to the "turning of stones into bread". And when, for example, Karl Marx declared the spiritual-cultural life to be a function or superstructure of the economic life, then here again we have an affirmation of the temptation of "turning stones into bread". Yes, materialism in every shape and form — theoretical and practical — is the temptation to win life out of that which has no life, or to explain the living through the lifeless, or to conceive of consciousness arising from the subconscious, or quality from quantity. The materialistic illusion entails the belief that the "how" produces the "why", as if oil colours and paintbrushes could paint pictures, string and wind instruments could create works of music, the substances of the brain could produce thoughts, and chemical elements through combination could bring forth the world with its stones, plants, animals, and human beings . . . Materialism is based on the fantastic thesis that inorganic matter creates life, that organic matter creates consciousness, and that consciousness is a condition of matter in which matter reflects itself to itself — where, therefore, matter acquires the capacity for reflecting itself and thereby produces the epiphenomenon of "inwardness" which is experienced as "consciousness". Thus it is maintained that the unconscious produces consciousness, passivity generates activity, darkness gives rise to light, and that which is dead gives birth to life! The temptation to "turn stones into bread" is obviously at work in the materialistic attitude of mind. The materialistic (or materializing) attitude turns beings into things. Thereby, however, the beings at the same time become "possessable" things, i.e. things which one can manipulate according to one's desires. To possess something means to be able to do what one likes with it, i.e. to have power over it.

The "will to power", in which Friedrich Nietzsche saw the basic urge for progressive development, is actually just as generally operative as the tendency toward intoxication (= diving down into the collective subconscious) and as the inclination toward materialism. In other words, the temptation to take possession of the beings of the world, to exercise power over them, is just as universal in the life of mankind as the temptations "to cast oneself down from the pinnacle of the temple" and "to turn stones into bread". They are basically "natural factors" in human life. And the coming to terms with these three "inherited tendencies" (the three temptations in the wilderness of the Son of God who became the Son of Man) consists principally in the fact that these three "natural conditioning factors" have to be countered by three moral-spiritual supernatural ideals, namely, the three vows on which all true spiritual life and all spiritual progress rests — the vows of obedience, poverty, and chastity. The assertion of the will to power is countered by the vow of obedience; the tendency to materialism is countered by the vow of poverty; and the urge to plunge down into the collective subconscious is countered by the vow of chastity.

These "vows" are to be understood in a more all-embracing sense than the traditional three vows of the religious orders. They are the concretized rules of life and behaviour relating to three ideals which embrace the whole of human existence. These ideals are not valid for monasteries and religious orders alone, but for every human being who strives for truth — indeed, for everyone who intends in a responsible manner to fulfill his life's tasks. Every human being whose primary aims are truth and goodness has thereby taken on the irrevocable duty of endeavouring to follow the path prescribed by the threefold ideal of obedience, poverty, and chastity. For how can one strive for knowledge of the truth without being prepared to bow before the reality of the outer and inner spiritual actuality and to obey its commands instead of one's own wishes and tendencies? A striving for truth presupposes on the one hand renunciation of arbitrary whims and on the other hand obedience in the encounter with reality. Without renouncing one's own assertive speaking, it is impossible to hear the voice of truth. Obedience is the path towards hearing the voice of truth. And the vow undertaken by those in religious orders of obedience to their superiors is the exercise or preparation for the faculty of obedient listening. The unqualified obedience of a chela (disciple) to the guru (teacher) in India signifies a similar exercise in preparation for pure hearing. The religious superior or the guru may in certain cases not be in the right; however, it is primarily not a question of whether he is in the right, but of the practice of the inner attitude of obedience as the path to clairaudience ("spiritual hearing") of the truth. It is the path of learning the silencing of one's own self in the encounter with another more highly developed person or being.

The second basic requirement, which the striving for truth brings with it as a prerequisite, is a condition of dissatisfaction, a hunger and thirst for truth, i.e. a condition of "poverty". For, just as one cannot pour any more liquid into a vessel that is filled to the brim, so also a spiritually rich person — a human being who is filled with one aspect of truth, or one system of ideas, and is fully contented with it — is no longer capable of grasping other aspects of truth or thoughts and ideas which do not fit into his system. The flowing in of revelations of truth presupposes an emptiness. This is why the first beatitude of the Sermon on the Mount says: "Blessed are the poor in spirit, for theirs is the kingdom of heaven." Moreover, this spiritual poverty does not in any way mean imbecility or a lack of interest, but rather an active yearning and striving for an ever more complete and deeper truth. It would be more meaningful to translate the words of the beatitude (*pauperes spiritu*) as "beggars for the spirit", instead of "poor in spirit". For a beggar is not only a man who has nothing, who is poor, but rather — and more especially — one who is conscious of his poverty and stretches out his hand asking for a gift. The meaning of the first beatitude is that the active consciousness of poverty is receptive for the kingdom of heaven. Only he who is conscious of the fact that all education and knowledge "of this world" is really poverty as regards essential revelation, is genuinely a "beggar for the spirit" in the sense of the Gospel. For he brings to meet that essential revelation the inner emptiness which it demands.

Again, the vow of poverty taken by those in monastic and religious orders is a way of practising non-possession, which leads to that "begging for the spirit" — to that "spiritual poverty" — which makes human beings capable of receiving the essential revelations of truth.

Similarly, the third vow of religious orders, the vow of chastity, is a way of practising a faculty and attitude of mind which is just as indispensable to the seeker for truth as "obedience" and "poverty". For an experience and knowledge of truth presupposes temperance or sobriety, a presence of mind which enables a person to distinguish truth from the intoxication of suggestion coming from sources belonging to the subconscious. Examples of the latter are represented by the slogans "blood and soil" (Nazi Germany) and the "collective class-consciousness" of communism, where it can be seen that they seek to rise up and dominate the entire consciousness of human beings. Through temperance or sobriety, the human being can distinguish between truth and these subconscious influences as surely as he can between sunlight and electric light. Unchastity is intoxication of every kind; and chastity is temperance or presence of mind, that is, knowledge and action in the sunlight of reason and conscience. Sobriety or temperance has, however, nothing in common with coldness; the warmth of enthusiasm, which the brightness of an enlightened consciousness and conscience brings with it, is the opposite of the sultry, feverish heat of intoxication. There exists on the one hand the warmth of enthusiasm and on the other hand the sultry heat which is caused by the dark abysses of the subconscious. Also the love between man and woman can be expansive and bright — or it can be strong and dark. It can enthuse or enslave. In the first case it is chaste; in the second unchaste. The Apollonian principle of enlightenment is present at all levels of human existence as a counterpart to the Dionysian principle of intoxication. The brightness of the former can increase to a state of rapture or ecstacy; the intoxication of the latter can boil up into frenzy. The foremost representative of chastity — yes, incarnated chastity itself — spoke the words of the Magnificat, the high hymn of bright enthusiasm. How can it be doubted, then, that true temperance is filled with sunlight, warmth, and life? So it is an error to see in so-called Dionysianism the source of enthusiasm and of the capacity to be enthused.

The events of world history (that is, its day aspect) are in their moral-spiritual essence the coming to terms of the three "vows" with the three "temptations in the wilderness". Wars are waged, countries conquered, peoples migrate, revolts and revolutions shatter the social order, new technological inventions and scientific discoveries cause profound changes in the economic life, the way people live, and the way nations fight wars. However, what is really basic to all this (from the standpoint of the biblical way of looking at world history) is the coming to terms between the three "temptations" and the three "vows" within the consciousness of human beings. One can see power and force in confrontation with service and free obedience, the eternal Babylonian tower of godless self-sufficiency of humanity using material technical methods in confrontation with a God-given participation in the coming down from above of the "kingdom of heaven and its righteousness", and the intoxication of volcanic outbreaks of passion in confrontation with the radiance of conscious selfhood. And the confrontation of these contrarily directed forces causes the whirlpool which we call "world historic events", and determines the strength, extent, and duration of these events. For just as whirlpools are caused by the meeting of two opposing streams, so do world historic events arise through the meeting and confrontation of the contrarily directed streams of the "temptations in the wilderness" and the "vows".

This is the moral-spiritual essence of what happens on the stage of day-consciousness, that is, on the "day side" of history. Behind and above it lies the field of operation of the "night side" of history. The latter is noiseless; its events take place in darkness and silence; they come and go like a "thief in the night" as far as human day-consciousness is concerned. This night aspect relates to the day aspect of history in a way similar to how homeopathy relates to allopathy. Whereas in the latter chemical substances work against specific symptoms of sickness, in the former chemically indistinguishable ("invisible") energies work, not against specific symptoms, but in support of the healing activity of the organism itself. The night history of mankind does not consist of a battle against evil, but in the turning of evil into good through a transmutation which works quite inconspicuously. In this sense it can be compared with homeopathy. It heals men in secret by preserving them from degeneration and by constantly giving rise to regenerating effects.

The key concepts for understanding the night aspect of history are "degeneration" and "regeneration". For, with their help, it is possible to understand the reality of history, that is, the cooperation of both the night and day aspects of history in their interplay. They are like two "eyes of thought", which make possible an overview or comprehension of revealed and of hidden historical happenings. We will concern ourselves now with considering these concepts and the realities of experience which correspond with them.

The concept of degeneration — the process we experience — is a gradual and step-by-step descent from an originally higher level to a lower one. Regeneration is the re-ascent to that higher level. The former is a transformation in the direction of hardening, with a corresponding loss of elasticity and of the capacity for adaptation; it is the path from the spiritual to the earthly. The way of degeneration is that of a gradual sinking into earthliness. It is a matter here of a process of gradual exteriorization. For example, when the experience of the breath of God becomes morality, and morality becomes legality, and legality becomes a system of outer customs and conventions — then the process of degeneration lies unveiled before us. "Spirit and life" arrive at the "dead letter". In this process of degeneration the "how", the technique, replaces the "what", the essence. Thereby the living organism goes the way of change into a corpse, i.e. the way that ends in a complete transformation of the living organism into a piece of the outer world. For the corpse is nothing other than the end result of a process of exteriorization of the organism. This is degeneration. Therefore degeneration is an expression of the generally prevailing force — biologically understood — of earthly gravitation.

The same is true of all other expressions of life (not only the biological ones) and of the spiritual life in every form. Oswald Spengler's historical prognosis of the inevitable "Decline of the West" into the morass of technology and technocracy is only a conclusion through analogy from the way of all natural things ("the way of all flesh") drawn with respect to the sphere of culture in general. Spengler drew the analogy from the natural and biological realm to the spiritual and cultural domain. And as in the former degeneration always has the last word, so Spengler concluded that in the latter also it will not be otherwise.

Spengler would be absolutely right and his prognosis unshakably sure if the natural process of degeneration, i.e. the force of "earthly gravity" (the force of transformation of the living and ensouled into the non-living — the corpse) alone governed everywhere. It is indeed at work everywhere and always, but it is not the only process at work. The natural operation of the degeneration process is from time to time interpenetrated by supernatural impulses of regeneration.

The operation of degeneration, which we have designated above as "earthly gravity", can be made clear with the help of the following example from physics:

Imagine an impulse of energy which causes a kind of swinging motion. This movement will sooner or later deplete itself, that is, it will of necessity gradually lose pace and come to rest, unless brought into movement again by a second impulse of energy. The system of repeaters operating in long distance telephone connections serves precisely the task of bringing the decreasing strength of the vibrations up to its original level. In this manner the audibility of the human voice is carried on over thousands of miles. Analogous to this is the law which governs every movement set going by an impulse — every movement which we call "fashion", every movement in politics or in the sphere of world-conceptions. All movements of a social, political, artistic, intellectual, and religious kind may indeed have different speeds of devolution, but one thing they have in common: if no reinforcing impulse is given after a certain time, they will inevitably exhaust themselves. A thing of motion or of life becomes a corpse unless "reawakening impulses" intervene. Impulses of regeneration, however, do actually intervene — precisely out of the hidden energy center belonging to the "night realm" of history and also to every individual biography. Thus, it was the spoken word of Jesus Christ heard by his disciples, it was his miracles which they witnessed, it was his Passion and Resurrection at which they were present, which made them into his disciples. However, it needed the event of Whitsun (the pouring out of the Holy Spirit) to make them into apostles. The event of Whitsun was the first reinforcing impulse, or we should rather say "reawakening impulse", which turned Christianity from a local happening in Palestine into a worldwide human concern of the first order. What economic, political, social, national, or psychological causes in the day-history sphere of mankind could cause and "explain" the Whitsun event? From which source in the visible world did the power stream which transformed a handful of men belonging to a Jewish sect into a spiritual world-conquering movement? Whence their sureness, their energy, their success? The event of Whitsun was the intervention of an impulse which brought Christianity onto the level of the original impulse of the Son of God becoming man. It was the first renewal impulse or "reawakening" coming from the realm of the night side of the history of Christianity and of mankind. The event of Whitsun was the first of a sequence of reawakening impulses which has kept Christianity alive through nineteen centuries.

For example, let us consider what happened in the fourth century at the time when the Church entered into an alliance with the Roman Empire and the influence of the latter became paramount. It was as if a dark cloud covered the sky. It even came to a point when the center of Christianity itself — Christ himself as the Son of God made flesh — was to a large extent veiled, and Arianism for a time achieved almost complete dominance. Then a strong fresh wind scattered the clouds and the sun of Christ as the Son of God shone forth again in the heavens as faith. Not only a Pleiad of great believers (with St. Athanasius at their head), and holy hermits such as St. Anthony of Thebes (the friend of St. Athanasius), and great priests such as St. Ambrosius and St. Augustine, were the fruit of this spiritual wind, but also — and especially — the Council of Nicaea with its wonderful creation of the Nicaean Creed, which to this day has lost nothing of its inspiring and enlightening force and effect. It became (and today still is) the banner around which the Christ-faithful Christians gathered (and today still gather), while the general run of believers in God, to which the pagans also belong, might make use of various other creeds. The Nicaean Creed is a formula of divine magic, and he who knows this is tempted to say: heaven and earth will pass away, but the words of this Creed will not pass away.

Further interventions of reawakening impulses out of the night sphere into the day sphere were brought by spiritual movements which culminated in widespread religious orders, or in their renewal. The impetus which underlay the great millennial-old mission of the Benedictine Order was the third intervention of reawakening after the Whitsun event. It was the Benedictine Order which fashioned the bridge from the Christian culture of antiquity across the barbaric floods of the folk migrations to the epoch of the great cathedrals and the great thought-constructions of Scholasticism. The Benedictine Order was the "Noah's Ark" which rescued Christian culture — together with the culture of antiquity, insofar as the latter had become taken up by Christianity — from the "flood" of the great folk migrations.

A further impulse of reawakening took place in the thirteenth century. There arose two great Orders — the Dominicans and the Franciscans — which brought with them a mighty impetus for fostering Christian thinking and the Christian feeling-life. A new springtime blossomed forth for Christianity. A renewed enthusiasm for a radical living of Christianity, inspired by St. Francis, and for a philosophically founded Christianity enlightened by thinking thought through to the last detail, inspired by St. Dominic, suddenly became active and took hold of the noblest hearts and minds of the time.

And yet the merciless, crippling influence of the law of gravitation — of degeneration — asserted itself, and during the course of the following centuries this enthusiasm gradually dried up. Then again there took place a streaming in of reawakening impulses in the sixteenth century. This expressed itself in a great movement of interiorization connected with the bringing into existence of the Jesuit Order through St. Ignatius of Loyola and his comrades, and also in the reformation of the Carmelite Order through St. Teresa of Avila and St. John of the Cross. There arose at that time a deep yearning for inwardness — for experience and understanding of Christianity at first hand. This yearning underlay a widespread meditation movement which then arose. Already during the lifetime of St. Ignatius hundreds of thousands of people practised his spiritual exercises (*exercitia spiritualia*). It was a matter in this spiritual training of awakening the whole human being to the reality of Christianity through inner experience. Through the meditative training people became more than pious; they became witnesses to the truth of Christianity, just as Paul, for instance, through his experience on the way to Damascus, became a witness to the Resurrected One. The constructive effect of pious devotion was not supplanted — rather, it became supplemented by an inner dramatic transmutation, or even complete transposition, of thinking, feeling, and the will through the practice of the spiritual exercises. Human beings emerged from the meditation training of the spiritual exercises to wholly devote themselves, out of their own deepest knowledge and conscience, to the redemptive truths of Christianity. What was usually experienced — more dreaming than awake — through pious devotion became in this experience of meditation a matter of burning conscience, a challenge to action, and an overwhelming awakening to the reality of redemption, the Redeemer and the saints. The consequence of this awakening to the reality of the truth of Christianity is the unshakable determination of an "eye witness".

The stream of meditative practice which rose up strongly in the sixteenth century and became widespread stood in the sign of the Gospel words: "From the days of John the Baptist until now the kingdom of heaven has suffered violence, and the violent take it by force" (*Matthew* xi, 12), or also in the sense of the Gospel summons: "Ask, and it shall be given you; seek, and you shall find; knock, and it shall be opened unto you" (*Luke* xi, 9). For it is a matter of the awakening of inner activity, the transformation by human beings of their own minds, the forming and reshaping of consciousness to make it capable of opening to the effects of divine grace, and cooperating with that grace. Thus human consciousness strove to become a co-worker with divine grace; it offered itself to divine grace as an ally. The people who were gripped by this reawakening impulse strove — in the sense of the parable of the entrusted "talents" — to ensure that the human faculties of consciousness (the talents entrusted to them) should bear fruit and increasingly become more useful for the work of the Lord.

The epoch of operation of the fourth reawakening impulse after the event of Whitsun is ordinarily designated as that of the Counter-Reformation. Actually this should not be understood as anti-reformatory, but as a true reformation. For the movement toward interiorization and spiritualization which arose then in the Church was indeed in a real sense *reformation*, and in no sense a process of outer revolt — destroying images and annihilating Church hierarchy, and doing away with spiritual orders and the three vows. A monastery, for instance, is not reformed by chasing out the monks, but by bringing in a more interiorized spiritual life — as was the case, for example, in the reformation of monastic life in the Carmelite Order proceeding from St. Teresa of Avila. The so-called Counter-Reformation and the so-called Reformation stand in the same relationship to one other as the spiritualization of monasteries stands in relation to their dissolution. The first was an impulse toward inner transformation; the second signified rebellion and "purge". The one meant "evolution", the other signified "revolution".

It was the impulse toward inwardness of a Christianity reawakened through meditation which rescued the Church from the storms of the so-called "Reformation", just as it was rescued by the Benedictine impulse from the storms of barbarism of the folk migrations, and just as the Nicaene reawakening impulse saved it from the earlier storms of the Arian "reformation".

During the following centuries — down to the present time — the law of earthly gravitation (of natural degeneration) asserted itself again. The intensity of meditative Christianity gradually lessened and what originally meant a dramatic transformation of the whole human being — of his thinking, feeling, and striving — ultimately developed into weekend retreats for the youth, for nurses, teachers, parents, and doctors . . . where lectures were held on moral and theological themes. Although in itself a good thing, this has little in common with the meditative training of an Ignatius of Loyola or a Teresa of Avila.

The ebb, however, goes before the flow. It would be highly tempting to characterize the preliminary signs and particular characteristics of a new impulse of reawakening in our time, but we must hold back in this respect. For, far too many people have definite views about it, and it is only right to leave them time, until actual events will themselves speak the last word on the subject, so that the various opinions will prove themselves to be either correct or false. In any case it is not necessary, because the task which we have set ourselves here consists in the clarification of the concepts "degeneration" and "regeneration" and in elucidating the factors of experience which are related to these words.

The results of our investigation may be expressed as follows. Degeneration is change taking place in the direction from life to death, from the living toward the corpse. It is the general rulership of the natural law of earthly gravity, which operates constantly. Regeneration, on the other hand, is the working of supernatural revivifying and reawakening impulses operating counter to degeneration. With the help of examples belonging to Church history, we can observe the reality of the working of the law of degeneration, and the repeated interventions of reawakening impulses from the "night side" of history. Thereby it is apparent that every impulse coming into the realm of earthly events (i.e. day history) out of the super-earthly realm (i.e. night history) necessarily exhausts itself in the course of time; it loses intensity, and is only kept alive thanks to occasional interventions of new reawakening impulses from the night side of history. This is true for the biography of mankind (world history) as well as for the individual biographies of human beings.

For example, Goethe was at work writing his *Faust* for a period of sixty years. This does not mean that he actually took sixty years to write the drama, but that he worked at it as long as he had periods of creative enthusiasm alternating with those of creative "dearth". In other words, the original impulse for the creation of this work, which he received in his youth, was given a succession of reawakening impulses which moved him to take up the work ever anew, after intervals of pause during which "earthly gravity" exercised its paralysing influence.

The rule of degeneration, and the reawakening impulses of regeneration, both in the biography of mankind and in the individual biographies of human beings, can be summarized briefly as follows: Suppose an impulse arises out of the depths of the "night side" of history and of life, which causes a living stream to flow in the realm of the "day side" of history and of life. After a certain time its intensity decreases under the growing influence of "earthly gravity". Then a new impulse breaks in from the night side and brings the sinking, foundering movement up again to its original level of intensity. This repeats itself several times. The movement with its tendency to fall into slumber, gets repeatedly reawakened — or, it could also be said that the death-inclined, dying movement is repeatedly raised up.

The law of the life-giving, revivifying breath of the spirit belongs to the most ancient store of knowledge of mankind. Moses' book of *Genesis* also begins with a description of the archetypal working of this law ("law" — in the sense of an eternal ordinance of God), and describes it as the "first day of creation". Actually *Genesis* does not describe it as the "first day", but as the "one day" (*jom echad*), which St. Jerome also has translated precisely according to the text as *dies unus* and not as *dies primus*. For it precedes time; it belongs in the realm of eternity. Time is sequential, but it arose initially on the foundations of — and in relation to — the juxtaposition of the two primal directions of movement of which the world consists, namely, the directions "above" and "below", which in *Genesis* are called "heaven" and "earth". Therefore the movement directed downward is called in the second verse "the deep", comprising "the waters" over which the breath of God (*ruach elohim*) moved. "Spirit" and "breath" are in Hebrew one and the same, just as *spiritus* in Latin and also *pneuma* in Greek can both be translated as "spirit" or "breath".

What we have described above as "earthly gravity" is, as the movement directed downward, called in the Mosaic story of creation "earth", "the deep", and "water" — that is, it is "gravity" in the sense of movement directed toward the fathomless deep (abyss) of passivity (water). And what we described above as the moving and life-giving breath of the spirit is, in the Mosaic story, the "spirit (or breath) of God moving over the waters". It is the mover, whereas the "waters of the deep" are what is moved. What St. Thomas Aquinas called the *primus motor*, the first stimulator of motion, is the life-giving and moving breath of God's spirit (*ruach elohim*) on the "first day" of creation. But as the first day of creation was not the first in a sequence of creative acts following one after another in time, but has more the meaning of the first foundation — i.e. it is fundamental to all existence — it is not then replaced by the "second day" or the "third day", etc., but is eternally present through and within them. It is therefore the case that the moving and life-giving breath of God's spirit is always active, and according to the above-mentioned law of repeated reawakening counters the influence of "earthly gravity" (i.e. that which gives rise to forgetting, sleep, and death).

Not only *Genesis*, but also the *Bhagavad Gita*, speaks of the law of repeated impulses of the divine spirit intervening in order to maintain the level of intensity of the original life-impulse of the world (there called *dharma*). It speaks of the law of the repeated appearance

of Avatars. It formulates this law (which is the reality of the first day
of creation in *Genesis*) as follows:

> Every time when dharma is expiring and unrighteousness is in
> ascendance, then I appear through birth. For the liberation of the good,
> for the destruction of those that do evil, for the setting up of righteousness
> upon the throne, I appear through birth from age to age. (*Bhagavad Gita*
> IV, 7–8)

Thus the teachings of the *Bhagavad Gita* speak of the law of
maintenance of the original basic impulse through repeated revivification of it from age to age, happening every time when it danger-
ously loses its intensity and consequently needs a renewal. Although
according to the teachings of the *Bhagavad Gita* these revivifying or
reawakening impulses are linked each time with a particular human
individuality — in whom these impulses are centered and from whom
they go forth — this specific conception changes nothing in the nature
of the law of repeated awakenings, which is the reality of the timeless
"first day of creation" by the spirit of God (*ruach elohim*) in history.

The spiritual thinking and feeling of India is so strongly permeated
and governed by a consciousness of the reality of the timeless
"first day of creation", that not only orthodox Hinduism — represented
chiefly by the *Bhagavad Gita* — but also Buddhism which is, as it
were, a considerably later "reformed" kind of Hinduism, likewise
definitely has the law of repeated "reawakening-impulses" as an
underlying basis. For, according to the basic Buddhist conception, the
natural course of the world is aging, sickness, and death; this means
degeneration. This is the natural way of the world, which is not a
path, but rather an unconscious gliding down of consciousness into
the realm of unknowing, that is to say — of forgetting, sleep, and
death. In contrast to this exists a path going in the opposite direction
to the "way of the world", like a swimming against the stream of the
world. Its steps are stages of awakening within the wide open spaces
of a world sunk in spiritual slumber. Over and against the sopo-
rific influence of this world stands the way of awakening. Calls
to awaken go forth from age to age originating from powerful
(*tathagatas*) Awakened Ones (*buddhas*), each of whom is the central
point of an awakening impulse valid for one particular epoch, and
who teaches the appropriate way, exemplifying it in himself. The
Buddhas represent awakening impulses for particular epochs, and
show the way leading to awakening which is suited to that epoch of
time. Therefore the Buddhist world awaits, after the fading away of
the awakening impulse carried by the last Buddha, Gautama, and
the noble eightfold path which he taught and exemplified — the

appearance of a new Buddha, Maitreya, who will bring a new awakening impulse, and will teach and exemplify a new path of awakening.

The periodic appearance of the Avatars, according to Hindu teaching, and the periodic appearance of the Buddhas, according to the Buddhist teaching, doubtless represent a specific manifestation of the law of repeated reawakening impulses, or the reality of God's spirit (*ruach elohim*) from the timeless first day of creation. Consciousness of this law lives not only in Hinduism and in Buddhism, but also in the third great religion — the younger of the world religions — namely, Islam. It lives especially strongly in Islam's more spiritually tangible form — Shi'ite Islam — whose spiritual depth and wealth was made available for the first time to western readers in a comprehensive manner by Henri Corbin, in cooperation with Seyyed Hossein Nasr and Osman Yahya in their work *Histoire de la philosophie islamique*, which appeared in 1964, published by Gallimard, Paris. In this work it is not merely stated, but also shown, that eastern Islam (Shi'ite Islam) is related to western Islam (Sunnite Islam) as the soul is to the body. For the latter is in fact legalistic, while the former actually expresses the way of interiorization. This interiorization comes to expression in the ascent from the other cycle of Prophets to the inner cycle of Imams. The former are proclaimers of the *shari'at*, the law of positive religion for an epoch, while the latter are initiators into the *haqiqat* (theosophy). The Prophet (*nabi*) proclaims and teaches, while the Imam enlightens and vivifies. The sphere of the Prophets encircles that of the Imams; it is the outer (*zahir*) over and against the inner (*batin*).

Correspondingly, the famous philosopher of Iranian Ismaelism, Nasir-e-Khosraw (eleventh century) taught: "Positive religion (*shari'at*) is the exoteric aspect of wisdom (*haqiqat*) and wisdom is the esoteric side of positive religion. Positive religion is the symbol (*mithal*); wisdom is that which is symbolized (*mamthul*). The exoteric is in constant flux in accordance with changing epochs, while the esoteric is a divine energy which is not subject to becoming" (Corbin, p. 17). The esoteric side of religion (of the prophetic religions), the *haqiqat*, is the sphere of eternal Mohammedan prophecy (*haqiqat mohammediya*) out of which from age to age prophetic revelations are sent out into outer history. The Prophets represent and mediate these periodic rayings out from the sphere of eternal prophecy; the Imams, however, who follow after the Prophets, reveal their inner (esoteric) significance. The Prophets proclaim, and the Imams initiate human beings into the inner secret of the prophecies. The Prophets bring down to human beings the revelation from the "sphere of eternal prophecy"; the Imams lift up the souls of human beings to the inner meaning of this revelation in the "sphere of eternal prophecy". The Prophets condense the revelation into "law" (shari'at), while the Imams interiorize the "law" right to its original essence. They transform "the letter of the law" into "spirit and life". So the twelve Imams are the revivers and life-preservers of the work of the seven great Prophets. Their missions follow one after the other. Toward the end of our aeon the twelfth Imam will be in full action; it will be the time of resurrection (qiyamat), when the inner significance (batin) of all earlier divine revelations will be completely illuminated.

Now, it is obvious that the law of a cyclical alternation of reviving, life-preserving "reawakening impulses" breaking into the "day history" of mankind is without doubt recognized as a fact in Islam. For we have here to do with the *fact* only, not with its varying interpretations: whether there were six or seven great Prophets, whether there are twelve or more Imams, how many Buddhas and how many Avatars there were, and so on. Alone the fact is of importance: that the spiritual life of mankind is maintained through the breath of the Spirit from beyond the human sphere, and that the great religions of mankind are quite conscious of this fact. It is the fact that is concisely expressed in the Christian Creed as follows:

Et Spiritum Sanctum, Dominum et vivificantem, qui ex Patre Filioque procedit . . . qui locutus est per prophetas ("I believe in the Holy Spirit, the Lord and giver of life, who proceeds from the Father and the Son . . . who has spoken through the prophets"). In Christianity the vivifying "reawakening activity" of the spirit (the "night side" of history) is not only acknowledged, but is also recognized in its essential nature to be the third Person of the eternal Trinity. This is the highest and most comprehensive insight into the nature of the law of consecutive "reawakening impulses", which stem from the night side of history and reveal themselves in the history of mankind. This law originates in the eternal Trinity itself. It follows that it is eternal and universal. But it is indeed not a mere "law", i.e. something resembling the laws of nature; it is the Person of the Holy Spirit. This means, however, that the enlivening reawakenings from the hidden realms of "night history" do not happen, as it were, automatically and indifferently. Discrimination rules in the enlivening reawakening activity of the Holy Spirit. Just because it is no mere "law", being much more than a law — as it proceeds from "the Holy Spirit, the Lord and giver of life, who proceeds from the Father and from the Son, who together with the Father and the Son is worshipped and glorified" — therefore it takes place with discrimination.

There are spiritual streams which degenerate without receiving a regenerating impulse; others again are kept going for thousands of years through a sequence of such impulses. There were (and are) actual "twilights of the gods", when whole world conceptions became powerless and torpid. Ultimately they are pushed out of the life of mankind as lifeless husks and are forgotten. And on the other hand there exist spiritual streams which become ever and again torn out of torpidity and exhaustion through enlivening, reawakening impulses. "Twilights of the gods" and "renaissances" takes place side by side in world history. But neither should be conceived of generally — so that, for example, when Hellenistic paganism with its gods perished, then it perished in its entirety. Its lifeless husk (the "straw", as it were) was recognized as such and cast out (i.e. "burnt"), while the "grain" (i.e. that which was worthy of living on) was awakened to new life. So it ·was that the world of the pagan gods experienced a real "twilight", while the seeds of wisdom of Greek philosophy sprout and grow again elsewhere — on other terrain — and celebrate their "renaissance". Who bothers today about Zeus? — while Plato and Aristotle are intensely present in all idealism and in all rational logical cognition. All thinking whose goal is truth, beauty, and goodness cannot avoid a meeting with Plato, and all thinking which strives to combine experience with reason carries further the life-work of Aristotle.

Friedrich Schiller once said: "World history is World Judgement". How true this is can most readily be seen when one considers the reawakening impulses from the realm of the night side of history, i.e. the rule of the Holy Spirit in the history of mankind. Under this rule, neither is the child thrown out with the bath water, nor is the water — because of the child — treated as an untouchable living being. This means to say, in the due course of "twilights of the gods" and "renaissances", what is worthy of life — indeed *all* that is worthy of life, and *only* what is worthy of life — is maintained and preserved by the reawakening impulses of the Spirit. When the Creed says of the Holy Spirit *Dominus et vivificans* ("Lord and giver of life"), it means that He is Lord of the decisions as to what is to be revived and what is to be left to the fate of all natural things — concluding ultimately with death. He is the Lord who bestows life and who also does not bestow life. He is the Lord and giver of life who not only bestows life but also makes the decision as to what is worthy of life. Yes, world history is World Judgement, which is the rulership of the life-giving Holy Spirit.

Spiritual-cultural history (viewed as a continuation of biblical history) is, therefore, the coming to terms in mankind of the three "temptations in the wilderness" with the three "vows". This is the domain of the "day side" of spiritual-cultural history. The "night side", on the other hand, consists in the rule of the Holy Spirit, in the sense of the rainbow of the seven eternally operating miracles of St. John's Gospel. Underlying these seven miracles are the timeless realities of the seven days of creation, and they have their "after image", so to say, in the seven sacraments. And just as the seven days of creation are all contained in the "first day", so does the miracle of the raising of Lazarus contain the other six miracles of which St. John's Gospel tells. Accordingly, the "law of repeated reawakenings" which holds sway in the spiritual-cultural history of mankind—which is regarded as a fact by all the great religions of mankind—is the timeless reality of the first day of creation, revealing itself in the miracle of the raising of Lazarus. The whole regenerating activity which works against the "natural process" of degeneration—culminating with death—is the constant revelation of the miracle of the raising of Lazarus in the history of mankind.

3. CAUSALITY AND MIRACLES IN THE SPIRITUAL-CULTURAL HISTORY OF MANKIND

The results, described above, of our considerations concerning the nature of the spiritual-cultural history of mankind, viewed as a continuation of biblical history, challenge us to think simultaneously in two dimensions: in the horizontal dimension of the chain of cause and effect (i.e. the dimension of causality), and in the vertical dimension of interventions from outside the causal chain (this being the dimension of miracles). Spiritual-cultural history thus appears as a cross formed out of causality and miracles. In other words, the spiritual-cultural history of mankind is the result on the one hand of the causes which are to be found in space and time, and on the other hand of the causes which are not to be found there, which are of a timeless and spaceless nature. The miracle, too, is a cause initiating effects in the domain of the chain of cause and effect, but it is a cause which is not itself an effect of another cause within this chain. It is a new cause, which appears in the chain of causality from outside this chain. It strikes like lightning from above into causally conditioned events. The lightning, after having struck, also becomes a cause having its effects within earthly events. However, in itself it is not caused by these earthly events but through things which must be sought above earthly happenings, among the inhabitants of heaven. A miracle is like the appearance of a new cause within the chain of the natural course of causes and effects. It is related to this chain in the same way as a stroke of lightning is related to things on the earth's surface into which it strikes.

The miracle is a vertically appearing cause within the horizontal sequence of causal events. The miracle, therefore, is in its nature not to be regarded just as an "unexplainable" and "astounding" thing, but as something belonging to another dimension of causality. For many things seem to us inexplicable, incomprehensible, and astonishing, without being for that reason miracles; they have simply not yet been investigated in the right way, and are reserved for a future method of research. They are secrets, but not miracles. Secrets and miracles are fundamentally different things, and should not be confused. The secret is in an unknown link within the chain of cause and effect, while the miracle is, in the realm of natural causality, an "uncaused cause". The miracle appears in the causal sphere — coming from the realm of pure morality transcending causally conditioned things — appearing, that is to say, out of the realm of freedom. So when the natural sequence of causality (for example in the sequence of generations) consists of father-mother-child, of which the father is the active cause, the procreative factor (*causa efficiens*), and the mother is the receptive factor (*causa materialis*), while the birth of the child is the result of procreation and conception, then the miracle in the generative sequence would be the "fatherless" conception by a virgin. Then the procreation, the effective cause, would be brought about by the power of a moral-spiritual (divine) intervention, and consequently the mother would be mother and virgin. For the realm of causality, every miracle is fundamentally an "immaculate conception" — a conception for which the father, the procreator, as effective cause, is not on "earth" but "in heaven". The immaculate conception and the virgin motherhood of Mary — "blessed among women" — is according to its natural structure like an archetypal phenomenon for all miracles. For it reveals, in the most essential and concise form imaginable, the intrinsic nature of a miracle as a vertical cause in the sphere of the horizontally linked chain of cause and effect.

Therefore, he who does not recognize the miracle of the immaculate conception, and the virgin motherhood of Mary, denies at the same time all miracles, and he who denies miracles in general, denies at the same time the free creativity of the Spirit, i.e. the creation of the world as an act of causation which itself is not caused. And he who does not recognize the creation of the world, also does not recognize God as the Creator. He denies the Fatherhood of God in the coming into existence of the world. Let the "demythologizing" modern theologians, who are addicted to "enlightenment", consider the following: if they want to be consistent, they have to cancel the first article of the Creed, "demythologizing" their faith in God the Father, the Creator. For "demythologization" carried to its conclusion yields nothing other than the "dialectical materialism" of Marxism. "Judas, what thou doest, do quickly; but if thou betrayest, at least do not do it with a kiss . . ."

The miracle as the vertical cause within the horizontally proceeding sequence of causality does not cancel the latter out; it simply adds an "uncaused cause" to the causal chain which then continues on according to its own laws. After the immaculate conception, Mary was pregnant and bore the child until it was ready to be born. When Therese Neumann of Konnersreuth lived for decades solely from the Holy Communion, it does not mean that she suffered a measure of hunger which for any other person would be deadly — that she hungered superhumanly — but rather that the measure of calories needed by her organism was taken in through other means than by an outer imbibing of nourishment. The daily expenditure of energy was replaced in her organism in the same way as in any other human organism; only that this expenditure was not replaced by the taking in of nourishment from without, but by a substance creating activity within the organism itself. We know today that matter is a condition of energy — that matter can be transformed into energy — and that, basically, energy can be transformed into matter. The miracle which happened to Therese Neumann consisted therefore in the fact that the "moral energy" of the holy communion condensed itself into the substance necessary for the preservation of the life of the organism. One could name this miracle (not the only one of its kind in history) — in comparing it with the immaculate conception — the miracle of the "immaculate nourishment". It is — from a physiological point of view — the conversion of the digestive needs of the organism from the taking in of nourishment from without, to a replacement of the expended energy by an *inner* process. As if a pool, whose water level was held constant through the influx of water from a ditch, now needed the influx no longer because, from the bottom of the pool, a spring had broken forth and begun to flow. The spring would then replace the influx of water from outside the pool.

Miracles are springs which open up within a world considered constant with respect to energy and matter.

On the other hand, the peculiar phenomena which are regarded as mysteries and riddles are not necessarily miracles. They may simply be things not yet understood. If inexplicability is the nature of a riddle or mystery, then the nature of a miracle is its "explainability" through the realm of morality and freedom, which relates to the realm of causality as the vertical relates to the horizontal. A forgiving or generous deed of love is more miraculous (being of the nature of a miracle) than a rocket flight to the moon or to Venus. For a deed of love is a revelation of a world of creativity and freedom, whereas the "miracle" of a flight to one or another planet is only an episode and achievement in the struggle for existence out of which it arose. This means to say that it is an episode in the development of power over nature beginning with the stone axe and continuing through to the moon flight. The achievement is impressive, but it is in no sense a growth of the human being or of mankind into the heights, depths, expanses, and essentialities of existence. The visit to the moon means nothing for the development of man's humanity, but signifies new possibilities in the sense of an extension of the power of man — as an unchanged being — over the outer physical world. In consequence of the successful flight to the moon, man will indeed have greater capacities in the sphere of making use of his physical environment but he himself remains the same as he was before.

It is different when it is a matter of a miracle rather than an achievement. The essential thing then is a becoming, not a getting or an accomplishing. The miracle which happened to Paul on the way to Damascus did not consist primarily in his having an extraordinary experience — that, namely, of a meeting with the Resurrected One — but in the fact that he, the enemy of the new spiritual movement, became its apostle. Also the essential factor of the event of Pentecost did not lie in the phenomena — the rushing mighty wind, the flames of fire, the speaking which each heard in his own mother tongue — but in the fact that the disciples became apostles. It is hardly necessary to mention that the archetypal phenomenon of all miracles — the Immaculate Conception and Virgin Birth — signified the "becoming" of the God-Man.

The miracle of the raising of Lazarus, also, was more than a revival of the body of a dead person. It was actually the coming into being of a new Lazarus who was, as it were, born anew — as the concrete answer to the question put to the Master by Nicodemus in his nighttime conversation. For both the newly born Lazarus and the nighttime conversation of Jesus with Nicodemus belong to the "night side" of Christianity. They belong to the hidden core of being of Christianity, which is the mystery of "becoming", i.e. the essence itself of all miracles. For the essence of a miracle lies neither in might nor in mystery — neither in extraordinary power, nor in incomprehensibility — but in the reality of the moral world order working down into the reality of the mechanical, causal world order. Every such "intervention" on the part of the moral world order into the realm of the mechanical, causal world order, whether it be the widow's mite or a raising from the dead, is fundamentally a miracle. Obviously miracles differ in their extent and effects, just as, say, a stroke of lightning differs from a spark — but both lightning and the spark are of the same nature. The archetypal miracle of the Creation, and the lighting up of a spark of faith in a human soul who had been captivated by the spell of the mechanical, causal world order, differ indeed in extent and range, but are essentially the same. For the *fiat lux* of the first day of creation and the *fiat lux* of the awakening faith in the soul are of the same essence. In both cases it is a question of the creative act of "Let there be light!" Thus, many miracles take place constantly in an intimate and private manner in the shadow and half-shadow of the lives of human beings and the life of mankind — large and small miracles. One could say: life is interwoven and impulsated by miracles, which for the most part go entirely unnoticed — let alone become evaluated and recognized. The days as they pass are not just "the trite everyday with its trifles and treadmill", but bear also the reflected glory of the first day of creation, eternally present. The world of miracles constantly shimmers through the shadow-world of the mechanical-causal world of everyday.

Pope John XXIII gave clear expression to the difference between these two aspects of the world and all events by saying at the reception of a large group of scientists that "it is not our task to make judgements about the methods and results of scientific research; our task lies in the sphere of miracles alone". In other words, the competence and mission of the Holy Father relates and limits itself to the moral world-order, which does not lie within the competence and scope of science. For the Creed of the Church is an avowal of the miracles of creation, redemption, and sanctification of the world; the sacraments are religious acts which have their roots in the miracle, are oriented toward the miracle, and are effective through the miracle. The Church itself lives and exists through the miracle of its foundation and the miracle of its repeated revivification. The modernizing theologians (that is, the "scribes" of our time) and the moralizing humanists (that is, the "Pharisees" of our time) — busying themselves with "demythologizing" in the sense of eliminating the miraculous and the supernatural, and reducing them to fit mere human reason and human morality alone — are basically heretics, apostates.

Christianity itself is a miracle, and whoever denies miracles, denies Christianity. For faith is actually a recognition of the moral world-order, and the conviction that this is primary over and against the mechanical, causal world-order. This means, however, that the miracle, as a manifestation of the moral world-order, is primary over and against the natural mechanical-causal course of things. The "kingdom of heaven" (the moral world-order) indeed reveals itself in "this world" (the mechanical-causal world), but it is not of this world. Christ's saying to Pilate: "My kingdom is not of this world", is valid also for Christianity and for the Church. Now the so-called "demythologizing" humanist theologists want to adapt Christianity and the Church to this world, to make it into a piece of this world. They call it "modernizing" — adaptation to the "spirit of the age" and its requirements, including its "progress". Thus Prof. Mag. Dr. Edward Schillebeecks, Professor of Dogmatism and Theological History at the University of Nijmegen (Holland), in answering the question: How did it happen that the Netherlands are in advance of the development within the universal Church? — made the following statement (in *De Tijd*, August 13, 1969): "The Netherlands were the first country where theologians, priests and laymen interested in religion approached religious problems from the aspect of humanist science and not from that of theology only. The inclusion of sociology, psychology and the humanist sciences made possible the breakthrough in general here in the Netherlands." A German theologian and priest "consoled" a friend of mine in a conversation by stating that the angels (including the archangels Michael and Gabriel) have *no reality* — according to the most recent and now apparently universally accepted theology. They are merely personifications of human soul-forces. And thus, and only thus, did an "angel" come with the annunciation to the Virgin Mary. It seems that psychology takes priority over the Holy Scripture and tradition.

This and similar methods and teachings of theology are clearly symptoms of apostasy from Christianity — which indeed works in this world, but is not of it, nor of the world of psychology and sociology. Christianity is not an "ideological superstructure" to psychological, sociological, and economic facts, but a revelation of the reality of the moral world-order in the realm of the mechanical, causal world-order. Whoever does not understand this — how can he be a "theologian" or "priest"?

The above examples only serve to demonstrate the fact that a strong movement is working within the Church which has chosen "this world" with its pretensions and demands. It seems that this movement is drawn with irresistible force to the human sphere belonging to the realm of time; it wants to be human (and humanistic) and up-to-date ("progressive"). Thereby it subjects itself to the laws of time, which is the path to inevitable degeneration, decline, and death. It is quite useless to argue with people of this trend — just as useless as to try and bring to his senses a man who is in love. They are in love with anthropology, and theology has no further attraction for them.

Strangely enough it happened that this movement surfaced right after the Second Vatican Council — the Council called together by Pope John XXIII out of a desire for renewal, i.e. to deepen, elevate, and expand the traditional inheritance of the Church. A tremendous misunderstanding then entered in; instead of a renewal of the Church in the sense of a deepening, elevation, and expansion of tradition, there arose a striving to revise the tradition, to "de-mythologize" it, to "simplify" it, to make it accord with the taste of modern culture. The pope who summoned the Council prayed the following prayer for it (September 23, 1959):

"May this Council bear rich fruit; may the light and power of the Gospel be more widely spread in human society; may new strength be given to the Catholic religion and its missionary activity; may we all gain a deeper knowledge of the teachings of the Church and experience a healthy growth of Christian morality . . . Renew in these our days Thy miracles, as a second Pentecost; and grant that the Holy Church, reunited in one prayer and more fervent than before, with Mary the Mother of Jesus and under the leadership of Peter, may extend the Kingdom of the Divine Redeemer — the kingdom of truth, of justice and of peace. Amen."

While the Holy Father prayed thus for the Council, the bishops, as representatives at the Council of their dioceses, gathered the human complaints and the suggestions for reform of their dioceses, to lay them before the Council. They acted like genuine parliamentarians — as delegates — reflecting more the complaints, needs, and wishes of people they represented than the timeless truths and duties of divine revelation.

Thus it happened that the "second Pentecostal miracle" hoped for and prayed for by the Holy Father — the proclamation by the World Council of a deepened, elevated, and expanded treasure of Church revelation — was replaced by a policy of "keeping in step with the times". The Council did not reflect the timeless inspirations of heaven, but rather the earthly needs, complaints, wishes, and demands of the age. It became a sort of "religious parliament" with a "progressive left", a "conservative right", and a "moderate center". Thus people spoke of a "democratization" of the Church, now breaking through. The "world" remarked with satisfaction: the Catholic Church is moving closer to us; yes, just a while and it will be part of us — the Council exudes a "fresh wind", the wind of a free and modern spirit! And a "fresh wind" did indeed blow from the Council. It blew up such problems as: the abolition of the celibacy of priests suddenly become pressing; the problem of mixed marriages with those of another faith; the problem of acceptability of the "pill" and other methods of contraception; the problem of "demythologization" of the Holy Scripture and of tradition; the problem of the Mass, in the sense of abolishing Latin as the liturgical and sacred language, and the substitution for it of many national languages; and many other problems associated with conforming to the spirit of the age at the cost of tradition. The "fresh wind" of the Council was not the wind of the Pentecost miracle in the Church, but a wind blowing out of the "world" into the Church—through a portal which had now been opened. It was not the effect of the Church on the world, but the effect of the world on the Church. Against the will and the hope of the now deceased Pope John XXIII and of his successor Paul VI, it happened that the Second Vatican Council became a door which opened to the world, but in such a way that the "world's wind" blew into the Church.

The Council for which Pope John XXIII prayed did in fact fail; it failed to fulfill the highest and most responsible task of the Church's leadership, to guard the "portal" where the way begins which leads to degeneration, to exhaustion, and to death (*hades*)—the "way of the world". This failure to guard the threshold of the portal opening up to the "way of the world"—which, as we have shown above, is nothing else and can be nothing else but the way to death—gives us cause to meditate on the primal ordinance of the Church, as expressed by its divine Founder (*Matthew* xvi, 18). I mean the range and significance of the words of Jesus Christ which the *Gospel of Matthew* quotes verbatim: "And I say unto thee: Thou are Peter, and upon this rock I will build my church, and the gates of hell shall not prevail against it". Firstly it is necessary to understand the text rightly, then to understand it within the context of the Gospel, and lastly to compare the insight gained with historical experience, including that of the Second Vatican Council.

What are the "gates of hell" which "shall not prevail" against the "rock" upon which the Church will be built? What is the meaning of the "gates of hell" (*portae inferi*)? As a "gate" has the meaning of an entrance and an exit, it is actually the beginning or starting point of a way or a tendency in a particular direction. "The tendency in the direction of hell" is, therefore, the significance yielded up by these words themselves. But what is this "hell" (*hades*) whose gates shall not prevail over the "rock"? *Hades* is not "hell" in the sense of *gehenna*, the final place of punishment, the "fiery pit" of the Apocalypse (xx, 14–15), but rather that which corresponds to the Old Testament *scheol*, that is to say, the underworld, the realm of the dead, the grave. Death and *scheol* or *hades* are corresponding concepts (*Isaiah* 38, 18; *Hosea* 13, 14; *Revelation* i, 18; vi, 8; xx, 13–14). Sometimes *scheol* appears to designate only the grave (*Genesis* 37, 35; 42, 38; etc.). In the simplest as also in the most comprehensive sense *scheol* and *hades* signify death. Thus it is clear that the sentence "and the gates of hell shall not prevail against it" (the rock) means that the tendencies in the direction of death shall not prevail against it (the rock).

The tendencies in the direction of death are nothing else than "this world" itself, i.e. the natural course of things according to the law of all-pervading and ever-present causality. They are the sum of the "broad way", that is, the general way of all natural things, leading to death. It is the way of forgetting, sleep, and death — of exhaustion which leads to a standstill. The "way of the world", the "broad way", leads only through exhaustion, decline, and degeneration to death, if the miracle of revival — the miracle of the raising of Lazarus, in general and in particular — does not take place.

Now, what is the "rock" against which the gates of death shall not prevail? Let us again proceed by means of a deeper contemplation of the Gospel text. Rock signifies firmness and durability in contrast to the mutability of sand, clay, and soft soil. In other words, it is the pictorial expression for the imperturbability of the inner security of faith, in the face of the influences of the world with its waves and winds. The storms, waves, and winds of the world have no power over it; unbending, unbreakable, and immovable it stands in the midst of the attacks and enticements of the temporal world.

Who and what is this Peter, this rock? It is a special faculty, a particular man, and a definite office. To have the faculty here required — the rocklike "unshakableness" of the surety of truth and of the redemptive worth of the divine revelation of Christianity, on which the Church rests — is the Petrine faculty of receptivity with regard to the vertically operative revelation of the moral world-order. This faculty was revealed in Peter through the answer which he gave to the question of Jesus Christ: "Who do you say that I am?" For the answer of Peter: "Thou art the Christ, the Son of the living God", was neither a confirmation of the opinions of the multitude that he was John the Baptist, Elijah, Jeremiah, or one of the prophets, nor was it the finding of a common spiritual denominator between them. It was independent of all that is "thought and heard" and also of all preceding cases (John, Elijah, Jeremiah, one of the prophets) which could be taken as a means of orientation. It was an insight striking like lightning from above, and related to all existent opinion and precedents of the past like the vertical to the horizontal dimension. It was not the result of anything learnt in space and time — anything heard, seen, or chosen by agreement with prevailing majority views or by way of pragmatic argumentation — but a directly revealed insight into the reality of the living God and His Son. It was uninfluenced by space ("flesh") or by time ("blood"). For that reason it was the expression of a characteristic, a faculty which was like a rock as regards the influences of space ("flesh") and time ("blood"), and could therefore be the foundation of the Church.

The Petrine faculty for openness to revelation from the objective moral world-order in the vertical dimension is the rock upon which the Church was to be built. And the bearer of this faculty was Simon Bar-Jona (Peter). "Blessed art thou, Simon Bar-Jona, for flesh and blood has not revealed this to you, but my Father who is in heaven. And I tell you, you are Peter (*Petros*), and on this rock (*petra*) I will build my church, and the gates of hell (*hades*) shall not prevail against it" (*Matthew* xvi, 17–18). This is the majestic proclamation and ordinance of the divine Founder of the Church. Here it is important to pay full attention to the fact that Christ's solemn statement is addressed to Peter alone and not to the twelve, i.e. not to the entire group of disciples. His opening words are, "Blessed art thou, Simon Bar-Jona" and not "Blessed are you, my disciples". And He does not refer at all to the "faithful multitude" who saw in Him "John the Baptist, Elijah, Jeremiah, or one of the prophets".

The "rock" upon which the Church is to be built is therefore neither the "faithful multitude", nor the group (council) of apostles, but Peter alone. So the Church — as intended by its divine-human Founder — is neither "democratic" (i.e. subject to the consensus of opinion of the majority of the faithful), nor "aristocratic" (i.e. subject to unanimity in the views and will of an elite of the "elders", meaning the council of bishops), but "hierarchic-theocratic" . . . that is: the final decision and therewith the highest authority is entrusted to one alone, i.e. Peter. Hereby it is not simply a question of the "Petrine faculty" or of the primacy of a bishopric, but of the individuality of St. Peter himself. Thus it is not a matter here of a statement with allegorical significance, as if — for example — by "Peter", all apostles were meant, or perhaps even any faithful Christian who like Peter recognizes in Christ the Son of God. No, it is stated, "Blessed art thou, Simon Bar-Jona . . ." and not, "Blessed are you, my disciples", or "Blessed are those who are like thee Simon Bar-Jona in surety of faith". Decisively and clearly the human individuality Peter is alone meant. This signifies that the holy apostle Peter received the task — the mandate to be Shepherd of the Church. This mandate brings with it the possibility of fulfillment, i.e. the constant presence of Peter through centuries of history. "Presence", however, means the kind of presence which makes it possible for Peter to let his voice be heard, make decisions, and carry out actions. Peter is the eternal Shepherd of the Church, who is present in every pope, makes decisions in him and speaks through him.

The third meaning of "rock" — besides the "Petrine faculty", and the constant presence of the apostle Peter as a human individuality — is the office or post of Shepherd of the Church. It is the post of standing between "heaven and earth", entailing the simultaneous representation of the world of miracles in the vertical dimension, and the world of historic evolution in the horizontal — as the sequential flow of causality. He who occupies this post is between time and eternity; he represents time to eternity and eternity to time. The pope is the guardian of the threshold between the eternal and the temporal, the absolute and the relative, and the unchangeable and the changeable streams of historic progress — whose duty and task it is to maintain these contrasts in harmony with one another. He is crucified on the cross of the "should" of eternity and "must" of time. His position is that of the total lack of freedom entailed through being bound by the ordinances of timeless truth on the one hand and by the demands of time on the other hand. According to tradition, Peter died in Rome on the cross, crucified with the head downward. This image of Peter crucified with the head downward is valid for all time, as it brings to expression the real nature of the papacy. Peter is crucified in the history of the Church through the centuries; in this he partakes in the destiny of his divine Master. This is Peter's "Imitation of Christ" in fulfillment of the three times repeated mandate given him by the Resurrected One: "Feed my sheep: and "follow me" (*John* xxi, 22).

Thus, the "rock" is the "Petrine faculty" of the infallibility *ex cathedra* — secured through the presence of St. Peter himself, and by the cross of Peter in the history of the Church. However, this cross is the "key to the kingdom of heaven", the power which brings about harmony between "heaven and earth". ("Whatever thou shalt bind on earth shall be bound in heaven, and whatever thou shalt loose on earth shall be loosed in heaven" — *Matthew* xvi, 19.) The infallibility *ex cathedra*, which the office of Shepherd of the Church brings with it, results from the summation of the three meanings of "the rock": the Petrine faculty of openness to the vertical revelation, the active presence of St. Peter as a mediator of that vertical revelation, and the spiritual cross of Peter — arising through the mission and duty of reconciling the ordinances of eternity with the demands of time. For a decision made and proclaimed by the pope *ex cathedra* is the result of consultation between the "worldly" responsibility for the ways and destinies of mankind represented by the pope, and the "heavenly" responsibility for the ways and destinies of mankind represented by Peter's mandate received from Christ. *Ex cathedra* is a state in which all arbitrariness is absolutely excluded, for the pope represents the whole of mankind and brings its requirements to expression, while Peter represents and proclaims the will of Christ. The result of this consultation is a decision and proclamation *ex cathedra*. This is always basically a "word from the Cross" — spoken in the state of being crucified, and born out of that state. Its authority is that of the Cross.

Now, in the times when the papacy was combined with worldly power the situation of inner crucifixion, and of "inner swooning" which it produces, was often too heavy a burden inwardly for individual popes, as human beings. Thus there arose attempts — impossible though this might be — at "flight from the cross": into politics, court life, the enjoyment of art and culture, and the intoxications of sex. Therefore certain popes, rather than suffering together with the crucified Peter, added more to the human side of his cross. But in the state which we have designated *ex cathedra* they could do no other than make decisions in and through the spirit of Peter. And it is a fact that no heresy has ever been proclaimed by the Holy See.

Now, within the last one-and-a-half centuries or so the human side of the papacy has been constantly improving and thereby the purity and holiness of the Holy See of Peter has been restored. This fact expresses itself outwardly in its being taken seriously by the whole world — the non-Christian and non-Catholic world also. In the world, in general, it is thought of and spoken of with respect. People look up to the Holy See and listen to the voice which speaks from it. Today no one would dream of suspecting the pope of secret political intentions or maneuvering tactics planned under cover of the mantle of religion and morals. Practically no one nowadays doubts the integrity of the pope.

Not unfounded, therefore, was the hope that the impulse of revival which Pope John XXIII expected from the Second Vatican Council would not this time come out of the periphery of the Church — as it did at the time of the Arian crisis (through Athanasius and the hermits), at the time of the barbarian invasions (through St. Benedict and his order), and at the time of the Reformation crisis (through the spirituality which surged up in Spain and culminated in the Society of Jesus) — but would now come from the center, the Holy See of Peter itself. I speak only of the hope, but do not allow myself to set up a prognosis of the intentions of the divine leadership of the Church. In any case the experience of the Second Vatican Council showed a spirit of compliance and a tendency to adjust to the pressure of what the times seemed to demand — this pressure coming from "the world" — so that one can only hope for more Petrine "rock-steadfastness" in future, whether proceeding from the pope himself or (as in the past) recognized, sanctioned, and supported by him.

Be that as it may, the Church has need again of an impulse of revival from the "night side" of history, a reawakening of its truth and love through a repetition of the call: "Lazarus, come forth!"

4. CHRISTIANITY AS THE PROCESS OF RESURRECTION IN THE SPIRITUAL-CULTURAL HISTORY OF MANKIND

The Creed ends with (and culminates in) the sentence: *Expecto resurrectionem mortuorum et vitam venturi saeculi. Amen.* ("I look for the resurrection of the dead, and the life of the world to come. Amen.") This sentence proclaims the fact that Christianity neither affirms the world as it is (for affirmation of the world is heathen), nor denies it (for denial of the world is the Buddhist-Hindu striving for liberation) — but aims and hopes to transform it. "A new heaven and a new earth" is the ideal, the goal, the task, and the hope of Christianity. The *vita venturi saeculi* is the life of the resurrected world which through Christianity is proclaimed, prepared, introduced, believed in, hoped for, and striven after. Yes, it is actually in its already apparent blossoms (e.g. the saints) the anticipation of the "life of the future world". The "future world" is one in which the moral order will have absorbed the mechanical-physical one — swallowing it and transforming it. Precisely this happens in the lives of saints. The lives of saints, that is, of completely Christian persons, is the process of transformation of physical-mechanical causality into spiritual and moral originality (i.e. from the preconditioned "natural" human being into the free "supernatural" human being). And this process of transformation is no mere private human event, but a human participation in the cosmic process of becoming of the "future world" of which the Creed speaks.

In other words, Christianity is the process of resurrection in the spiritual history of mankind and the world. This means that all the forgotten truth and love, all the sleeping truth and love of the past, will be remembered and reawakened; and that all bearers, proclaimers, and participators in all truth and love, who have passed through the gate of death, will come again to speak, act, and be influential. The history of Christianity is the history of the resurrection of all the past, insofar as it was united with truth and love. It is a question, however, of resurrection, not of repetition or return — that is to say, it will be a transfigured, Christianized return, not just a breakthrough of reminiscences of the past lurking in the subconscious. Of course there actually is something like the "eternal recurrence" of which not only Friedrich Nietzsche, but also Solomon in *Ecclesiastes* speaks. The formula of Solomon: "There is nothing new under the sun", also signifies that everything which appears to be new has existed before and consequently only appears to be new. But Solomon, in contrast to Nietzsche, meant "eternal recurrence" as the end of all wisdom, as a deeply pessimistic diagnosis of the world as it became after the Fall. And just for that reason the book of Solomon the Preacher, with its pessimistic diagnosis, is the foundation for an expectation of redemption and salvation. Solomon, in describing the great imprisonment of spirit in the world, tossing and turning "from vanity to vanity" on the wheel of eternal repetition, points forcibly toward the necessity for redemption. Just as the correct diagnosis of a disease calls for the physician and his healing methods, so does the book of Solomon the Preacher demand the Messiah and his salvation. The first chapter of St. John's Gospel is the answer to Solomon's burning question, hidden behind his wall of pessimism. It is different with Nietzsche. He ardently affirms the "eternal recurrence", which for him is not a prison but eternity. Thus he says enthusiastically:

> – Oh! how should I not burn for Eternity, and for the marriage
> ring of rings — the Ring of Recurrence? Never yet found I the
> woman by whom I would have children, save it be by this
> Woman that I love: for I love thee, O Eternity!
> *For I love thee, O Eternity!*
> (trsl. A. Tille, rev. M.M. Bozman, Everyman Library, 1958, p. 204)

This "burning" for the "marriage ring of recurrence" of Nietzsche is, in Solomon, unspeakable sorrow about the same ring; and in Buddha it is *tanha*, the thirst for life which fetters men to the "wheel of existence" with its eternal repetition of birth, sickness, old age and death. And the eightfold path taught by Buddha was the way of liberation — offered by him out of compassion for mankind — from slavery to the "wheel", or the "ring of rings" spoken of by Nietzsche.

Oswald Spengler, also, believed himself to have made a "Copernican discovery" in proposing the thesis (in his work *Decline of the West*) — and illustrating it by numerous examples — that all cultures pass through the same stages as they grow old and in the end perish. A kind of eternal repetition or "eternal recurrence" holds sway, says Spengler, in the cultural history of mankind. And his message tells that in his opinion the culture of the West is in the process of repeating this decline and fall. Nothing new exists under the sun!

Now, there has been in our age also a discovery of a new world — analogous to that of Columbus — of the subconscious hidden behind the waking day-consciousness. This was discovered by Freud and more deeply researched by C.G. Jung. This discovery sheds new light on the symptoms of "eternal recurrence". It consists in the following: behind the ordinary consciousness of "why" and "wherefore" a perspective is opened up into a world comprising on the one hand a cloudless unending heaven of superconsciousness, and on the other hand an abysmally deep sea of subconsciousness. This ocean of the subconscious, whose edge (or coastline) phenomena Freud investigated and regarded generally as a reservoir of sexual energy (libido), can also be compared with an underground sea of glowing fluidic lava, whose flow manifests in volcanic eruptions and its ebb in earthquakes. Be that as it may, whether one compares the sea of the collective subconscious with the horizontal rhythm of the ebb and flow, as in the ocean, or with the vertical rhythm of the ocean of glowing lava enclosed within the earth — whether we tend to view the thing neptunianly or volcanically — in both cases it is a matter of the dominating image of an ocean with its rhythm of ebb and flow. For the ocean of the collective unconscious has its rhythm of ebb and flow, that is, the interchanging sequence of the reason-ruled day-consciousness of human beings, with the flood of irrational impulses working out of the realm of the subconscious. So, for instance, the First World War from 1914 to 1918, and the revolutions and civil wars which immediately followed it, are not explicable in terms of rational day-conscious events. The First World War broke out like a catastrophe of nature; it was not the deed of the clear day-consciousness of one person or of any group of people. It was the consequence of a flooding over of consciousness by the tide of a rising subconsciousness or, in other words, the First World War was a collective psychopathological phenomenon.

The tides of the rising subconscious which flood consciousness — the rising psychic past, the "recurrence" of the past (untransformed) — all this is the opposite of resurrection, which is the reappearance of a transfigured past. Thus it happened that the peoples of Western Europe found themselves in a psychological state in which it seemed to them that they had to defend civilization from the onslaught of barbarism — just as fifteen centuries earlier their ancestors had to defend the order, the way of life, and the customs of the Christian Roman Empire against the barbarians from beyond the Rhine. The peoples of France, Belgium, Italy, and England experienced once again the horror and fear which their ancestors in Gaul, Italy, and Britain had felt in the face of the ravaging hordes of Goths, Alamanni, Vandals, and Huns. The French and Belgians fought for "civilization" — the word which not only in the press was most often mentioned as their aim, but also lived in the minds of soldiers and ordinary people. And the British spoke and thought of their adversaries as "Huns", and projected onto Kaiser Wilhelm II the image of Attila, leader of the Huns.

The peoples of North and South America participated in the recurring reminiscences of the ancestors they had in common with Western Europe.

As regards the European East (the peoples of Russia) — its Western part (namely, the Poles, Lithuanians, White Russians, Letts, Estonians, and the Russian inhabitants of Western Russia as far east as Moscow and Petersburg) — were gripped, with the force of a hallucination, by rising reminiscences of the sinister strangers (the "silent ones") who, coming from the West heavily armoured, overpowered land after land of the Slavs, Prussians, Lithuanians, and Baltic peoples, reduced them to slavery and held them in check by means of fortified castles, everywhere taking possession of their holy earth and using it for their unholy purposes. In short, the reminiscence of the general impression of the thousand-year-long expansion eastward took hold of the minds of a portion of the Russian peoples and kindled in them a warlike spirit. These peoples, in contrast to those of the West, were not fighting for civilization, but for their soil and independence, for their very existence. But the more easterly lying realms of the Russian empire were not gripped by this reminiscence. So it never came to a national war of the Russian people. Psychologically it was a war of the West Russians against the Germans. A large part of Russia remained psychologically uninvolved, and only took part in the war because of their traditional loyalty to the Tsar — so much and so long as that had validity. Unlike the French, for instance, for whom the war was a concern of every single member of the folk-community, a large proportion of the inhabitants of those parts of Russia remote from the fighting zone was psychologically unconcerned, seeing in the war a matter of the government only (represented by the Tsar), but not their own concern. Therefore the Russian monk Grigori Rasputin represented not only his own but also the point of view of the people to whom he belonged (he came from Siberia), when he condemned the war and pushed for an immediate peace with Germany.

The psychopathological condition into which the Germans fell in the First World War was brought about through the actualization of the latent reminiscences of the ancient Teutons. It was primarily the spirit of the "Hermansschlacht" in the Teutoburg Forest against the Roman legions which inspired the people. There rose up the old hate of the Teutons against the Romans which gave the armies breaking through Belgium into France such a mighty thrusting power. Each marched off against the "hereditary enemy" into the land of the "hereditary enemy". And this enemy became actual and up-to-date. It did not originate from school history books, but out of the waves of the flooding over subconscious which called up the past and allowed the present to be seen only in the light of the past. No military drill can explain the psychological fact that, for example, shoemakers and tailors from Mainz and Hildesheim, postmen from Berlin, and farmers and peasants from East Prussia were suddenly transformed in masses into warlike heroes who, storming to the attack, overran fortified positions of the enemy. It was the old heroism, Germanic heroism, which arose in them out of the subconscious, making those conscripted — and also those freely volunteering representatives of the most various and peaceful vocations — into heroes. For it is a fact that the German armies on all fronts at the beginning of the war — until the war turned into trench warfare — possessed an almost irresistible thrusting power.

This was true as much on the West front as on the East front. Yet it was a different reminiscence arising from the subconscious which inspired the German fighters in the East. It was the reminiscence of the thousand-year-long pioneering march eastward, when "the German sword won soil for the German plough" (from Hitler's *Mein Kampf*). The old contempt for the Slav (= *slave*) peoples, and disregard for their rights of possession as heirs of their forefathers, resembled all other forms of the colonizing pioneer spirit. This was apparent, for instance, in America and Australia, where it was taken as self-evident that the white immigrants had every right to the land of the natives, because they would make better use of it, and where they gasped with anger when the natives had the impertinence to defend with weapons their "rights" to misuse their land in a wasteful manner!

This anger was all the greater when the peoples of the "hereditary colonial realms" (in contrast to France which was the "hereditary enemy") not only put up resistance, but even dared to go over to the attack themselves. Thus, anger at the impertinence of the "slave-rabble" who went to war against the master-race ordained by destiny to rule over them was the driving force of the German wars in the East.

The Second World War from 1939 to 1945 was a continuation and intensification of the play of driving forces from the First World War, whereby in Hitler they had reached a focal point of highest concentration. He was the center of that consciousness, flooded over by the subconscious, in which lay his whole might and the secret of his role as leader (*Führer*).

The two world wars are an example of the tragic "recurrence" of the past out of the ocean depths of the collective subconscious — tragic for all peoples. Such a "recurrence" may be no less tragic for an individual person. This tragedy is exemplified in the case of Friedrich Nietzsche's destiny. For in him — this wonderfully gifted man, through his innate capacities obviously predestined for all things noble and lofty — we can see the tragic "recurrence" of the drive which underlies all mankind's subconscious life, which can be described as the "evolutionary drive" in the sense of the serpent's promise in Paradise. "Ye shall be as gods." What took place in his case was this: a human being, moved by the urge to reach the foundations of human existence, penetrated to the depths of the subconscious, where the primal will of evolution (the primal drive designated by the Bible as: "Ye shall be gods") holds sway — and could do no other than to let this urge take over his consciousness. It took possession of him, and he became the mouthpiece of the abysmal will: "Ye shall be as gods". The "recurrence", not of the vision, but of the essence of the tree of knowledge (i.e. of the primal beginnings of mankind, of the Fall into sin), displaced Nietzsche's own consciousness and "possessed" him. The author of *Beyond Good and Evil* and of the *Antichrist* was no longer Friedrich Nietzsche. It was the reminiscence from that layer of the subconscious containing the serpent's teaching which had taken possession of his mind. The displacement of consciousness by the subconscious went so far that the former was entirely pushed aside, and imbecility set in. The madness in which Nietzsche's great adventure ended was not personally deserved; nor was it brought about by addiction to a personal lust for power, position, and greatness. Nietzsche was a sacrifice to the superhuman force of the collective all-human subconscious, which came to a kind of volcanic eruption in him. And what broke through there was the archaic evolutionary drive itself, belonging to the most archaic layer of mankind's subconscious. Here lies the most general and most hidden drive working in the subconscious of man: this is the impulse and promise given by the serpent in Paradise. In this sense

Nietzsche's tragic destiny is of invaluable worth to mankind. For, he who has ears to hear and eyes to see can perceive in this example the reality and essence of the primeval temptation of man, and can thereby gain the insight that evolution with its struggle for existence and its survival of the fittest is not and cannot be the divinely purposed path. This insight, however, calls forth inevitably the demand and desire for the great repentance (*metanoia*) of evolving mankind, corresponding in the deepest sense to the parable of the Prodigal Son. To such a repentance, to such a conversion, mankind is called by the fatal experience of Nietzsche, which was not in vain. Whoever understands this cannot think of him without gratitude.

The "recurrence" of the past, experienced in two world wars by all peoples, and the "recurrence" of the archaic past in Nietzsche's individual destiny, are not "resurrections". For resurrection is the reappearance of a transfigured past, i.e. of that past which has eternal value. All truth and all love from the past have eternal value — and it is this which has the capacity for resurrection. Thus the first, apostolic era of Christianity was that of the resurrected, transfigured religion of Israel. In this era Christianity sloughed off all that was time-conditioned and of merely local or national significance for Israel. But what still lived in it of universal (catholic) significance and timeless value was revived with new life and radiated like the sun for all peoples of mankind. Thus the amazing miracle occurred that Moses and the biblical prophets became teachers for mankind; they become the "circle of stars" around the sun of Christ, so that when the Temple and Jerusalem had been reduced to rubble and ashes, the transfigured spirit of Israel rose to rulership over the minds of the peoples of the Roman Empire and beyond. The City of David and the Temple of Solomon were destroyed, but the Psalms which had been created there were sung, prayed, and meditated by all the world. Abraham, Isaac, and Jacob were venerated in Britain, Gaul, and Hellas as holy patriarchs. And all peoples joined in the hymn of Israel: "Holy, holy holy is the Lord God Zabaoth (Lord of Hosts)".

The second epoch of the history of Christendom was marked by the fact that a strong impulse, foreign to the religion of Israel, arose within it. This was the great yearning and thirst for renunciation of the world and for solitude with and for God. The hermit's existence, out of which the monastic life later developed, arose in the Christian Church as a new ideal of the path to the life of truth. The "desert Christianity" of the hermits differed from the "Christianity of congregations" (that is, the life of the Church). It was inspired more by the Gospel words: "Since John, the kingdom of heaven is taken by force" and "Seek and you shall find, ask and it shall be given unto you, knock and it shall be opened unto you", than by a trusting expectation of redemptive grace through the treasured gifts of the sacraments, bestowed by the liturgical observances of the Church. One became a hermit through an unquenchable yearning, gripping and dominating the whole human being, to experience through inner discipline the reality of the kingdom of heaven — to become a witness of its reality and thus to live a Christianity of firsthand experience. The hermits were no reformers; they were loyal to tradition and did not doubt the truth of the Church tradition and the redemptive effect of its sacraments. But they wanted to experience and live what they believed, in the solitude of the desert — for the "world" with its noise and colourfulness was a hindrance to them on the path of profundity which is necessary for the transformation of faith into experience.

Now, the transformation of faith-by-hearsay into immediate individual experience is the essence and heart's desire also of Indian-Tibetan spirituality. Similarly, it is the concern of Yoga, of the Vedanta, and of the way of Buddhist meditation. There, also it is not a question of a lack of faith in tradition, but of a striving for experience of that which tradition teaches, in order to become a witness to the truth of the tradition. This could only be realized in the solitude of meditation and the stillness of the hermitage. Thus there arose, alongside the congregations of the faithful Buddhists and Hindus, a stream of solitary witnesses to the spirit, who enjoyed high esteem in the eyes of the faithful people. Yes, this esteem reached in time so high a level that the hermitages of solitary wise men became places of pilgrimage, to which thousands of pilgrims trailed yearly. And the writings set down by hermits became the most widely known and appreciated commentaries on, and supplements to, the Vedas, or the recorded words of the Buddha.

The revival of hermitism in Christianity which, as we said, was foreign to the spirit of the religion of Israel — the latter being based wholly on family and community — was not in any way the result of an "Indian influence" on Christianity. Neither St. Anthony of Thebes nor St. Paul the Hermit had been influenced at all by India. The same is true for St. Jerome and all other hermits (the Irish-Anglo-Saxon hermits included) of whom history has related anything definite. No, Christian hermitism arose out of a profound need of the soul — namely, the need to personally experience the truth of the tradition. And the fact that this need is at the same time the living core of Hindu-Buddhist spiritual life, only makes it more plausible that the eternally valid kernel of Hinduism and Buddhism reappeared in transfigured form — that is to say, was resurrected. Its transfiguration consists in this: the ideal of redemption of the self from the world became the ideal of the redemption of the world; the striving for eternal rest in *nirvana* became a striving after unity with the living God of Abraham, Isaac, and Jacob; and the yearning for deathlessness in the world beyond became the hope for resurrection in this world.

The Christianity of the hermits, as the essential core of Indian spiritual life resurrected within Christianity, was no passing phenomenon limited to a few centuries only. Today it still lives with all the intensity of its youth. Though it may not be deserts and thick forests into which one can retire into an undisturbed solitude nowadays, there are still people who have found or created in the deserts of the great cities and among the thickets of the crowds a solitude and stillness of life for the spirit. And as before, their striving is devoted toward becoming a witness for the truth of Christianity. The way into the depths has not led them to an individualistic brand of belief, but has given them unshakable security in the truth of the Christian revelation as transmitted and taught by the Church. They known the truth of the following: *Extra Ecclesiam non est salus* ("there is no salvation outside the Church"); the Holy Father is not and cannot be the mouthpiece of an ecumenical council; the Holy See alone can make decisions in questions of faith and of morals — a majority of the bishops cannot do so, and even less can a majority of priests or congregations do so; the Church is hierarchic-theocratic — not democratic, aristocratic, or monarchic — and will be so in all future times; the Church is the *Civitas Dei* ("the City of God") and not a superstructure of the will of people belonging to the Church; as little as the shepherd follows the will of the herd does the Holy Father of the Church merely carry out the collective will of his flock; the Shepherd of the Church is St. Peter, representing Christ — his pronouncements *ex cathedra* are infallible, and the power of the keys of the kingdom of heaven belongs to him, and him alone. In other words, those who become solitary in order to seek profundity may reach on their path of spiritual experience to the unshakable insight that the dogmas of the Church are absolutely true. And so it can happen that, as they did at the time of the Arian darkening of the Church, the "hermits" of today may again come to the assistance of the Holy See, leaving their solitude to appear as witnesses to the truth of Peter's Throne and its infallible teaching. In those times it happened that St. Anthony of Thebes left the desert and hurried to Alexandria to support St. Athanasius with the weight of his moral authority — St. Athanasius who became the standard bearer for the divinity of Christ. The darkening which today is described as "the present crisis of the Catholic Church" can lead to the necessity for the solitary sons of the Church to hurry to the aid of the Holy Father, the most solitary of solitaries, in order to save the Church from the abyss toward which she is moving . . .

Now, the resurrection within Christianity of the Hindu-Buddhist spiritual life, to which the Church owes the arising of the whole monastic movement and the founding of religious orders in late antiquity, was not the last event of its kind in Church history. Others followed according to the law that all truth and love of the past which have timeless values are called back out of the realms of forgetting, sleep, and death into the daylight of Christian spiritual life through the call which from age to age reminds, rouses, and awakens. Through this call sounding forth from Him who is the Resurrection and the Life — saying: "Lazarus, come forth!" — the most noble and valuable aspects of pagan antiquity were also resurrected. The Platonic-Aristotelian treasury of thought arose radiant in transfigured form and inspired great spirits of the Church to take up the *philosphia perennis* ("perennial philosophy"), in which lay the task of lifting up the chalice of pure human thinking in sacrificial offering to divine revelation. For this was the essential aim of the Scholastics: the raising up of the chalice of crystal-clear human thinking upon the altar of the Godhead — the Godhead manifesting in divine revelation.

The difference between the Scholastics and the pre-Christian Greek philosophers consisted in the fact that the former were directed toward grasping by means of thought the revelations of Scripture and tradition, while the latter had the task of comprehending the world as God's creation. Now, as both the world and Holy Scripture are a revelation of the same Author, it became a basic conviction of the Scholastics that thinking directed toward the world and thinking directed toward revelation could not contradict each other. The logic which reveals itself in the world and through the world can be no other than that of the revealing and incarnated Logos by whom "all things were made, and without whom not anything was made, that was made" (*John* i, 3). Thus it happened that thinking in Christendom became held in high esteem, and a tremendous work of thinking was carried out within Christianity — an activity and achievement which surpassed by far in intensity and range that of the pre-Christian ancient philosophers. It was the resurrected philosophy of pagan antiquity — Christianly transfigured — which lived again so powerfully.

Martin Luther, who turned his back both on scholastic thinking and on the way of inner training of the monastic life, had well understood that these two paths of spiritual striving were foreign to the original (that is, in Christianity, the earliest) apostolic epoch — that

they had entered in later. However, in his reformative zeal—aiming
to cleanse original Christianity from "additions"—he failed to perceive the fact that Catholic Christianity brings with it the resurrection
of all timeless values of the past. What he looked upon as "works of
men", as "the doings of monks" and as "playing with thoughts"—and
thus rejected—was in reality no less God's work than the original
revelation; it was the miracle of resurrection of all truth and all
love out of the past: remembered, wakened, and raised up by the call
ringing out in the history of Christendom of "Lazarus, come
forth!"

For the history of Christianity is not that of adjusting to world
progress—it is the story of the return of the Prodigal Son, i.e. mankind, to the Father's house. Its path is not so much a forming of the
future as a resurrection of the past—not indeed the mere return of the
past, but the reawakening of its eternal core of truth in all its greatness
and nobility. As the Fall of man into sin was a descent from the
heights of consciousness of the everlasting Presence of God, so does
the way of re-ascent lead through the same stages by which the descent was made—that is, through the stages of a resurrection of the
past. And the future of the world, its end, the Last Day, is not the final
triumph of the progress of natural evolution, but the state of resurrection of the whole of the past. The Last Day is no specific "day" of the
last year of the world, but is the ever present process of resurrection
which culminates in the resurrection of the eternal "first day of creation". It is the primal creative Word: "Let there be light" which forms
the essence of the Last Judgement. Yes, the world passes away—and
simultaneously it is resurrected. The eternal creative Word: "Let there
be light" is the Alpha and Omega, the first and the last, and the
eternally present (*Revelation* xxi, 6).

Thus the first is also the last, and the "first day of creation" is the
Last Day, the day of universal resurrection. Therefore the history of
Christianity—moving in the direction of the Last Things, toward the
future—is at the same time the history of the reawakening of the past,
i.e. the resurrection of the total past, insofar as truth and love have
dwelt therein. So gradually there will revive in Christendom the forgotten, deeply sleeping, and perished treasures of wisdom and sacrificial deeds of the past—right back to the primeval revelation and the
paradisiacal state of mankind. Thus all truth and all love of all times
will have their home in the Church of Christ, which will then be the
all-embracing (catholic) unity of all things and all beings who are
striving for timeless values—in the sense of realizing the ideal of one
Shepherd and one flock. The words of the Creed: *Credo in unam,
sanctam catholicam et apostolicam Ecclesiam* ("I believe in one, holy

catholic and apostolic Church") receive their full significance when the Church becomes universal (catholic) not only in space but also in time, i.e. when it embraces not only all peoples of the present, but also times of the past. This happens, too, when in the course of the history of Christianity the past is gradually resurrected. There sounds out ceaselessly in the history of Christianity the awakening voice of Him who is the Resurrection and the Life, and who promises to be with us even unto the end of the world, saying: "Lazarus, come forth!"

PART TWO

THE TEN COMMANDMENTS

The Revelation on Mt. Sinai

INTRODUCTION

THE CLOUD UPON THE MOUNTAIN

In the second book of Moses (*Exodus*) the world-historic event of the revelation and proclamation of the Ten Commandments is depicted. There it is described how a thick cloud covered Mt. Sinai, and thunder and lightning accompanied the proclamation of the Ten Commandments. The people of Israel stood at a distance while Moses entered into the darkness in which God was (*Ex.* 20:21). Out of the darkness of the cloud, which covered the top of the mountain, Moses emerged, descended the mountain and proclaimed the divine commandments to the people.

Out of the cloud which lay over Mt. Sinai he brought down the Ten Commandments and communicated them to the people in human language and with a human voice. Moses "condensed" that cloud, pregnant with revelation, which lay over the mountain, into the sentences of the Ten Commandments. They were a *crystallization* made comprehensible and accessible to human beings, of what took place in the "darkness of the cloud, in which God was", whereby the thunder and lightning of divine correspondences became translated or concretized into human, earthly language as the Ten Commandments. This is indicated in the biblical text itself, where it says with respect to hallowing the sabbath: "For in six days the Lord made heaven and earth, the sea, and all that is in them, and rested the seventh day; therefore the Lord blessed the sabbath day and hallowed it" (*Ex.* 20:11). Here the heavenly-divine correspondence underlying the commandment of hallowing the sabbath is expressly indicated. The heavenly-divine archetype of the seventh day of creation is to be reflected in the earthly-human realm. Thus the Bible provides a key towards understanding the mystery of the cloud upon the mountain. Figuratively speaking, the Ten Commandments were "condensations" distilled from the cloud, which contained the divine-cosmic correspondences of the Ten Commandments intended for the earthly-human domain. The cloud consisted of the cosmic-divine archetypes of the earthly correspondences or reflections which are the Ten Commandments.

The third of the Ten Commandments — that of hallowing the sabbath — is no exception here. The Ten Commandments represent an organic unity, and just as the third commandment is an earthly-human correspondence or reflection of a cosmic-divine archetype, so it is with each of the Ten Commandments. All ten are condensations of the cosmic-divine content of the same cloud upon the mountain; all are earthly-human correspondences or reflections of heavenly-divine archetypes. Since the proclamation of the Ten Commandments is a matter not of human but of divine legislation, their justification cannot be sought in the earthly-human realm — nor in human morality, or in social relationships — but in the sphere of the cosmic-divine world-order, "in the cloud" which lay upon the mountain. The Ten Commandments must be an earthly-human reflection of the *moral world-order*. Accordingly, in order to be able to understand them and to properly appreciate them, it is necessary to spiritually climb to the top of Mt. Sinai with Moses and there to enter into the darkness of the cloud "in which God was".

In order to grasp that the Ten Commandments are *really of divine origin*, it is necessary to trace back once again the words of the stone tablets upon which the Ten Commandments were carved, to their original language of thunder and lightning in the cloud upon the mountain.

I

"I AM THE LORD YOUR GOD"

UNITY IN THE DECAD

All Ten Commandments presuppose one fundamental commandment: that of recognizing the revelation of the Lord. In order to understand that the Ten Commandments really are a reflection of the divine world-order and have their source in God, let us first take a look at the Hebrew esoteric tradition.

> Ten are the numbers out of nothing, and not the number nine, ten and not eleven. Comprehend this great wisdom, understand this knowledge, inquire into it and ponder on it, render it evident and lead the Creator back to His throne again . . . The appearance of the ten spheres out of nothing is like a flash of lightning, being without an end, His word is in them, when they go and return; they run by His order like a whirlwind and humble themselves before His throne . . . because the Lord is one and there is not a second one, and before one what wilt thou count? Thus it is written in the *Sepher Yetzirah*, the book of creation.
> (Published in the original Hebrew and translated by Isidor Kalisch New York: L. H. Frank, 1877, pp. 14–16.)

The *Sepher Yetzirah* is the oldest document of the Hebrew esoteric tradition (Cabbala). Although opinions about its age vary widely, all agree that the *Sepher Yetzirah* is older than the *Zohar*, the book of illumination, which contains the most comprehensive description of the teachings of the Cabbala, and whose origin is placed in the thirteenth century A.D. In any case, the *Sepher Yetzirah* is without doubt an ancient and authentic source of the Hebrew esoteric tradition, and faithfully reproduces the tradition's fundamental conceptions. Above all, the idea of the *qualitative meaning of number* belongs to its basic conceptions.

According to this conception, which was also that of the Pythagoreans, number and the operation of counting did not mean the endless quantitative increasing of [the number] one. Thus, it is not a matter of the proliferation of number, but of the stages of the process of the *analysis of oneness*. Oneness or unity encompasses all numbers, and all numbers should be reduced back to unity. Thus counting consists of two operations: the analysis of unity, i.e., dissecting oneness into its elements; and synthesis, i.e., reducing back to oneness, in that its parts or elements, after they have been analytically separated, are seen together again as a unity. For synthesis after completed analysis is the essence of knowledge obtained by thinking — the becoming conscious of unity in differentiation. Qualitatively speaking, the entire cycle of counting consists of two parts: making explicit the implicit structure stemming from unity, i.e., separating out the concepts, ideas, and ideals, which are contained in oneness, and then reducing the qualitative numbers thus derived back to their original unity by thinking and seeing them together.

Correspondingly, the first commandment — "I am the Lord your God, who brought you out of the land of Egypt, out of the house of bondage; you shall have no other gods before me" — is number one and is the oneness or unity which is the basis of all Ten Commandments. Ten is one separated into parts, and the 613 precepts of the Torah represent a further stage of the explicative analysis of the Ten Commandments.

Reduction to ten or oneness is called "theosophical addition". It consists in building the cross-sum of a number. For example, in the case of 613 (6 + 1 + 3) it is *10*. Ten is, in fact, the first stage in the process of enumeration where the number one is not lost sight of among the units. For, ten is the stage of differentiation of oneness at which oneness is again present. As the *Sepher Yetzirah* says:

> The decade of existence out of nothing has its end linked to its beginning and its beginning linked to its end, just as the flame is wedded to the live coal; because the Lord is one and there is not a second one, and before one what wilt thou count?

> (Ibid., p. 16.)

Thus, just as "the flame is wedded to the live coal", so is unity ("oneness") visible in the decad ("ten-ness"). There beginning and end coincide. For this reason in the qualitative mathematics of the ancients ten was considered to be one, just as twenty was considered to be two, thirty as three, etc. In antiquity it was self-evident that numbers had the significance of concepts, ideas, and ideals, and not just the significance of mere enumeration. One signified: unity and oneness; two: two-ness, polarity, opposition; three: three-ness, peace, harmonizing the contrast of duality; four: the four-ness of causality, i.e., *causa efficiens, causa formalis, causa materialis*, and *causa finalis*; five: five-ness, the principle of making use of causality, of creative work by primary causes, the principle of *freedom*;

six: six-ness, the principle of choosing between two opposing directions; seven is the chooser himself, the individuality; eight: the eightness of righteousness, i.e., the harmony between the two four-nesses of higher and lower causality; nine: the nine-ness of the tertiary peace of the threefold overcoming of opposites; and ten is the original oneness in the ten-ness. In this sense the Ten Commandments are comparable to ten flaming tongues of one and the same fire, that of the commandment of acknowledging the revelation of the Lord.

II

"YOU SHALL HAVE NO OTHER GODS BEFORE ME"

THE COMMANDMENT OF ESSENTIALISM

The human being is faced with the choice between two basic attitudes or outlooks: that of existential Being (existence) and that of essential Being. According to the choice he makes, he becomes either an existentialist or an essentialist. That is, he either becomes someone who, with regard to his foundation in Being and his descent out of Being, is more or less "orphaned", or he will be someone whose yearning and striving relates to his origin in Being. The latter is alone, but never lonely, while the "existentialist" is never alone, since he experiences the necessities of life and destiny in common with everyone for whom worldly existence is considered to be the only reality. However the "existentialist" is at the same time lonely; he knows no higher reality other than his own self, which together with the other human selves is "thrown" into existence. Even if he joins some group or "alliance" of selves — for political, social, or humanitarian purposes — nevertheless he basically remains alone with his own self. For loneliness is not the absence of society, but the *condition* where one's own self is the highest and final thing that there is, above which and behind which there is nothing. The human being whose life of soul has its center and apex in the self knows no trans-subjective, sphere of being higher than the self — the sphere out of which his own self has come and which is its true home.

"Self" here does not relate to the empirical self, which is a mere *mental image* formed on the basis of bodily impressions and the memories thereof, one's own temperament, character, inclinations, etc., all drawn together as a comprehensive *abstraction*. Rather, it refers to the real self of the individual, to the reality of his *center of being*, comprising the rememberer in remembering, the thinker in thinking, the feeler in feeling, the willer in willing. *This* self is no abstract mental image, but the concrete reality of the inner identity, which like a thread, brings together into a unity the continuity of all life experience. The real self of the human being — not the mental image of one's self — is the inner "Lord" which stands *above* the changing conditions of the life of soul with its moods, inclinations, wishes, and kaleidoscope of mental images; and (normally) it rules over them. This self is the kernel of the life of soul, its constant center. It is a part of *Being* within the tumultuous inconstancy of the life of soul, within the changing conditions of the soul's existence. Consequently the self stands at the threshold of two worlds: the world of external existence and the world of Being transcending the self. The existential human being experiences the self in its relation to the external world of existence; the essential human being experiences it in its relation to the world of Being above the self. For the existential individual the self is experienced at the summit of the process of internalizing the world of existence; it emerges at the completion of this process. For the essential individual the self is the point of departure for a course leading into the realm of Being, representing the path along which the individual becomes ever more essential.

Angelus Silesius meant this path when he said: "Man, become essential!" Becoming essential begins with the self and leads through stages of an increasing deepening and interiorization, leading to the ultimate — primal — inner sanctuary to the source of Being of selfness, to *God*. For God is not *external* to the self, but *transcendental* to the self. He is the innermost of the innermost, more inward than the inner sanctuary of one's own self. Just as the self is the inner "Lord" of the life of the soul, so is God the Lord of all selves. St. Augustine meant this when he said: "God is more I than I myself am". This saying of St. Augustine gives a concise, all-embracing characterization of essentialism as the basic attitude of the human life of soul directed to the reality of what is above the self. God is thereby not any "thing", an object of knowledge or belief in relation to a subject (knower or believer). Rather, He is above and beyond the separation of subject and object. He is trans-subjective and trans-objective.

Certainty of the reality of God, which is called faith, is not founded on what is empirical and not on proofs which derive from empiricism, but is due to the reality of God who transcends the self. For His reality makes itself known through a breath that wafts through the self like a native wind. This is not knowledge, since no object is thereby known by the knowing subject; it is more that the self, the subject, is *known* and knowingly permeated by the higher Being. The self becomes an object of the permeating cognition of One who is higher, who is above the self. That the human being, as soon as he awakens to consciousness, carries in himself the certainty that he is known by God, is also the fundamental tenet of the entire epistemology of Franz von Baader, a deeply religious thinker who may be considered to be a representative of the spiritual stream of "Essentialism".

Now the fundamental tenet of the entire spiritual stream of Essentialism is: Just as the self is the center and "Lord" (*Kyrios*) of the life of soul of the human being, so is God the Lord (*Kyrios*) over the self and is the center of all selves. God, as the Sun of Eternal Being, radiates into existence His rays of Being, the individual selves, in His image and after His likeness.

The powers of soul (thinking, feeling, and willing) acknowledge the self and its revelation, conscience, as its "Lord" — except in the case of madness, moral idiocy, or intoxication. Likewise the self acknowledges as its Lord the God who transcends the self; and it acknowledges His revelation, which stands *above* the individual conscience as the "conscience of consciences". This, which towers above the individual, human self and its conscience, and is experienced and recognized as such, is worshiped by the self and the powers of soul subordinate to it as *holy*. For what is holy to the self is that which on the one hand is not foreign to its true nature, and yet on the other hand is experienced as towering above it, as standing higher.

The fundamental law of Essentialism is alignment towards what is holy, i.e., towards worshiping the God who transcends the self, not the god who is alongside or external to the self, and certainly not the god who is below the self. It is not in the realm of existence, but in the realm of Being, that Being which towers above the self, that what is holy is to be sought and found. The horizontal plane of existence, everything which the breadth of space and the course of time offer, can become a diversion and hindrance on the path to the God who transcends the self. An exodus out of the "house of bondage", from the land of the manifold worshiping of many gods, who all lay claim to being honored by the human self, must precede the revelation of the God who is above the self. The revelation of Him who is Being — "I am the I am" (*Ex.* 3:14) — has to be preceded by an exodus and by wandering through the desert. Thus the exodus out of Egypt and the wandering in the desert preceded the revelation on Mt. Sinai. For Egypt was the epitome of all kinds of worship of the elements of existence in space (sun, moon, and stars) and in time (fertility, the power of procreation, life and death, natural evolution), i.e., those very things which work as necessities of nature and represent what is coercive about worldly existence.

Egypt was the "house of bondage" not just because of the compulsory labor which the Israelites had to endure, but also because of the worship — prevalent throughout the land — of the compelling necessities of existence, the "gods" of material being. The exodus of the Israelites out of Egypt was for this reason an unprecedented revolutionary event: a multitude of human beings wanted to go forth into the desert in order to worship there the God who is not to be found in material existence — the God whose name is "I am the I am" signifying "*He who is*" — and to bring Him sacrifice. For this was the reason given the Pharaoh for the exodus into the desert. The resolution which was put to the Pharaoh was just as much an unprecedented presumption, as if for example today several hundred thousand workers in Soviet Russia were to petition the government to be permitted to emigrate, in order, for example, in the Gobi desert to immerse themselves not in the "absolute truth" of dialectical materialism or in the problems of how to increase socialistic production, or in the task of the education of the new communist human being, etc., but in order to devote themselves there in the wilderness, far from the collective farms, the communes and factories, far too from the control of the all-ruling party apparatus, to devote themselves to contemplating the God transcending the self — He who is more *essential* than all the activities and problems of communism and capitalism, of states and nations, of production and the dictatorship of the proletariat. Just as the Soviet Union would reject this petition as madness, so too the Pharaoh rejected the petition of the people of Israel as crazy. The totalitarian regimes of today hardly differ from those of three thousand years ago. The "house of bondage" three thousand years ago and the "house of bondage" in our time are very much the same.

However, the reality of the "house of bondage" in the present is much broader and more comprehensive than just the social-political structure of a state. It expresses itself in all thinking, knowing, and believing that is *deterministic*. One lives in and belongs to the "house of bondage" when one believes that the chain of cause and effect — causality — absolutely determines the present, and that the entire future can be nothing other than the result of past and present causations. That is, if one believes that no causes arise anew in the chain of cause and effect, arising from the realm of moral and spiritual freedom, striking in like bolts of lightning — in other words, if one believes that there are no miracles. Whoever does not believe in miracles, i.e., in the reality of the coming into existence of *new* causes from the moral-spiritual realm, that person is imprisoned in the "house of bondage". The prisoners of this "house" consider, for example, heredity to be something higher and more powerful than the spiritual-moral freedom of the human being. For them heredity is a god before whom they bow down. The human being is determined by heredity; heredity created him — thus speaks the deterministic thesis. Then again others see in the influences of the stars, as they are, let us say, given by the birth-horoscope, as powers that determine the human being and the course of his destiny. The stars are their "gods" before whom they bow down. Innumerable human beings worship "natural evolution" as their "goddess". For them "natural evolution", with the help of the struggle for existence and the resulting survival of the fittest, has brought things so far that the highly complicated nervous system and brain named "human being" (*homo sapiens*) came into existence. All such human beings bow down before the guiding forces (i.e., "gods") of existence. They do not worship the God who transcends the self. On the contrary, they pay homage to the forces outside of and beneath the self, whether they be "above in heaven" or "below on the earth", or "in the water under the earth". They are all in "Egypt", in the "house of bondage", for they serve the "gods" of existence and do not acknowledge "He who is", the God of Being. They have not gone forth from the "house of bondage" into the desert in order to experience the reality of the God who transcends the self, whose name is "He who is". For, the encounter with the reality of the God who transcends the self is only possible in the "desert", i.e., outside of the sphere of influence of the other "gods", the gods of existence.

For this reason the first commandment of Essentialism says: acknowledge the God who transcends the self, the God of Being, that no other gods (*elohim aherim*) be acknowledged as gods next to him. As "He who is", God has a claim on the being of man, on his self, i.e., He has a claim to undivided devotion on the part of the center and essence of the whole consciousness of the human being. This is not the case when, for example, the human being, ascribes a leading role to the urges of the sex drive, ("libido") to the extent that he sees in the manifestations of cultural and spiritual life merely forms of sublimated libido. The human being who takes such a position does not worship the God of Being but, in fact, the ancient goddess Venus (Aphrodite or Astarte). In his thinking and aspiration he is dominated by the power of the goddess Venus; he is a "worshipper" of the goddess Venus and is a believer in Venus, even if he is "scientifically enlightened".

Likewise a human being may be ever so scientifically enlightened, yet he is nonetheless basically merely a *worshipper of Mars* if he sees in the struggle for existence and in the resulting "class struggle" or "race struggle" the ruling power of evolution. The ancient gods reappear in the present in disguised form, indeed even the inhuman Moloch is again present in the form of collectivism. Just as before he demands today also human sacrifice. The collective — state, national, and class collectives — once again demand the sacrifice of the "first born". That is, the inheritors or those who are entitled to inherit, and those individuals who stand out as individuals, all become sacrificed for the sake of the collective. The collective demands the sacrifice of what is individual, and the sacrifice of individualities for the sake of the collective is still taking place on a large scale. The old Moloch cult of the Canaanites and Carthaginians lives today in the form of the "worship" of the various collectives: the state, the party, the nation, etc.

The point is not whether the "other gods" correspond or do not correspond to the reality of existence. Rather, the point is that they do not derive from the sphere above the self, but instead from the spheres of existence beneath and outside of the self. They enslave the self and block its path to true freedom — freedom in God, who "is more I than I myself am". They do not lie on the "vertical line" of increasing interiorization, the line of development which progresses from subjective conscience to the conscience of the world, from the individual self to its very own source — that from which all selves radiate out.

God is not a phenomenon that exists alongside other phenomena. He is the very source of "selfness", more intimate and more inward than the most intimate and most inward that we know — the self. For this reason the entire world of phenomena and the whole conceptual world of appearances and also language itself, insofar as it relates to things, all are inadequate with regard to knowledge of the God who transcends the self and with respect to bringing Him to expression. Only in the language of the self, i.e., in the language of conscience, can one think and speak about God. It is in this language that the first commandment of Essentialism, as it was proclaimed by Moses, should be heard, understood, and acknowledged, namely the commandment:

I am the Lord (YHVH, Yahveh), your God, who brought you out of the land of Egypt, out of the house of bondage" (*Ex.* 20:2).

In other words:

I am "He who is", who transcends your self, who has freed you from the bondage of existence. Therefore you should not fall back into the bondage of existence by subordinating your self to the forces of existence. Or, in the language of Moses: "You shall have no other gods before me" (*Ex.* 20:3). The "other gods" do not represent an alternative alongside "He who is". They relate to the God who transcends the self as the periphery does to the center, as the relative to the absolute, as existence to Being. Here it is hardly a matter of a choice, just as in life in general there is no point in a choice between the reality of the self and, for example, wind and rain or other forces of the external world.

Wind and rain are peripheral; they are incidental. The voice of conscience of the self is central; it is *essential*. In the case of the contrast between the central and the peripheral, between the essential and non-essential, it is not a matter of choice but of discrimination. Likewise, with regard to the first commandment it is not a question of choice, but of discrimination — discrimination between what is essential and what is non-essential. He who discriminates between them *has* chosen. And yet such discrimination has to take place with the head *and* heart, not just with the head alone. Otherwise the danger constantly threatens of falling away from the God who transcends the self, who reveals Himself as the conscience of the world, and the temptation threatens of worshiping a god beneath and outside of the self, i.e., *another* "god".

So it happened at the end of Moses' forty day stay on the top of Mt. Sinai in dialogue with the voice of the conscience of the world. Those at the foot of the mountain followed the collective will of the people (the *"volonté général"* of Jean-Jacques Rousseau, *"vox populi, vox dei"*), which Aaron also yielded to. They collected contributions of gold jewelry and made from them the so-called "golden calf", the idol of a golden bull. With respect to this archetypal phenomenon of "falling away", it is not a question merely of the victory of inclination — preferring the sense-perceptible and material to what is super-sensible and purely moral — but of something deeper and more significant. It is actually a matter of an insurrection of the collective will of the people asserting itself against the aristocratic-hierarchical order which Moses represented. Moses *proclaimed* what was revealed to him on the top of Mt. Sinai; he did not interpret the collective will of the people, which awoke in those at the foot of the mountain. This interpreting was Aaron's doing, the subsequent high priest, who during Moses' forty-day absence had to take upon himself the responsibility of being leader of the people. While Moses above on the mountain stood before God who was giving the revelation, Aaron stood below at the foot of the mountain confronted by the collective will of the people. And while Moses translated the divine revelation into the language of human concepts and ideas, Aaron translated the content of the collective will of the people into the language of concepts and ideas related to worship of the divine in a cultic way. The result was the "golden calf" and the singing and dancing of the people in a circle around the statue.

What was the nature of the need and yearning of the will of the people that was satisfied in this manner? It was the basic need, the very first kind of democratic striving, to worship something higher and to obey it — something which one has willed oneself, projected and created from one's own will. This is an incarnation of the collective will intrinsic to the people, which therefore has authority *because* it is an incarnation of the collective will of the people. It was the yearning to see the highest authority not in a proclaimed *revelation* "dogmatically enforced", received and passed on by Moses, but in the collective will of the people, which is convincing precisely because it is present in all members of the people. Its commandments do not say "*you shall*", but instead, "*we want*". The "conscience of God", revealed to the chosen few and proclaimed by them was replaced by the "god of the will". The conscience is, as is well known, a burden of coercion to the will, a load difficult to carry. Thus the jubilant dance of the people around the golden statue — expressing their relief at their "liberation". The collective will of the people not only chose its own "god" as leader but, moreover, *created* itself. The democratic freedom of the collective will of the people went this far! "This is the god which led us out of Egypt" professed the people at the altar of the god of the collective will. It is therefore the collective will of the people, *our* national god and leader, who led us out of Egypt — this was the belief and the profession of faith (*Ex.* 32:4) which were spontaneously taken up by the people. This belief and this profession of faith were the result of completely democratic proceedings. It was the resolve of the majority of the people, which itself created its highest bearer of authority and, after creating it, pledged obedience to it.

Everything that happened regarding the people's decision in favor of the god of the people's will was therefore completely in the spirit of democratic freedom. However, a deeper intention and significance was behind these proceedings. In fact, a *magical* significance and a *magical* intention corresponding to the law of the "technology" of magic was hidden behind them. For magic — the forerunner of science — has the same goal as the latter: to increase the dominion of the will over nature (including human nature). Correspondingly magic also has its "technology" and its "laws". For example, in our time a machine created by men, the computer, plays an increasingly leading role by solving problems and giving answers to questions — almost like the oracles of antiquity. Thus it carries out the functions of elements of human will and intelligence which were programmed into it, just as in antiquity elements of will and intelligence were, so to speak, "programmed" into visible and invisible entities that were worshiped as leaders and gods.

In matters pertaining to folk-gods, the collective will of the people was projected into the self-created "god", so that the latter was, so to speak, "ensouled" by the will. And the more will power and phantasy that was "invested" in the god, all the more did it become effective and all the more stronger did its dominion become over the people who had created it. The magical fundamental law of creating and ensouling a leader, i.e., a "god" (called an *egregore* in the French magical tradition), is the following. There must be present, first of all, a collective willing, which through collective, intellectual fantasy creates an image (a thought-picture or an external image, with the help of collective contributions, offerings of valuables, jewelry, etc.). This picture (or image) should be the result of collective contributions of all members of the corresponding human community (the nation, brotherhood, party, etc.). It should be the result of voluntary offerings *from everyone*. In the case of an outer image which is to summarize and incorporate the collective will, everyone concerned must make donations of gold, silver, and other precious materials — materials that represent what is most valuable to the human beings of the given community. The more offerings that are given over for the creation of the image the stronger its influence and authority will be. The outer image, as well as the "thought image", should be intensely enlivened, ensouled, and "magnetised" (French: *aimanté*) so that it becomes magically *effective*. For, to the extent that psychic energy has been put into the picture or image and, so to speak, "stored up" in it, to that extent does it give off energy in the sense of influencing the attitude of the people, even to the extent of healing their illnesses. The collectively created picture or image, in order to retain its effectiveness, must be regularly "charged" again and again — similar to an electric battery. This purpose is served by the repeated practice of the cult, which culminates in the bringing of offerings — offerings of objects of value, animal offerings, and in certain lands (like Mexico and Carthage) even human offerings.

The magical law of creating a "god" and preserving its ability to be effective was exactly adhered to by the people of Israel at the foot of Mt. Sinai. First of all the collective will of the people was made known, which Aaron believed that he had to submit to, since he did not dare to oppose his individual will to the collective will of the people. Then a visible expression of the collective will of the people was created, which not only was a symbolic representation of this will, but also summarized and concentrated it. The entire folk donated golden objects of jewelry which were melted down together, and the figure of a bull was shaped from the melted gold. Further, there was erected before the idol of the bull an altar upon which animal sacrifices were made, while the people moved around the idol, dancing in a circle, and sang it songs of praise, thus collectively "magnetising" it further. Significantly, after Moses had come down from the mountain and had broken the stone tablets to pieces, and after he had three-thousand people killed by the Levites as a punishment, he reversed the magical "god"-creating operation of the collective will of the people by having the "golden calf" ground down to powder and by ordering the people to drink the powder in water. This meant that what the collective will of the folk had projected out of itself was taken in again by the people.

The turning away from the God who was revealed and proclaimed, in favor of the self-chosen and created god is, as it is depicted in the Bible, the original phenomenon of all stages and forms of falling away from the truths of revelation in favor of the collective will of the people, which usually comes to expression as the demand for being in tune with the "spirit of the times". Every time that this demand appears, there is an "Aaron" who gives way to it and a "Moses" who breaks to pieces the "stone tablets" of the timeless law, which then, after the disillusionment of the people has taken place, are written anew by the God who reveals, without changing one iota of the timeless revelation. This is essentially the story of falling away from the "timeless tradition" under the pressure of the collective will of various groups of people within the Church, opposed to whom stands either a yielding Aaron or a Moses breaking to pieces the tablets. For, excommunication in the history of the Church is fundamentally the repetition of the breaking to pieces of the stone tablets of the timeless law in regards to those who have fallen away. Those reforms in the history of the Church which did not serve the deepening of the understanding of the revealed truths and the ennobling of morals, but merely took place due to a giving in to the collective will of the people of the Church, are the repetition throughout the millennia of Aaron's deed. On the other hand, those reforms and renewals which aim at and effect a deepening and intensification of life within the transmitted revelation, repeat through the millennia the restoration of the stone tablets broken to pieces, "The tablets were the work of God, and the writing was the writing of God, graven upon the tablets . . . The Lord said to Moses: Cut two tablets of stone like the first, and I will write upon the tablets the words that were on the first tablets" (Ex. 32:16, 34:1). And these new tablets also contained "the words of the covenant, the ten commandments" (Ex. 34:28). The restoration of the tablets did not entail any yielding to the collective will of the people who had rebelled against the aristocratic — theocratic order. And it did not involve any alteration of the law of the renewed covenant inscribed on the restored tablets. Rather, the Ten Commandments graven upon the original tablets remained unaltered on the news ones.

In the Sinai-revelation, in the turning away of the people of Israel and in the renewal of the covenant through Moses' intercession, as well as in the restoration of the stone tablets, we see the original phenomenon of dogma — its nature and its coming into existence. It was a significant event in the spiritual history of humanity when, amidst the world of myths and the cults of mythical figures which comprised the cultic-religious life of various peoples towards the end of the second century B.C., the formless, and timeless God revealed himself in the desert of Sinai as "He who is". Indeed, the ancient religions were of a mythological nature, with both central and peripheral myths and mythical figures, but they had no dogmas, i.e., no obligatory articles of faith. The mythical traditions could be — and were permitted to be — freely interpreted, for they were no end in themselves. What was important was that their stimulating power and their effect suggestive to cultic practice make themselves felt. It was different with that primal dogma which was proclaimed at the revelation on Mt. Sinai: "I am the Lord (YHVH), your God . . . you shall have no other gods before me". For three thousand years this has been repeated daily by the faithful in the form: "Hear, Israel, the Lord (Adonai), our God is one". It has been received into the Christian Creed as the first article of faith: "*Credo in unum Deum, Patrem omni potentem, factorem coeli et terrae, visibilium omnium et invisibilium* — I believe in one God, the Father, the Almighty, maker of heaven and earth, and of all that is seen and unseen". What was new with regard to the primal dogma of monotheism was not that the manifoldness of existence derives from the oneness of He who is Being, or that the true God is one, but that this became a dogma, an article of faith. What this dogma proclaims was already known to the spiritually advanced adherents to the mythologizing religions, the initiates of "paganism". They had generally penetrated through the veil of the mythologies to insight into the truth of the *one* God — which anyone will admit who is familiar with the writings and fragments attributed to Hermes Trismegistus, the Pythagorean fragments, the writings of Plato and the Stoics. Also the many "esoteric" writings, which have their roots in the mythological writings of the Vedas — the Upanishads — have as their main object knowledge of the *one* God of the world. However, what is first found in the mythologizing religions, in so-called "paganism", *at the end* of the step-by-step path which leads from existence and its forces to Being and Essence, this was proclaimed to the shepherd people at the revelation on Mt. Sinai as an *article of faith*, a dogma. What the philosophers, the mystagogues, and the pupils of the mysteries — as adherents to the mythologizing religions of paganism — were accustomed to knowing at the end of their path, this was directly proclaimed by Moses in the Sinai desert to the shepherd people without a preparatory schooling. The "omega" of the path of experiential knowledge of the ancient mysteries became the "alpha" of the Sinai-revelation for the community of the faithful of Israel.

Dogma is, in essence, not a commandment which silences the active knowing of thinking and insight but, on the contrary, a gift from heaven that *orientates* this activity towards knowing the truth. It is not a prohibition against thinking and researching, but a command and a summons to orientate thought and research towards divine truth. Dogma is like a star in the heaven of eternal Being which shines, ever-radiating and inexhaustible, into the world of temporal existence. It stimulates, impels, and guides human beings to the genius who makes insight possible to them — this being *moral logic*, the logic of divine wisdom. Moral logic, which comes about in the human being from the union — or even fusion — of the thinking of head and heart, is capable of grasping the truth of the dogmas founded on revelation. This takes place when the human being resonates together with the Logos, "all things were made through Him, and nothing that was made was made without Him" (*Jn.* 1:3). The logic of the Logos illuminates dogma through and through. In His light dogma radiates with the clarity of the sun.

The primal dogma which was proclaimed at the Sinai-revelation exhibits all essential prerequisites, conditions, and dangers of a dogma's development and proclamation. The fundamental prerequisite for the arising of a dogma is revelation, which may be unique or also may repeat itself in different ways. The Sinai-revelation was unique in that it took place before the eyes of all the people of Israel, but with respect to the content it was a repetition of the intimate revelation which had been given to the patriarchs Abraham, Isaac, and Jacob. Moses, too, had received the revelation in an intimate manner previously (in the burning bush). The Sinai-revelation differed from previous revelations in that it was a public event and was directed to all the people of Israel. "And the Lord said to Moses, 'Thus you shall say to the people of Israel: You have seen for yourselves that I have talked *with you* from heaven" (*Ex.* 20:22). To the entire new community of faith that was founded through the Sinai-revelation was addressed this revelation.

Thus the very first dogma was not founded on a private revelation but on one intended for the entire community of faith. Here we see already present before us that which is essential to the *ex cathedra* proclamation, namely, revelation directed to the entire community of faith. Also essential is that dogma is independent from the collective will of the community of faith. It must not be determined or influenced by popular consensus, and it must not be changed or made plausible by majority decision. Yet that very thing happened — and it was a warning for future millennia — when Aaron yielded to the collective will of the people of Israel. The "golden calf" was made and took the place of the dogma of the God of Being. The "golden calf" came about not through doubt in the revelation proclaimed through Moses, but to make it plausible. Was it not the power of procreation that increased Jacob's family in Egypt to a people which became plentiful enough and strong enough to depart from Egypt in defiance of the Pharaoh? Is not the figure or image of the bull an expression of the power of procreation *par excellence*? And did not the God who revealed Himself on Mt. Sinai, the same God who had revealed Himself to Abraham, promise Abraham that his descendants would be as plentiful as sand on the seashore? Thus, the God who spoke to Moses and whose name is "He who is" became, in the interpretation of the collective of the people, the God of procreation, who manifests Himself in the power of procreation. However, the God who transcends the self could only be approached in the "thought language" of the self, moral logic, and His name was therefore unable to be spoken. (Even today the name of God — YHVH — is not spoken, but instead *Adonai*", meaning "Lord", is said.) He was understood by the people of Israel at the foot of the mountain of revelation as the "golden calf", as the force of sexual procreation exerting its power over the self.

Thus the occurrence on the top of Mt. Sinai, and also that at the foot of the same mountain, signifies a warning for all time to come, namely, that the interpretation of any dogma founded on revelation must be subject to the same authority that proclaims the dogma. Dogma may not be given over to the collective intellectual capacity and interpretive inclination of the people or the community of faith, nor even to its priesthood (Aaron and the Levites). It may not be interpreted, or reinterpreted, in a democratic manner, otherwise its *otherworldly truth* will be turned into *truth of this world* — and the "God who is Being" ("I am the I am") becomes a "golden calf", a symbol of the power of procreation. And the Son of God, the eternal Word of the Father, becomes the "simple man from Nazareth" who represents the model for the "solution to the social question", etc. Dogma must retain its original revelatory character and entails a summons to life of the heart (*sursum corda*) — raising heart, thought, and endeavor to *its* level. Further, dogma ought not to be made plausible on a human level to the extent that it becomes re-evaluated according to human-social values. Dogma comes from above and calls down below. This can never be allowed to be reversed, in which case dogma would merely bring to expression the "common denominator" of the people's or theologians' opinions concerning faith.

The very first dogma of the Sinai-revelation was proclaimed to the people in the same language in which it had been imparted to Moses. It was not by making it known in a vision or in a dream, or in "dark riddles", or in images drawn from the realm of material existence, but directly from "mouth to mouth" (*Num.* 12:8), i.e., by way of direct speech from self to self, that is, in the language of the self, the language of Being. It is significant that over a thousand years later, the new revelation of the Gospels also used the essential language of the self. The God of Being ("He who is") revealed Himself to Moses as "I am the I am" (*Ex.* 3:14). This was followed by the "I am" sayings in the *Gospel of St. John*, which reveal Christ as the "I am": "I am the Vine, you are the branches", "I am the Way, the Truth and the Life", "I am the Door", "I am the Bread of Life", "I am the Good Shepherd", "I am the Light of the World", "I am the Resurrection and the Life", and also "I and the Father are One".

The words "I am the I am" ("He who is") of the Mosaic revelation are like a seed or germ which by the time of Christ had ripened through stages of growth — to blossom and to fruit. It was a festive moment in the spiritual history of humanity when Jesus Christ — after He had rejected various answers by His silence — put the question to His circle of disciples: "Who do you say that I am?" and Peter gave the answer: "You are Christ, the Son of the living God" (*Mt.* 16:15–16). At that time the new community of faith, the Christian Church, was founded. The "See of Peter" received for all time the task and mission to be the guardian of the revelation which stems "not from flesh and blood", but "from the Father in heaven". The answer that Peter gave was not pieced together from the people's views reduced to a common denominator, nor was it the result of a discussion with the circle of disciples — for the latter were silent — but it was the expression of a lightning-like insight into the mystery of the "I am", i.e., Him who asked the question.

Just as Moses was the receiver of the Sinai-revelation as well as its proclaimer and authoritative interpreter, so also Peter, following the event at Caesarea Philippi, became the receiver, interpreter, and proclaimer of the teaching of the Church. This is the significance, the task and mission of the "See of Peter", the highest authority in the Church of the new covenant.

The Greek-Orthodox Eastern Church, which rejected the authority of the "See of Peter" and decided in favor of the ecumenical council as the single highest authority, considered itself bound only to the resolutions of the first seven councils. In consideration of the split between the Churches, the further development of the Eastern Church is fundamentally impossible, since, according to its own understanding, further ecumenical councils cannot take place. For this reason the Eastern Church remains stuck at the stage of development — as far as teaching and practice are concerned — which was reached by the Church in the tenth and eleventh centuries. Thus we came to a *circulus vitisus*. Only a council which represents the entire undivided Church would make possible further development in the sense of deepening and clarifying traditional teaching and practice. But such a council presupposes unity between the Eastern Church and the Roman Catholic Church — a unity, however, which does not exist.

As a result of this standstill, the Eastern Church did not take part in the great development of the theological and philosophical schooling of Scholasticism; and it was unable to benefit from the fruits of the cultural and moral development which matured and ripened through the spiritual orders (Benedictines, Carmelites, Dominicans, Franciscans, and Jesuits — to name only the largest ones); and further, as it had to leave canonization to local and national practice, it has consequently had to forego the universal validation of canonizations. The price of falling away from the "See of Peter" in favor of the conciliary principle is all this and much more. Do Catholics of today, who place their hopes in the conciliary principle and in the "decentralization" and "democratization" of the leadership of the Church, want the same destiny for their Church as that which has befallen the Eastern Church? This is the destiny of disintegration and standstill, i.e., disintegration into several national and regional, independent churches, and standstill in the development of dogmatic, moral, and exegetic theology. For this follows unavoidably due to the reinterpretation of the words of Christ: "You are Peter (*Petros*), and on this rock (*petra*) I will build my Church, and the powers of death (gates of *Hades*) will not overcome it" into: "You are the rocks, and on these rocks I will build my Church and the gates of death will not overcome them". A second reinterpretation is that of the thrice repeated mandate to Peter: "Feed my sheep" into a mandate to the circle of disciples: "Feed my sheep". It is these two reinterpretations which must underlie belief in the primacy of the council.

These questions, which are of vital importance for the Church, arose, and also already found their answers, in the primal phenomenon of the founding of the first monotheistic community of faith through the revelation on Mt. Sinai. Already then the problem of authority had arisen — whether it should be accorded to majority decision or to an individual authorized or chosen from above — and the decision was made in favor of the individual. Even then the problem had arisen, which presented itself in the conflict between revealed dogma (the article of faith obligatory for all) and the ability to comprehend it, and in addition the intellectual inclination of the people of the faith: namely, the problem of whether it is permissible to adapt the teaching to the demands of the majority of the faithful — and the decision was made in the sense of the invariability of dogma. Here the question of "rule of the people versus hierarchical order" was clearly decided in favor of the latter. The events on Mt. Sinai are the archetype and model of hierarchical order. On the top of the mountain the voice of the God who is Being rang out — speaking to His chosen one the infallible commandments — while at its foot the people worshiped the creation of their own will as their god.

III

"YOU SHALL NOT MAKE FOR YOURSELF A GRAVEN IMAGE"

THE LAW OF UNIMAGINABILITY AND INCOMPARABILITY AS THE BASIC CONDITION FOR THE REVELATION AND KNOWLEDGE OF BEING

The introductory prayer of the Mass of St. Pope Pius V contains the following text from the forty-second Psalm:

> Send Your light and Your truth to lead me forth, to guide me up Your holy mountain and into Your tabernacles. (*Emitte lucem tuam et veritatem tuam; ipsa me deduxerunt et adduxerunt in montem sanctum tuum, et in tabernacula tua*)

This prayer contains — as many of the Psalms do — indications about essential facts of spiritual life and mystical experience, having to do, namely, with two paths: the path of light or the path of the day, and the path of darkness or the path of night. These two paths also play a role in theology, where one speaks of positive theology, for example that of Thomas Aquinas, and negative theology, for example that of Dionysius the Areopagite (the so-called "pseudo-Dionysius"). (Concerning the controversy about the person of Dionysius, Monsignor Darboy, who was archbishop of Paris, makes a very convincing case for the authenticity of the writings ascribed to Dionysius the Areopagite. See his introduction to the collected works of Dionysius, translated by Darboy from Greek into French (1932). Positive theology proceeds from the supposition that increasing and elevating the human being's power of conceptualization along the path of analogy leads to those conceptions which signify the greatest possible approach to the essentially inconceivable Being of God. Negative theology, on the other hand, proceeds from the supposition that the human being's power of conceptualization is fundamentally incapable of grasping the Nature of God. For negative theology, therefore, every idea — lofty and spiritual though it may be — nevertheless remains a mental picture which intrudes between the individual and the reality of the Being of God, and thus obscures the reality of the Nature of God. The path of negative theology leads to mysticism as the living experience in the human soul of the revelation of the Being of God. In contrast, the path of positive theology leads to "symbolic" knowledge of God, i.e., to grasping His Nature by way of images or metaphors through the elevation of ideas and concepts. The latter is the path of the progressive *approach* of human reason and conceptual power to the Being of God.

Both of these paths are based on a difference in the spiritual predisposition of human beings as determined by destiny. Some cannot do otherwise than to see in the creation the revelation of the Creator, His work, which proclaims Him and is His image and likeness — in the sense of the words:

"Heaven and earth are filled with your glory." (*Pleni sunt coeli et terra gloria tua.*)

Others yearn in dark silence for the revelation of the Being of God. In other words there are *day-souls*: those who in the brightness of the light experience the visible and invisible things and beings of the world as revelations of God. And there are *night-souls*: those who in the lightless and soundless depths of Being, where there is no light other than the light of conscience and where there is no voice other than the voice of conscience, sense the reality of the Being of God. The Franciscan St. Bonaventure and the Carmelite St. John of the Cross, can be considered outstanding representatives of these two orientations. To St. Bonaventure the entire world of visible and invisible things and beings was "like a mirror full of lights representing divine wisdom, and like burning coals radiating out light (*si patet quod totus mundus est sicut unum speculum plenum luminibus praesentantibus divinam sapientiam et sicut carbo effundens lucem*)". (II *Sententiae* 9.) For him the world was the "other Holy Scripture"; its beings and facts were symbols to him which reveal God just as the words of the Bible do. And just as the Holy Scripture has a literal meaning which is historical and factual, so too the "book of creation", i.e., the world, initially has a "literal meaning", behind which — just as in the case with the Holy Scripture — a deeper moral, theological, and mystical meaning is hidden. Therefore, just as a perceptive mind, the ability of penetrating to the heart of the matter, makes it possible to go beyond the literal meaning of Holy Scripture to its moral, theological, and mystical sense, so also there is an experience of the world and of life, a beholding through the light of the Logos "which is the light of mankind", which transforms experience of the creation into a revelation of the Creator. It transforms whoever experiences it into a *seer* who perceives not only the world of the senses, but also the supersensible world — the world of souls, the world of the angelic hierarchies — this latter world being full of light, bearing immediate witness to God. The world of the senses, the kingdoms of nature, testify to the all-pervasive wisdom of God, whereas the angelic, soul world *represents* this wisdom in that it lives from and in this wisdom.

The message of St. Bonaventure was this: that the world of visible and invisible things can be seen in and through the divine light and that this kind of seeing strengthens, confirms, and deepens the truth of revelation. Experience of the world in the light of grace is a support for faith.

The path and experience of St. John of the Cross, the author of the work *The Night of the Senses and the Night of the Spirit*, are different. John of the Cross renounced "experience of the world in the light" and strove for the experience of meeting God in the darkness of the senses and the spirit without ideas and images. For him it was not the mirroring of God in the world that was important, nor the images and analogies which vouchsafe experience and support and confirm faith. Rather, it was the encounter of the being of the soul with the being of God, i.e., with the reality of God Himself, with the *truth* of God that was important. This is not possible through seeing or knowing. It can only happen in the reciprocal permeation of the love of God and of the love of the soul. And this can only take place in the complete absence of images and ideas, in the "night of the spirit". The "night of the spirit", in which the immediate experience of the loving permeation of the soul by the Being of God can take place — the most direct experience imaginable — is in fact not darkness but absolute light, which blinds because of its abundance and therefore is experienced as darkness. It is the radiance of the reality of God — the truth of God — which permeates and envelops the soul of the human being.

Let us now turn again to the forty-second Psalm: *"Emitte lucem tuam et veritaten tuam: ipsa me deduxerunt et adduxerunt in montem sanctum tuum, et in tabernacula tua"*. This means: let me experience life and the world in Your light, and envelop and permeate me with the darkness of the direct revelation of Your essence, Your reality, the truth of Your Being itself. The experience of the world and of life in Your light and the truth of Your Being will lead me forth from the narrowness of my own self-consciousness and give me the all-encompassing view from on high of the world of experience ("guide me up Your holy mountain") and transpose me into the inner presence of God and the condition of union with Him ("Your tabernacles," *tabernacula tua*"). The "holy mountain" and the "tents or tabernacles of God" characterize the goals of the two paths — the "day path" of light and the "night path" of darkness and night — as they are, for example, represented by St. Bonaventure and St. John of the Cross. The goal of the former was ascent, the elevation of the spirit to behold the world in divine light, so that it would appear as the revelation of God. The goal of the latter was descent into the depths of the human being, where it encounters the Being of God directly and where the Being of God and the being of man mutually permeate one another. Seeing the world as a revelation in the light of God is the condition of the soul upon the "holy mountain", and the intimate, inner experience of God indwelling the soul is the condition of being in the "tabernacle of God". These two conditions are the *light of God* and *truth of God*, as they are designated in the forty-second Psalm.

Now, the Sinai-revelation — according to its spirit as well as its text — expressly emphasizes the *truth* of God, i.e., the pictureless unimaginability of God on the path of the "nocturnal" experience of God in the darkness of the spirit. This is clear not only from the words: "You shall not make for yourself a graven image, or any likeness of anything that is in heaven above or on the earth below, or that is in the water under the earth" (*Ex.* 20:4), but also in the characterization of the nature of the "prophet" Moses as given in the twelfth chapter of the book of *Numbers*. There we read: "Hear my words: if there is a prophet among you, I the Lord make myself known to him in a vision, I speak with him in a dream. Not so with my servant Moses; he is entrusted with all my house. With him I speak mouth to mouth, clearly and not in dark riddles; indeed, he beholds the form of the Lord" (*Num.* 12:6–8).

In other words, "He who is" revealed Himself *directly* to Moses in the clear light of day-consciousness, without symbolic dreams and visions. He spoke with Moses *directly* and revealed Himself to him, as He is (in "His form", as Luther translates it). This means, however, that in the sense of the two paths, characterized above as the day-path and the night-path — or the path of light and the path of truth — the revelation of God to Moses took place on the "path of truth". This is also confirmed in the book of *Deuteronomy*, where it is written concerning Moses: "And there has not arisen a prophet since in Israel like Moses, whom the Lord knew face to face" (*Deut.* 34:10).

This knowledge was therefore reciprocal and two-sided — a direct approach of God to the human being, and of the human being to God — a mutual permeation. For this reason both declarations in the Bible could be made, namely, that in contrast to other prophets, Moses knew God directly (*Num.* 12:6–8), and that he was known by God like no other prophet (*Deut.* 34:10). Both were *one* process of reciprocal approach, which meant the disappearance of any possible distance, including the distance, which "seeing or beholding in the light" presupposes. In Moses' case what is present is actually the revelation of God in "His truth", and not the revelation in "His light", signifying God's revelation in the sense of St. John of the Cross and not in the sense of St. Bonaventure.

Now, everything indicates that the path of the Israelites' community of faith was fundamentally the same one which Moses went. For Moses' path of destiny, as well as that of the people of Israel's, was determined by the wandering in the desert. It was a *desert path*. Just as Moses had to go into the wilderness, to Mt. Horeb, where he experienced the first revelation of the God who is Being ("I am the I am"), so the community of the people of Israel had to flee out of Egypt into the desert, where they were allowed to experience the revelation on Mt. Sinai and became the community of faith of Israel. It was in the wilderness that Moses experienced the first revelation of God in the burning bush, and it was again in the desert that the community of Israel experienced the revelation on Mt. Sinai. And only after wandering in the desert for forty years were the people of Israel allowed to enter into the promised land. However, Moses did not cross the Jordan, but crossed the threshold of death. *His* "promised land" lay on the other side of the threshold of death. The people of Israel prepared themselves for the future encounter with the expected Messiah in the promised land; Moses was granted this meeting in the disembodied state. It took place in the scene of the Transfiguration on Mt. Tabor in the accompaniment of Elijah. Peter, John, and James were present as witnesses to this encounter. They experienced not only the meeting of Moses and Elijah with Christ, but also the conversation that Christ had with the two prophets. Thus Moses and Elijah were not hindered by death from meeting the living Messiah come down to the earth. They spoke with the Living One, as did other Israelites who had the opportunity to do so at that time. Moses and Elijah were granted the opportunity to converse as "living ones" to the Living One. So great was the impression of them as "living ones" made on Peter, John, and James that the disciples suggested building three tabernacles on the top of Mt. Tabor: "one for Jesus, one for Elijah, and one for Moses" (*Mt.* 17:4). Thus to the three disciples they appeared to be just as much alive and living as Jesus.

The wandering in the desert of the people of Israel under Moses' leadership meant more than the migrations of a shepherd people. It arose from the inner necessity pertaining to the path of withdrawal and purification. Egypt, with its cities, buildings, temples, and cultic services had to be forgotten so that a purification from its influence could take place. The path through the desert was a schooling, an inner preparation for the revelation whose precondition is "emptiness of soul" with regard to memories, images, and thoughts. Just as only an empty glass can take in new liquid, so only a soul which has become empty is able to receive a new revelation. And the wandering in the desert of the people of Israel under Moses' leadership was just such an "emptying" by way of preparation for taking in the new revelation. This journey did not have the goal of reaching the promised land, Canaan, for two weeks would have been enough to get from the eastern boundary of Egypt to Canaan. That the wandering lasted forty years was not conditioned by the distance to the goal of the journey. Rather, the wandering in the desert was in a certain sense an end in itself. The loneliness of the desert was to be the decisive, direction-giving experience for the entire future spiritual path of the "chosen people". For the twelve tribes of Israel were chosen as representatives of humanity to set an example by treading the desert path of experiencing the pure revelation of God without "pictures and images". They were chosen that humanity be taught, and that it might live, the path of pure intuition, i.e., knowledge of God exempted from the power of thought and imagination. This path of inner certainty is founded on *nothing*. It is the path of pure *belief*, in the sense of Christ's words: "Have you believed because you have seen me? Blessed are those who *have not seen* and yet believe" (*Jn*. 20:29). The preparation for this power of belief was the path through the wilderness, which the twelve tribes of Israel went with Moses. The path through the desert taught them that unimaginability and incomparability are *the* preconditions for the revelation of God and for knowledge of His Being.

Human beings who tread the "desert path" or "path of night" are compared by St. John of the Cross with adults who walk without need of support; they are not carried. They forego the many "comforts" — dreams, visions, the sun-like blissful moods that are bestowed, and other sorts of "comforts" — which correspond to the embraces and caresses according during childhood. An adult endures the tediousness and the unpleasantness of life out of his inner strength, while the child must be entertained, comforted, and encouraged. In this sense St. John of the Cross understands the way of purification through the inner desert as a path for mature souls who are strong enough to bear the tediousness, stillness, and loneliness of the "night of the spirit". Nevertheless, these souls also have need of being strengthened, encouraged, and cheered up. It is one of the experiences which every human being who treads the "desert path" knows, that at night, in the condition of sleep, something happens which gives him again and again new strength to endure and not to despair. The night, which seems to be just as desert-like, unmoving, and dark as the "night of the spirit" experienced during the waking consciousness of day, in time transforms itself into a giver of strength of soul and courage of spirit for the human being. It is as if something received as a kind of after-effect from the heavenly choirs of the spiritual hierarchies was actively giving new life and strength to the soul (and often to the body, too) of the awakened wanderer. The result is renewed courage for life and the temporary disappearing of any lack of hope. This strengthening is not due to a dream or any kind of instruction during dreaming, but purely and simply to the *condition* resulting during the night. Despondency, or even despair, simply disappears by itself, and one is reinvigorated and strengthened to continue the "path through the desert". It is not arbitrary to compare this after-effect of the night with the miraculous nourishment of manna, to see here an analogy with this feeding of the chosen people in the desert during their wandering through the wilderness. For the nocturnal strengthening that one experiences is to be experienced anew every night; it cannot be "stored up" for the following days as a content of memory. In the sunlight of day-consciousness it "melts", as it were. It loses its strength. The analogy between the experience of the invigorating effect or "feeding" in sleep, which the human being who "wanders through the desert" can have, and the feeding with the divine manna, of which the Bible reports, goes even further. It extends also to "taste" and "colour". In the Bible manna is designated as the bread of heaven or of the angels (*Ps.* 78:23–25), which like dew or frost covered the immediate area surrounding the Israelites' camp in the morning. It was white and consisted of seeds in the size and shape of coriander seeds. It tasted like honey cake (*Ex.* 16:31).

Now, the strengthening effect of the night, which can be given to the spiritual "desert wanderer", is experienced as "white" and perceived as "sweet" ("sweet" in a similar sense as is said about sleeping "sweetly"). "White" and "sweet" is the overall impression which is experienced upon awakening, the result of the integration of countless, tiny, uniform entities, somewhat in the sense of the *petites perceptions* of the philosopher (and mathematician) Leibniz. (Leibniz, *Nouveaux Essais sur l 'entendement humain*, III, 1.) In "pneumatism" these play a similar role to the smallest particles (*corpuscula*) in physics, i.e., which are invisible because of their smallness and for that reason are not noticed, which, nonetheless, can have great significance and influence. The totality of these tiny impressions (*petites perceptions*) leaves behind upon awakening the overall impression of "whiteness" and "sweetness", and their multiplicity and uniformity make well for a comparison with "coriander seeds" (*Ex.* 16:31).

Also, their combined effect is strengthening, i.e., refreshing and nourishing. Thanks to them one is strong enough again to take up and continue the "desert path" with its monotony and lack of stimulation — wandering "without pictures and images", without dreams and visions.

It must be emphasized that we are speaking of the *analogy* between the strengthening effect of sleep (as this can be experienced by those such as St. John of the Cross who travel the "desert path") and the manna of the biblical report. Here it is not a matter of an *identity* in considering the concrete reality of this biblical miracle. Biblical miracles are not to be understood merely as symbolic pictures for psychological and spiritual experiences. On the other hand, it would be a mistake to consider manna simply as the sugary substance which the lice who live on the tamarisks of the Sinai peninsula secrete as fine grains. The analogy referred to here opens up the possibility of contemplating the moral-spiritual dimension of "heavenly sustenance". This is not something simply to be marvelled at, but also to be *understood*. Nevertheless, to understand something by way of an analogy which can be experienced in the moral and psychological domain does not signify that it is not also possible for it to take place as a concrete event in outer reality. The Bible does not speak just in symbols, and not just about facts, but about facts that are at the same time symbols. Thus the forty-years' wandering in the desert of the chosen people under the direction of Moses is factual and symbolic at the same time. It signified preparation for the revelation of God, who is unimaginable and incomparable. That is, it prepared for the revelation of God in His truth and reality.

As a *fact* the wandering in the desert was an historical occurrence, as a *symbol* it is an expression of the timeless law of the necessity of purification and the "emptying of consciousness" as precondition for the revelation of God in His truth. The Sermon on the Mount expresses this through the beatitude: "Blessed are the poor in spirit, for theirs is the kingdom of heaven" (*Mt.* 5:3).

IV

"YOU SHALL NOT TAKE THE NAME OF THE LORD YOUR GOD IN VAIN"

THE UNUTTERABLE NAME OF GOD

In the depth-language of moral logic, i.e., in the language of the Old and New Testaments of the Bible, the words, concepts, and ideas bound up with "names", "giving names", "naming", and "calling by a name", have a deeper meaning with respect to knowledge of beings and of their activity. In contrast, the widespread, superficial language of today — the clear and transparent language of the intellect — generally refers to appearances only and does not penetrate to the essence of things.

Thus, let us consider the following passage in the Bible, where it says: "And out of the ground the Lord God (*Elohim*) formed every beast of the field and every bird of the air; and He brought them to Adam to see what he would name them; and whatever Adam called every living creature, that was its name" (*Gen.* 2:19). This does not mean that the human being invented designations for the beings of the animal kingdom, and even less that he classified them according to genera and species — along the lines of the system of Linnaeus — but rather that he received and fulfilled the divine mandate to determine the *vocations or missions* relative to the human being of the living creatures hierarchically subordinate to him. For, in the language of the Bible, "name" means "mission" or "activity of being", and "naming" is the magical act of determining the vocation or mission of a being. For example, the new name that was given by God to Abram ("exalted father"), namely Abraham ("father of a multitude"), is to be understood only in this sense. "No longer shall your name be Abram, but your name shall be Abraham; for I have made you the father of a multitude of nations" (*Gen.* 17: 5).

Using and misusing a name is a very serious matter when one considers that the animal names were given according to God's mandate by the not-yet-fallen human being. Even more so is this true for the names of human beings that were given by God, like the name Abraham, or the name John, which was proclaimed by the Archangel Gabriel to Zacharias, the father of John the Baptist, when he was serving as priest in the temple (*Lk.* 1).

How is it, however, with the *name of God*, the name whose misuse is expressly forbidden in the Ten Commandments? "You shall not take the name of the Lord your God (*Eloheha*) in vain; for the Lord (YHWH) will not hold him guiltless who takes his name in vain" (*Ex.* 20:7).

Who can give to the highest of all beings His actual and effective name? Only God Himself can do that. Revelation is the only possible source of knowing about the name of God, i.e., His name is that which He gives Himself. No human being, not even the wisest, can name God (in the biblical sense) in such a way that the name would be no mere designation but real and effective. This is impossible for the following reasons. There is a name, a word, and a concept in the use of human language, namely the word "I", which only makes sense when it is used by the speaker himself for naming or designating himself. It would be meaningless if it were to be used by someone else for indicating "me" myself. Only the person himself can designate himself as "I". It is the same with regard to the name of the God who transcends the self ("I"). The God who transcends the self is, so to speak, the sun whose single rays are the individual "I's" and He is, in the sense of St. Augustine, "more I myself than I myself am". Now, if the name "I" is misused when it is not used by the speaker himself, it is all the more misused when the name of the God who transcends the "I" is used by someone other than God Himself. For the human being God is not a "He", not a "You", and not an "It". He is not a being existing externally in relation to the "I" of the human being, and the latter is also not His own "I". Just as a ray of eternal being may not identify itself with Eternal Being, so also the human individual "I" may not identify itself with the source of its being. And yet it ought not view the source of its being as something foreign, something existing external to its "I"-ness. For, although a ray is not the sun, it is nevertheless sun-like through and through, and cannot experience itself otherwise than as the raying-in of the sun of Eternal Being into the realm of temporal existence. In order to be permitted to utter the "name" of God—in the biblical sense, i.e., truly and effectively— without misusing it, the human being would have to be in the position of speaking it in the same way as he speaks the word "I". At the same time, however, he would have to speak it in such a way that in doing so the primal source and archetype of all "I"-ness, i.e, of spiritually internalized participation in being, is meant and invoked. Thus the prohibition in Judaism against uttering the actual and effective name of God, and therefore no human being—not even Moses—would have invented or given this name. It was revealed to Moses—in fact by God Himself—as is clearly said in the text concerning Moses' summons at Mt. Horeb (*Ex.* 3:13–15). There it is stated:

> Then Moses said to God: "If when I come to the people of Israel and say to them, 'The God of your fathers has sent me to you,' and they ask me, 'What is His name?' What shall I say to them?" God said to Moses: "I AM THE I AM (EHIYEH ASHER EHIYEH [אֶהְיֶה אֲשֶׁר אֶהְיֶה])." And He spoke further: "Say this to the people of Israel, 'I AM (EHIYEH [אֶהְיֶה]) has sent me to you.' "
>
> God (ELOHIM [אֱלֹהִים]) spoke further to Moses: "Say this to the people of Israel, 'The Lord (YHVH [יהוה], the God (ELOHIM) of your fathers, the God of Abraham, the God of Isaac, and the God of Jacob, has sent me to you. This is My name for ever, and thus I am to be remembered throughout all generations."

The name of God which was revealed to Moses corresponds completely with the Being of the God who transcends the self ("I"). The name "I am the I am" is not the name which Moses gave God, but on the contrary it was given and revealed by God Himself. It is, then, of such a kind that it cannot be used in the sense of "He" or "It" but only in the sense of *transsubjective* Being. It contains no analogy, no likeness or image from the entire realm of existence, except for the analogy with the "I am" experience of the human being. The most intimate, intuitive experience of the human being, that of "I am", is the only "image and likeness" which it contains.

In fact, two names were revealed to Moses—one name that is absolute: "I am the I am" or "I am"; and a second, the name of the God of Abraham, Isaac, and Jacob, YHVH, which is to be His name for ever and which, "to His remembrance", is to be valid throughout all generations. Thus was revealed to Moses the timeless, absolute, and cosmic name "I am", and also the name valid for historical time, the name of the "God of the fathers", YAHVEH (YHVH).

"I am" is the name for the realm of eternal being, while the name Yahveh is meant for the realm of temporal history, i.e., for the realm of existence. (YHVH, as is now generally recognised, is spoken "Yahveh" and not "Jehovah"—the latter having arisen through incorrectly reading YHVH.) Yahveh is the name for the "upper" partner of the covenant: Israel—Yahveh. It contains within it and also reveals the meaning and nature of the divinely willed mission of Israel, the "chosen people"—historically actually "the people of Yahveh". The *tetragrammaton*, the name composed of four letters, contains the secret of fatherhood, motherhood, childhood, and the family. The four letters (Yod-Hé-Vau-Hé) represent this four-foldness. Yod stands for the eternal masculine, eternally active and creating; the first Hé for the eternal feminine, receiving and nurturing; Vau for the eternal child, ever born and reborn; and the second Hé for the principle and archetype of the family community.

"Therewith is the name EHIYEH (אֶהְיֶה) the name which God gives Himself in the first person; it relates to the subjective aspect of divine being. And the name Yod-Hé-Vau-Hé) (יהוה), given in the third person, relates to its objective aspect which was revealed to the people of Israel," writes Francis Warrain about the two names, the author of the work *La Théodicée de la Kabbale*, which is the deepest and most comprehensive investigation of the teachings of the Cabbala concerning the names of God and the system of the ten Sephiroth.

According to de Pauly (the translator of the *Zohar* into French and an expert concerning this text) the name EHIYEH indicates God's dominion in heaven, and the name YHVH God's sovereign power on earth. (Francis Warrain, *La Théodicée de la Kabbale*, Paris 1949, p. 87.) In other words, the name EHIYEH ("I am") is the name of God in heaven, in the realm of eternal Being. And the name YAHVEH ("He who is") relates to material existence, the realm of becoming, i.e., the world of earthly and historical events. YHVH is the name for the "God of the fathers". Thus it is also the holy banner of the "covenant of providence" underlying the mission of the descendants of Abraham, Isaac, and Jacob — to become and to remain the "people of Yahveh", which mission culminated in the appearance of the Messiah.

The two names of God EHIYEH ("I am") and YHVH ("He who is") are, in Hebrew, forms of the verb to be. In fact, they are in the future tense which, however, in Hebrew means not just the future, but also (and much more so) *duration, permanence*. EHIYEH is the form of the future (duration) in the first person and YHVH "He is, he was, and he will be".

The name "I am" (EHIYEH) was unutterable because there was no legitimate speaker for this name. On one occasion it was spoken, and concerning this occurrence the *Gospel of John*, written in Greek, reports Jesus answering the ironical question of the Jews:

"You are not yet fifty years old, and have you seen Abraham?" Jesus said to them: "Truly, truly, I say to you, before Abraham was, I am." So they took up stones to throw at him; but Jesus hid himself, and went out of the temple. (*Jn.* 8:57–59)

As far as the name "He who is" (Yahveh) is concerned, the high priest was allowed to speak it reverently once a year at a celebration in the temple, in the Holy of Holies. Otherwise, instead of the unutterable name the substitute name ADONAI ("Lord") was used, also while reading the Holy Scriptures. Only the high priest in the Holy of Holies of the temple was allowed to speak the name YHVH during the festive divine worship without this being a misuse of the name of God. For, in the consciousness of the world characterized in the Bible the spoken name meant releasing the *summoning power* contained in it, thus signifying a magical invocation. And therein lies the possible serious misuse of the holy name. For this reason Martin Buber understands the revelation of the name Yahveh in the third chapter of *Exodus* above all as proof of the fact that the Lord did not have to be summoned, but is always present with His power and help. Therefore he translates the name YHVH as "I am there". The Everpresent One does not have to be summoned.

"YHVH, the God of your fathers, the God of Abraham, the God of Isaac, and the God of Jacob, has sent me to you. This is My name for ever and thus I am to be remembered throughout all generations" — this was the mandate to Moses concerning the name YHVH. It was not said that with this name you are to *call* to Me for all time, but to *remember* Me for ever and ever. It is the name of God for inner, meditative use, not for external speaking or any kind of magical use. However, even the inner, meditative use of the name of the "God of the fathers and of the descendants for all of time" can be subject to misuse. This is especially so once the secret of the name has been recognized — the secret bound up with the significance of the historical mission which finds its expression in the name YHVH. What then, is the meaning of this historical mission?

The name YHVH bears within it the divinely willed mission to create and preserve a special people through the powers of reproduction and heredity, a people which finds itself a stranger to those in other lands and fundamentally in opposition to all other peoples. For this people is to be the bearer of a living tradition, borne by heredity, of the covenant with YHVH, nurturing the hope that through this covenant redemption from the consequences of the Fall will take place at some time. The significance of reproduction and heredity can be clearly seen from the text of the Ten Commandments in the sentences concerning the nature of Yahveh's justice and mercy:

'For I, the Lord (YHVH), your God am a jealous God, visiting the iniquity of the fathers upon the children to the third and the fourth generation of those who hate me, but showing mercy to thousands of those who love me and keep my commandments" (*Ex*. 20:5–6).

There is no talk here of single souls, of individualities; it is justice and mercy for the *generations* of the stream of heredity. This understanding of justice and mercy stands in stark contrast to the idea of justice and mercy as it is understood as the law of *karma* in India and Tibet (and now, increasingly, in Europe and America too). For the law of karma is oriented to the single soul, the individual, not to the generations of descendants. The idea of karma is founded on the proposition: "What you *sow*, you will reap". The consequences of what one has caused through one's deeds will be experienced by oneself and not by others, such as, for example, one's descendants.

Thus the law of punishment for sins and of reward for righteousness which is proclaimed in the Ten Commandments is a moral law working through heredity and reproduction. Here the blood which flows through the generations is the bearer of the curse of sin and of the blessing of righteousness.

In short, the name of the "God of the fathers", with which one is to remember for all time the God of Israel who led the people of Israel out of Egypt — the name Yahveh — reveals and contains the moral law of retribution and selection which holds sway in reproduction and heredity throughout the generations. This law was proclaimed and expressly meant only for the chosen people, because this people had the mission of preparing for the appearance of the Redeemer of all of humanity. The Redeemer of all of humanity is the *causa finalis* of the existence and destiny of the chosen people — indeed, He is the very reason for the choosing of this people. And the name YHVH signifies historically the sanctification of reproduction and heredity. Reproduction and heredity are made holy through the name Yahveh (YHVH).

However, insight into the special relationship of Yahveh to procreation and heredity can lead to misuse of the holy name of God. On the one hand the name of God can be misused by calling Him forth in the sense of a magical invocation. On the other hand it is misused if in the forces of reproduction, procreation, and heredity the holy name itself is sensed instead of the reflection of this name (the reflection being the divinely willed mission and task). In this case the God of Israel Himself becomes viewed as a reflection or a kind of "religious superstructure" of these forces. Instead of seeing the original divine ideal in the forces of the sexual life, the sexual becomes projected onto the divine itself. If this happens, the same thing is repeated which took place at the foot of Mt. Sinai with the worshiping of the "golden calf" — the bull that was conceived of as divine. (Indeed, at that time the procreative and reproductive power itself was raised up to the "God who led us out of Egypt".) This would be a kind of "Freudian interpretation" of the religion and mission of Yahveh. This is the other great misuse of the name of God. However, "the Lord (YHVH) will not allow to go unpunished whoever misuses His name" (Ex. 20:7).

V

THE USE OF THE NAME
OF GOD IN MEDITATION

We have seen that two names were revealed to Moses on Mt. Horeb: "I am" (אֶהְיֶה —EHIYEH) and "He who is" or "He who is Being" (יהוה — YHVH). The first name refers to timeless existence, the second to temporal existence, i.e., to the historical mission of the people of Israel. The second name designated the God of Abraham, Isaac, and Jacob, the first name He who says of Himself: "Before Abraham was, I am", as it is stated in the *Gospel of John*, i.e., He who is timeless and does not relate to one people and its historical mission. The name "I am the I am" is the answer to the question of *humanity*, whose representative Moses was; it was actually the answer directed to Moses and meant for him. The name YHVH was the answer which was meant for the children of Israel. For Moses, who was summoned with this name by the "angel of the Lord" from the burning bush, received the revelation (which then followed) both as the representative of humanity and the one who was given the task of creating a new people from the descendants of the three patriarchs and of leading them out of Egypt.

The exodus from Egypt was the *birth* of the people of Israel. They consisted of the descendants of the sons of Jacob and other slaves of the state of Egypt who joined them and departed together with them. The people that was led into the wilderness by Moses was a rather colourful mix of different familial and tribal traditions. In addition, God's revelations that had been imparted to the patriarchs were not identical with the revelation to Moses at the foot of Mt. Horeb. For God did not reveal Himself to the patriarchs as YHVH, let alone as "I am" (EHIYEH), but as "SHADDAI" (שַׁדַּי ter), the "Almighty One". This name corresponds to the level of the comprehension and revelation of God at that time. SHADDAI was used whenever it was a matter of convincing the human being that for God nothing is impossible (*Gen.* 17:1; 28:3; 35:1; 43:14; 48:3; 49:25). And it was with this name that God revealed Himself to Abraham, Isaac, and Jacob.

In the account concerning Jacob (*Gen.* 31: 13; 33: 20; 35: 1; and 46: 3). God's name EL (לא te), which means "the Strong, the Exalted, the Superior One", is used.

The names of God which are used in the Bible represent stages of the progressive revelation of the Being of God, adapted to the human power of understanding. They denote stages of the increasing interiorization of the human power of understanding, and at the same time those of the progressive revelation of aspects of God's Being (progressing in the direction of interiorization).

Along the path of internalization the name "SHADDAI" ("Almighty One") corresponds to the first, lowest level of understanding of God. It does not go any further than the morally indifferent concept of "might" and "being able to do everything". Comparing this, for example, with the words of the old Russian prince Alexander Nevski: "God is not in might, but in truth and righteousness" (*Ne w sile Bog a w prawd*), one understands, then, how great a step in the interiorization of the knowledge of the being of God this interpretation of St. Alexander Nevski signifies. In this connection it must also be mentioned that one of the most amoral and barbarous men of our time, Adolf Hitler, often expressly appealed to the "Almighty One".

The name EL ("Strong One", "Exalted One", "Superior One") represents a further stage in the interiorization of the knowledge of God's being. For here it is not a matter of might or omnipotence, but of the higher hierarchical *order of rank* — God's exaltedness in comparison to the human being. The name EL forms the beginning of several other names which express exaltedness — for example, EL-HAÏA, the "Living God". It also forms the last syllable of various angelic names, for example, Michael, Gabriel, Raphael, Uriel. EL expresses the attitude of looking up and worshiping one who is higher in order of the hierarchy of being. The name EL presupposes a feeling of reverence and dignity in a hierarchical sense, a feeling within man for the Divinity of God's Being. This is more than a mere acknowledgement of a power superior to man. Reverence signifies a more interior relationship to God than mere fear before the power of the Almighty. And yet Moses, to whom the highest stage of the names of God, the name EHIYEH, was revealed, had first of all, as a go-between in relation to the Egyptians, to serve the revelation of God which corresponds to the name SHADDAI — beginning with the magical struggle by means of the rods transformed into snakes, followed by the ten plagues, then by the destruction of the Egyptian army in the Red Sea. All these events were a revelation of God under the name "SHADDAI" ("Almighty One"). The Pharaoh and the Egyptian people were to learn what it meant to oppose the will of the Almighty One.

They learned through experience that the Hebrews had the God "SHADDAI" on their side.

It is scarcely necessary to say that Moses himself possessed a much more intimate and inwardly deeper knowledge of God than that which he had to represent in Egypt. This is certain if one considers the following. When Yahveh wanted to destroy the people of Israel because of their turning away from Him and on account of their worship of the golden calf at the foot of Mt. Sinai, Moses asked that he, instead, be blotted out from the book of life rather than that the people of Israel be destroyed. Thus he attained pardon for the people of Israel. In his sacrificial willingness a deeper understanding of the divine expressed itself. Here it was not a question of omnipotence, but of love and readiness for self-sacrifice. Under which name had God made Himself in this dialogue, the result of which was that God did not destroy the people of Israel? known to Moses? Was it not the highest name that was revealed to Moses, knowledge of which burned in his soul a fire, the name which once in the distant future was to be legitimately spoken by Him who said: "Before Abraham was, I am?" Since Moses had declared his readiness to die for the people, he was, together with Elijah, found worthy to take part in the dialogue on Mt. Tabor with the Transfigured One — the bearer of this name — about His mission to die for humanity.

On the other hand, only the One who had chosen Abraham, as father of the people in which He wanted to appear, could propose to Moses that he replace Abraham to become the patriarch of a new people. And was not the "I am, before Abraham was" simultaneously the One who chose and appointed Abraham to be the father of the people in which He wanted to incarnate as a human being?

The most mysterious name of God, the name "I am" (EHIYEH), which was revealed to Moses, is in truth the name of Christ before His appearance as the Son of Man. In the dialogue of Moses with God which led to the pardoning of the people of Israel, Moses addressed himself to Christ "Who was in the beginning with God and was God" (*Jn.* 1: 1).

There is a name of God in the Bible and in the tradition of the Cabbala which unites the two names of the highest level "I am" (EHIYEH) and "He who is" (YHVH), in that it is a part of both. This is the name JAH ([יָהּ]). The name JAH is not often mentioned in the scriptures. It appears in the song of Moses: "The Lord (JAH) is my strength and my song, and He has become my salvation" (*Fortitudo et laus mea JAH, et factus est mihi in salutem*) (*Ex.* 15: 2). The name JAH represents the principle of redemption for the period of time from the destruction of the temple until the coming of the Messiah.

The Psalms contain the instruction: "Let this be recorded for a generation to come, so that a people yet unborn may praise the Lord (JAH)" (*Scribantur haec in generatione altera, et populus, qui creabitur, laudabit JAH* (Ps. 102: 18).

And in the book of the prophet Malachi the following prophecy is given: "Behold, I will send you Elijah ('My God is JAH') (*Mal.* 4: 5). This refers to the prophet whose name itself contains this name of God, which in the time of preparation for the coming of the "Anointed One" of God, the Messiah, is to be called upon and revered.

Generally the name JAH is understood as the contraction of the tetragrammaton YHVH. However, a mere contracting of the unutterable and holy name for the reasons of making the pronunciation easier (bearing in mind that it was not allowed to be pronounced at all!) and remembering it (who would be able to forget the holy name of God and want to simplify it?) is, unthinkable. A contraction of the name of God could have the sole significance of emphasizing that which is most essential in the name in order to intensify meditation on it. In this sense the name JAH is the sacred ideogram and the sacred phonogram of the Incarnation, which is contained as intention and inclination in the name JAH. This name brings to expression ideogrammatically as well as phonogrammatically the will of God for redemption. And truly for human beings this can be considered most important within the complete divine name YHVH, hence the contraction of YHVH to YH (Yod-Hé) = YAH or JAH. Here, likewise, is the reason for the traditional view that this name was particularly meant for the time of the preparation for the coming of the Messiah and for he who prepares the way (Elijah).

According to the *Zohar* the name JAH is the most mysterious of all the holy names. It designates the source of the divine stream where "the Yod gives its light to the Hé, which grants nourishment to the world below". The union of Yod with Hé is the origin of the divine stream of blessing. If one only considers that the Yod signifies the original, creative oneness and the Hé the sign for the breath of life, one will be inclined to see the image for the name JAH in the radiating sun — in the "sun of compassion" which shines for the just and the unjust alike. And it was this aspect of God, which reveals itself under the name JAH, with which Moses effected the pardoning of the people of Israel.

The name ELOHIM is the name of God as the One who completed the work of the creation of the world in six days. In the first chapter of *Genesis* it appears thirty-two times, while the name YAHVEH ELOHIM is mentioned for the first time in the second chapter of *Genesis* (*Gen.* 2: 4).

The singular of the name ELOHIM [אֱלֹהִים] is ELOHA [אֱלוֹהַ re] and it seldom appears in the Bible. One finds it in *Deuteronomy*, in the book of *Job*, in *Isaiah*, and in the book of *Kings*. It consists of the name EL and the last two letters of the name YAHVEH. The name ELOHA has the meaning: "Master" (in the sense of Master of the work of art which is nature, Creator of nature). In this sense the riddle of the plural, which the name ELOHIM expresses, can also be solved. The name ELOHIM can be understood as the "many-sided mastery of the Master, which reveals itself in the creative work of the creation". This understanding of the name ELOHIM goes beyond the explanation that we have in the name ELOHIM merely a *pluralis majestatis*. It also does justice to the decidedly monotheistic view of the Bible, which the literal translation of the name ELOHIM as "Gods" contradicts, though, in fact, it would be linguistically correct. For it is not a question of a multiplicity of creators but of an astonishing and unimaginable many-sidedness to the Creator which reveals itself in the work of the creation of the world. For this reason the Cabbala speaks of thirty-two paths of wisdom, which is grounded in the fact that the name ELOHIM appears thirty-two times in the account of creation in the first chapter of *Genesis*.

Here it is not a question of thirty-two "Gods", but of this many paths of wisdom upon which the all-encompassing wisdom of the Creator reveals itself in the work of creation. Therefore it is more correct to see in the name ELOHIM not a multiplicity of originators of the creation, but the many-sidedness of the creative wisdom of the *one* Originator.

In turn, the name ELOHIM can also be used correctly or improperly. The correct use of this name would be as a meditation on the manifoldness of the wisdom of God as it reveals itself in the creation — thus a meditation concerning the thirty-two paths of wisdom. In contrast, misuse of this name would consist in the analytical dissection of the Godhead into a multiplicity of independent gods, which was the general rule with the pagan peoples. It was not without reason that the word ELOHIM was also used for the gods of the pagan religions, indeed even for those human beings who were members of a court of justice. The Bible reports numerous oft repeated cases of the misuse of the divine name ELOHIM in connection with the decline into polytheism — especially in the cult of the "Baalim" (plural of Baal) and also in the cult of Baal and Astarte (the Phoenician goddess Astarte or Ashtoreth, equivalent to Ishtar of the Assyro — Babylonian peoples).

ELOHIM is doubtless the unity within the multiplicity of the revelations of the mastery of the Master in His creation. Just as the image of the radiating sun corresponds to the divine name JAH so the image of the *rainbow* corresponds to the name ELOHIM. The idea of unity within multiplicity, or of the harmony of the many under the union of leadership is expressed clearly in the name ELOHIM SABAOTH and YAHVEH SABAOTH which are both translated as "Lord, God of Hosts" (*Dominus Deus Sabaoth*). This name relates to God as the apex of the pyramid of the hierarchical world order—as the head of all hierarchies: the angels, archangels, principalities, powers, virtues, dominions, thrones, cherubim, and seraphim. To see God as the Highest One above the choirs of the spiritual hierarchies signifies enhancing God's exaltedness. Indeed this cosmically exalted reverence fills the Christian cathedrals, too, when the formula sounds:

(*Sanctus, sanctus, sanctus Dominus Deus Sabaoth. Pleni sunt coeli et terra gloria tria. Hosanna in excelsis.*) Holy, holy, holy, Lord, God of Hosts. Heaven and earth are filled with Your glory. Hosanna in the highest.

The name ADONAI (אֲדֹונָי), which is usually translated as "Lord" (*Dominus, Kyrios*), is the experience of the God of Hosts—God seen through the choir of the divine hierarchies as their superior. It is the name ADONAI which is spoken in place of the name YHVH and is substituted for YHVH when the scriptures are read. The vowel signs for ADONAI were therefore placed under the consonants of the name YHVH. Thus arose the word JEHOVAH. (Sometimes the vowel signs for the word ELOHIM are placed under the name YHVH, resulting in the name JEHOVIH.) Generally, however, the name of God YHVH is replaced by the name ADONAI which designates God in a certain sense as the "Master of the house"—the "house of the world". ADONAI is essentially and by rights the possessor and ruler of the world, the "Lord of the World". The world is His, and all beings of the world are His servants—not because His omnipotence compels them (that would correspond to the name SHADDAI) or because He is superior to the beings of the world (that would correspond to the name EL), but because He *is* the eternal *Lord* and because His glory convinces all beings to commit themselves to Him, to serve Him, and to be obedient to Him.

What the "Lord of Hosts" (ELOHIM SABAOTH) is in the heavenly world, is the "Lord" (ADONAI) in the world of nature, the world of facts and events.

A deeper understanding of the names of God in their inner context is scarcely possible without knowledge of the traditional teaching of the ten Sephiroth, which occupies a key position in the Cabbala. The word *sephirah* (plural: *sephiroth*) means "number". Here it is not a matter of number in a quantitative sense, but rather in the sense of the opening sentence of the book *Sepher Yetzirah*:

> YAH [JAH], the Lord of Hosts [YAHVEH SABAOTH], the Living God, King of the Universe, Omnipotent, All-Kind and Merciful, Supreme and Extolled, who is Eternal, Sublime and Most-Holy, ordained (formed) and created the Universe in thirty-two mysterious paths of wisdom by three Sepharim, namely: (1) S'for; (2) Sippur; and (3) Sapher, which are in Him, one and the same.

(*Sepher Yezirah* I, 1 [published in the original Hebrew and translated by Isidor Kalisch, New York: L. H. Frank, 1877, p. 14]. These Sepharim or three words of similar expression signify: (1) number, calculation or idea; (2) the word; (3) the writing of the word. The idea, word and writing (of the word) are signs to man for a thing, and is not the thing itself; to the Creator, however, idea, word and writing (of the word) are the thing itself . . . [footnote by Kalisch, p. 50].)

Here the concept of number signifies the "mode of creation". By way of analogy, just as one can say that for *knowledge* there are various categories (Aristotle put forward ten categories), so do the Sephiroth in a certain sense depict the ten categories of creation. The Sephiroth are the stages of transition ("connecting links") between the Creator and the created world, between the Absolute and the relative world. The Sephiroth portray in their totality the paths of transition from the archetypal, which is in God, to the moral, and from the moral to the factually real. Thus the system of Sephiroth (the so-called "Sephiroth Tree") is divided into four spheres of existence (named "worlds") — the world of emanation (*olam ha atziluth*) — the world of creation (*olam ha briah*) — the world of formation (*olam ha yetzirah*) — and the world of activity (*olam ha assiah*).

These four worlds correspond to the four letters of the tetragrammaton (Yod — world of emanation, Hé — world of creation, Vau — world of formation, and the second Hé — world of activity).

The ten Sephiroth, which belong archetypally to the world of emanation, nevertheless extend into all four worlds. The three highest ones, namely the *crown* (Kether), *wisdom* (Chokmah) and *intelligence* or *understanding* (Binah) belong exclusively to the world of emanation; the next three, namely *mercy* (Chesed) [also named *majesty* (Gedulah)], *power* (Geburah) [also called *judgment* (Din)], and *beauty* (Tiphareth) belong to the world of creation; the next three, namely *victory* (Netzach), *glory* (Hod), and *foundation* (Yesod) belong to the world of formation and the last, tenth

Sephirah, the *kingdom* (Malkuth), which is the realization of the nine higher ones in the world of activity, is the only one belonging to the world of activity.

The ten Sephiroth are grouped together in the form of a tree, which is therefore named the *Sephiroth Tree*.

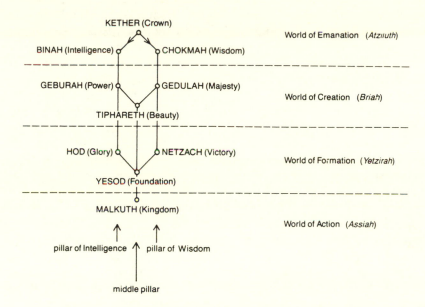

The four Sephiroth Kether (crown), Tiphareth (beauty), Yesod (foundation), and Malkuth (kingdom) form the trunk of the tree (which is also designated as the "middle pillar"); the other six Sephiroth to the right and left sides are called "branches". They represent, next to the "middle pillar" the "right pillar" and the "left pillar". The "right pillar" is the pillar of wisdom or the pillar of mercy, while the "left pillar" is the pillar of intelligence or the pillar of severity. The Sephiroth wisdom, mercy, and victory form the pillar of mercy (compassion), while the Sephiroth intelligence (understanding), power (judgment), and glory build the pillar of severity (righteousness). The "middle pillar", which represents the synthesis of mercy and righteousness, consists of the Sephiroth crown, beauty, foundation, and kingdom.

The Sephiroth Tree is also related to the *primordial man* (Adam Kadmon). The three uppermost Sephiroth crown, wisdom, and intelligence (understanding) form the head, mercy and power the two arms, beauty the trunk, victory and glory the two hips, foundation corresponds to the sexual organs, and kingdom corresponds to the feet.

The first Sephirah, the crown, is the initial and highest of all divine manifestations. "It is", says the *Zohar*, "the principle of all principles, the secret wisdom, the most exalted crown, with which all diadems and all crowns are decorated." (*Zohar*, III, 288b.) The divine name which corresponds to it is EHIYEH ("I am") because it is Being. For this reason, too, the first Sephirah has been named the "Supreme Point" (or simply "the Point"). "When the most Mysterious wished to reveal Himself, He first produced a single point. (*Zohar*. I, 2a.) As long as this point of light had not proceeded forth from the Eternal, the Unlimited (*Ain Soph*) was still unknown and spread no light at all." Out of this unity of the Eternal proceed two *parallel* principles — appearing to be opposites, yet in reality inseparable. These are a masculine or active principle, which is called *wisdom* (Chokmah), and a feminine or passive principle, that is usually translated *understanding* or *intelligence* (Binah). Wisdom is also called the *father*, for it is said that it *begets* all things. Understanding is called the *mother*, as it is written: "You are to name understanding *mother*" (*Zohar*, III, 290a). From this mysterious and eternal union a *son* is begotten who, being a true expression of the original, takes on the characteristics of the father and mother, and thus serves as a testimony to both. This son of wisdom and understanding who, on account of this "double inheritance" is also called the First-Born One, is *cognition* or *knowledge* (Daath)". (Adolphe Franck, *Die Kabbala oder die Religions — Philosophie der Hebräer* [translated from the French, revised and enlarged by A. Gelinek, Leipzig, 1844, p. 137].)

Here, we would like to add a very remarkable passage from the *Commentary to the Zohar* by Moses of Cordova:

> The first three Sephiroth — crown, wisdom, and understanding — must be seen as one and the same thing. The first represents *cognition* or *knowledge*, the second *the knower*, and the third *that which is known*. In order to explain this identity one must know that the knowing of the Creator is not like that of created beings; for with them, knowing is different from the subject of knowledge, and it relates to objects which again are different from the subject. This is indicated by the expressions: thinking, the thinker, and that which is thought. In contrast the Creator is simultaneously knowing, the knower, and that which is known. In fact, *His* manner of knowing does not consist in Him directing His thinking to things that are outside of Him; in that He Himself thinks and is knowing, He knows of everything and sees everything which is. Nothing exists that is not one with Him and which does not subsist in His own substance. He is the prototype of every being, and all beings are in Him in their purest and complete form, so that the perfection of created beings actually exists in the mind of that Perfect One who, in the process of begetting them, united Himself with

them, and to the extent to which they distance themselves from Him, they also fall away from that perfect and exalted state. Thus the form of all varieties of being in this world is in the Sephiroth, and that of the Sephiroth is in the Source from which they flow. (*Pardes Rimmonim*, 55a.)

The entire system of the Sephiroth can also be represented as three triangles which are united together and summarized in the tenth Sephirah, the kingdom, as their fulfillment. The first triangle (pointing upwards) is such that its neutral point (the synthesis of the other two points) is the crown, and its active and passive polarities are wisdom and understanding (intelligence); it belongs to the world of emanation. The second triangle, pointing downwards, is formed by the polarities mercy (compassion) and judgment (severity) together with their synthesis, beauty. The third triangle (also pointing downwards) contains the Sephiroth victory (Netzach) and glory (Hod) as polar opposites, and their synthesis is to be found in the Sephirah foundation (Yesod). This third triangle belongs to the world of formation (Yetzirah), just as the second triangle (Gedulah, Geburah, and Tiphareth) belongs to the world of creation.

The last and tenth Sephirah, the kingdom (Malkuth), brings to fulfillment the harmony of the nine higher Sephiroth in the world of activity (Assiah).

The names of the ten Sephiroth were translated into Latin by Athanasius Kircher, S.J., in his work *Oedipus Aegyptiacus* as follows:

Kether	– Summa Corona
Chokmah	– Summa Sapientia
Binah	– Intelligentia sive Spiritus Sanctus
Chesed (Gedulah)	– Misericordia
Geburah (Pachad/Din)	– Timor
Tiphareth	– Pulchritudo
Netzach	– Victoria
Hod	– Honor seu Gloria
Yesod	– Fundamentum
Malkuth	– Regnum

The ten names of God are sometimes assigned to the ten Sephiroth in the following manner:

Kether	– EHIYEH ("I am")
Chokmah	– JAH or YHVH
Binah	– ELOHIM or YHVH–ELOHIM

Chesed (Gedulah)	– EL
Geburah (Pachad/Din)	– ELOHIM–GIBOR ("Mighty One")
Tiphareth	– ELOHA or YHVH
Netzach	– YHVH–SABAOTH
Hod	– ELOHIM–SABAOTH
Yesod	– SHADDAI or EL–HAÏA
Malkuth	– ADONAI

Most probably these are also the ten mystical names of God of which St. Jerome speaks in his letter to Marcella. They may serve as a stimulus for meditative work — meditation being "thinking with the head and the heart".

VI

"REMEMBER THE SABBATH DAY, TO KEEP IT HOLY"

THE LAW OF TURNING WITHIN

The system of the names of God and the Sephiroth which were treated in the preceding chapter can provide an opportunity and a stimulus for thinking them through meditatively (i.e., for the kind of thinking in which head and heart resonate together). The system of the ten names of God and the ten Sephiroth represents a schematic program for this work, one which can play the role of a schooling in meditation concerning the rulership of God and the stages and paths of His revelation in the Bible and in the spiritual history of humanity. It has, in fact, already served as a schooling in meditation in the Cabbalistic tradition. Of course, it is not a matter of accepting the teachings of Old Testament mystical theology or of becoming a "believer" in the Cabbala. On the contrary, it is simply a matter of taking seriously the results of profound meditation on the Old Testament – results acquired through generations of human beings throughout the centuries – in order to think these results through and examine them on the basis of their fruitfulness. Since the Old Testament is part of Holy Scripture, of the the Bible, the Cabbala ought to be taken just as seriously for understanding the Old Testament as mystical theology is for understanding the New Testament. The Bible is a whole, and its understanding encompasses the results of the research and meditation of all those who have made such research and meditation their concern: church – teachers and theologians, Cabbalists and Hasidists. Someone who is serious about fathoming all of Holy Scripture to its depths, and on a level worthy of it, will scarcely allow himself to ignore the *Sepher Yetzirah* or the *Zohar*, just as little as he would ignore, for example, the "Miscellanies" of Clement of Alexandria or the *Homilies* and *Commentaries* of Origen on the Gospels.

The word *meditatio*, which is also sometimes used in the same sense as *consideratio* (for example by St. Bernard of Clairvaux), indicates the heightened wakefulness of the capacity for insight — not only on the level of thinking (ability to discriminate), but also on the levels of feeling (capacity for intuitive feeling) and the will. In other words, meditation is the turning within of the soul which is restlessly devoted to the search for truth. At the same time, meditation is a turning away from the outside world and its concerns, influences, after-effects, and memories thereof.

A master of meditation, contemplation, and prayer, St. Bernard of Clairvaux, says:

> Meditation (reflection) first purifies its own source, i.e., the soul, from which it arises. Then it regulates the inclinations, directs activity, moderates excess, shapes morals, makes life honest and regulated, and mediates knowledge of divine as well as human things. It is this which replaces confusion with order, checks the inclination to lose oneself in uncertainty, gathers together that which is dispersed, penetrates into that which is hidden, discovers that which is true and distinguishes it from that which merely appears as such, and brings to light fiction and lie.
>
> Further, it is meditation which determines beforehand what is to be done and which brings that which has been done to consciousness, so that nothing remains in the soul which is in need of clarification and correction. Likewise, it is meditation which enables misfortune to be foreseen even when misfortune prevails and which, during happiness, makes it possible to preserve an attitude of not being dejected. It is the source of courage on the one hand and of prudence (*prudentia*) on the other. (Bernard of Clairvaux, *De Consideratione* I, 7. He wrote this treatise between 1149 and 1152 for Pope Eugene III.)

Further, concerning the difference between meditation (reflection) and contemplation (beholding), St. Bernard says the following:

> Pay attention to what I mean by meditation (reflection). One should not conceive of meditation as being synonymous with contemplation in every respect. In fact, contemplation presupposes the truth that is recognized as certain, whereas use is made of meditation (reflection) for finding this truth. Understood in this sense it seems to me that contemplation can be defined as true and certain intuition of the spirit of any reality whatsoever, or also as grasping that which is true and which eliminates doubt. As far as meditation is concerned, it is the intensive effort of thinking, the striving of the soul in the search for that which is true. Nevertheless, it is customary to use both designations indiscriminately, whether one is dealing with meditation or contemplation. (Ibid. II, 2.)

The Holy Abbot from Clairvaux sees the fruits of meditation in the four virtues, which are the basis not just for the life of the monks of a contemplative community or order, but also for all life worthy of being called human. In other words, every one who strives "to know what he does" ought to dedicate a certain time to turning within, a time for observing and judging from a higher vantage point his life and his endeavors. In order not merely to be swept along by life's flow, but to be in a position to direct it creatively, one has to be able to periodically rise up out of the stream of daily life.

If one expresses this truth in biblical language, one obtains the words of the commandment: "Six days you shall labour, and do all your work; but the seventh day is a sabbath to the Lord, your God" (*Ex.* 20: 9–10).

While one dedicates the greater part of one's time to the stream of daily life, comprising work, duties, and concerns, a seventh of the time ought to be consecrated to *turning within,* to rising up out of this stream. Meditation is the "hallowing of the sabbath". It signifies the fulfillment of the command to turn within for inner reflection. Meditation, contemplation, and prayer all belong to inner reflection or "hallowing the sabbath". They are stages of the spiritualization of thinking (meditation), feeling (contemplation), and the will (prayer). Spiritualization is the goal and meaning of turning within — the hallowing of the sabbath.

Genesis expressly indicates that the rhythm: creating — turning within mirrors the divine work of creation and rest. The resting which follows the work of God's creation is a spiritualization of the preceding work of creation. Thus *Genesis* reports that after the completion of the work of creation on each one of the six days, "God saw that it was good (*tov*)". That is, the Creator interrupted His work of creation after each "day" and thus established the divine archetype of meditation, setting the divine example of turning within. In the divine-moral evaluation of the completed work of creation, where "God saw that it was good", there took place an interiorized repetition of the creative work completed that "day".

> And God saw everything that He had made, and behold, it was very good. And there was evening and there was morning, a sixth day (*Gen.* 1: 31) . . . And on the seventh day God finished His work which He had done, and He rested on the seventh day from all His work which He had done" (*Gen.* 2: 2).

The great rest of the seventh day consisted of the interiorized repetition of the entire six days' work in the form of *blessing*: "God blessed the seventh day and hallowed it" (*Gen.* 2: 3).

Thus we see in the creation, as *Genesis* reports it, the harmonizing together of three divine resonances: God creates through His Word; God practices turning within during which confirmation of the value of the created works takes place; and God blesses the work during the interiorization, the turning within which follows upon the creative activity. And just as the Word is inseparable from the Creator's work of creation, so the Holy Spirit is inseparably connected with the result of the Creator's repeated turning within. Therefore: Creator, the creative Word, to realization the will of the Creator, and turning within which confirms the creative activity of the Father and the Word, and the Holy Spirit who brings to illumination the meaning and value of the created works in the divine turning within, all belong inseparably together.

The world was created from the Father through the Son and was blessed through the Holy Spirit. The blessing after God's turning within belongs just as much to the account of the creation of the world as does the creation itself out of the Father's will through the Word that carried out and brought to realization His will. In other words, *turning within* belongs just as much to the fundamental truth and the divine law of the world as does its coming into being from the creative will of the Father through the creative Word of the Son.

The rhythm of creative activity and turning within — a rhythm founded by the Godhead — forms the basis not only of Moses' account of the creation but also of the wisdom of India. The latter teaches the universal cosmic law of the alternating creative activity of the Godhead of the world and its turning inward. There are the "days" of the Creator (*Brahma*) and the "nights" of *Brahma* — alternating periods of the creative breathing-out and the internalized breathing-in of the World Creator, which are named *manvantara* and *pralaya*. And this divine-cosmic rhythm is understood as the model and archetype, and also the cause, of the rhythm of breathing. This is the main reason for the practice of conscious breathing in yoga. It is nothing other than the conscious experience of the alternating conditions of turning towards the outside and turning towards the inside, i.e., activity and turning within, deed and meditation. In the language of the Bible, the former is participation in the creative work of the world, while the latter is participation in the occurrence of inner internalization — the "celebration of the world sabbath".

St. Bernard of Clairvaux, speaking from his great experience, convincingly presents the significance of turning within as absolutely necessary for bringing to realization and maintaining a way of life truly worthy of a human being. The traditional wisdom of India teaches the cosmic-metaphysical significance of withdrawing into oneself, turning within. The modern English researcher and philosopher of history Arnold J. Toynbee discovered and clearly presented the universally valid psychological-cultural-historical law of repeatedly alternating "withdrawal" and "returning" in the spiritual life of humanity.

Toynbee proceeded from the comparative study of individual biographies of the representatives of the creative minority who exert epoch-making influences on the cultural life of society. He then observed analogous effects of the law of withdrawal and returning in the development of human society itself:

> With regard to society and its relationship to the creative human being, we can describe the attitude and activity of the creative human being with the words withdrawal and returning. Withdrawal makes it possible for the personality to assess its own powers; these powers would perhaps remain slumbering were they not to be set free for a time through tensions within society. A withdrawal of this sort is sometimes a voluntary step; sometimes, however, it is also forced through circumstances which lie beyond the creative human being's sphere of influence. In any case they signify an opportunity, often the necessary precondition for the transformation of this human being or "anchorite". In Greek such a hermit signifies nothing other than "one who goes his separate way". However, wandering in loneliness can serve no purpose, and perhaps makes no sense at all, if it is not thought of as a preparation for the return of the "transformed" personality into society from which it proceeded. With regard to this world around us, it is indeed a question of the homelands from which the human social animal cannot part himself permanently, if he is not to deny his humanity itself and, to use Aristotle's words, "becomes either an animal or God." Returning constitutes the essence of the entire action and gives it its meaning. (A. J. Toynbee, *A Study of History*, Hamburg 1949, p. 229.)

Toynbee sees in Moses' lonely ascent onto Mt. Sinai a significant link between withdrawal and returning:

> Moses climbs the mountain at Yahveh's command in order to enter into contact with Yahveh there. The command is directed to Moses alone, while the rest of the children of Israel must keep themselves at a distance. However Yahveh's intention was to send Moses down again so that he should proclaim the new law to the people who themselves were unable to come and could not receive the communication. (Ibid., p. 230.)

In the fourteenth century A.D. the Arabian thinker Ibn Khaldun gave us a report about the prophet's experience and his mandate. This report also strongly emphasizes the return to the world (after the withdrawal from it has taken place):

The human being's soul is inclined to take off the apparel of its earthly nature so that it can transpose itself into the angels' being for at least a single moment, which comes and goes as quickly as the blinking of an eye. Then the soul returns to its earthly nature, as soon as it has received a message in the world of the angels which it can take back to its own human world. (Ibid)

Further, Toynbee indicates the significant succession of withdrawal and return in the life of Jesus, which also finds its expression in the expectation of the reappearance of the Resurrected One from His Ascension into heaven. After the great withdrawal of Ascension, the return — the Reappearance — is to take place. He also points to the life of the apostle Paul who after his sudden conversion on the way to Damascus went into the Arabian desert for three years. Only afterwards did he meet the apostles and disciples in order to take up his work. The life of St. Benedict is similar. He lived alone for three years before returning to society to become the head of a group of monks, first in the valley of Subiaco, and then on Monte Cassino. In the life of St. Gregory the Great his retreat also lasted three years. Then he began to convert the pagan English, was called back to Rome, held various church offices, and finally became pope (590–604).

Siddhartta Gautama, the historical Buddha, lived for seven years in retreat, the fruit of which was his enlightenment under the Bodhi tree and the resolve to share his insight with his fellow human beings, which made him the central focus and head of a brotherhood and founder of one of the great world religions.

In the life of Mohammed (570–632) withdrawal and return formed the prelude to two decisive turning points which can be determined in the course of his life. The first turning point, which led to a strict monotheism, happened after an approximately fifteen-year period of retreat, during which he led the life of a caravan merchant trafficking between the Arabian oases. The second stage, that of proclaiming an all-encompassing religious–political law, began with his "emigration", the *Hegira* (*Hijra*). He withdrew from his home oasis, from Mecca, to the oasis Yathrib, which since then has been called Medina (*Medinat-el-Rabi*, meaning "the city of the prophet"). This period of turning inward is perceived by Mohammedans as such a decisive turning point that they derive their reckoning of time from it — their year 1 begins with Mohammed's flight from Mecca. Seven years later he returned there, this time as lord and master of half of Arabia.

The essential teaching of all of these historical realities consists in the fact that the creative life and creative activity of human beings is founded on the succession of periods of turning within and turning outwards, of sabbath days and work days, of meditation and action. One cannot breathe out if one has not first breathed in. Similarly, one cannot be creatively active if one has not first received or awakened the necessary power, insight, and enthusiasm by turning within — in meditation, contemplation, and prayer. The essence and the secret of creativity is, in the final analysis, the power and ability which one owes to the blessing of the seventh day, the world sabbath.

VII

"HONOR YOUR FATHER AND YOUR MOTHER"

THE LAW OF CONTINUITY OR OF THE LIFE OF TRADITION

1. The divine foundation and archetype of fatherhood and motherhood

The most precious and most necessary experience that the human being on earth has from earliest childhood is that of love, specifically of parental love, without which he or she would not at all be able to begin life's course and remain living. As is well known, the newborn human child is not able to live unless loving, caring, and protecting hands receive and accept it. Nourishment, warmth, and protection — already given before birth in the mother's body — continue to be needed by the child in various forms after birth too. Moreover, the child needs to be heard and to hear the voices of other human beings. For the child's development as a human being language is necessary; it needs exchange, communication, interaction — all fundamental for the first stirring of thinking, understanding, and being understood. In the course of this continuing concern for the unfolding of the child's body and soul after birth, the distinction between mother-love and father-love begins to show itself more and more clearly. The tendency of mother-love is to maintain its enveloping quality in order to "bear" the child further until the ripeness of maturity. On the other hand father-love inclines to stimulate and speed up the child's development and independency. Father-love sees in the child the "heir", i.e., the future continuator of his life's work — fighting for the same ideal and continuing work upon the same task. Mother-love remains true to the image of the original mother-child relationship during the pre-natal period — enveloping, protecting, and sustaining the child. Thus mother-love strives to protect the child from life's roughness, to preserve the child from every disappointment, every sorrow, to wipe away every tear and transform it into a smile. The love of the mother holds the child in her embrace pressed to her heart, for decades on end—perhaps until death and beyond. Embracing the child is not foreign to father-love either, but it happens comparatively seldom— during the festive moments of an inner meeting of hearts, in mutual acknowledgement, in gratitude, or in being proud of one another.

Parental love, i.e., love bestowed by father *and* mother, represents the most valuable and meaningful experience of the human child on earth. Parental love is the dowry that it carries throughout life, the capital investment of soul-warmth and light from which the human being can live his whole life through. Yes, parental love makes the human being capable of comprehending or having a presentiment of divine love in a natural way by means of analogy, and therewith of understanding the depth and truth of St. John's words: "God is love, and he who abides in love abides in God, and God abides in him" (I *Jn*. 4:16). For, as God is love, so is the foundation and archetype of all love—including parental love—in God.

If all fatherhood has its origin and foundation in God, if therefore father-love essentially corresponds to the love of God the Father (as all Christians believe, even those, the Protestants, who have separated themselves from the stream of living tradition—the Church), never-theless one cannot leave aside the question as to whether motherhood and, correspondingly, mother-love also have their foundation and origin in the Godhead. Or ought one to deny that mother-love is rooted in the divine and has its archetype in the divine, and esteem father-love alone as being worthy of a divine archetype?

In the life of prayer and devotion of the tradition of the Church a categorical answer to this question is to be found. Indeed, acknow-ledgement of the maternal principle is of fundamental significance in the religious practices of Catholic and Orthodox Christians. Thus, the practice of praying the rosary has for centuries been intrinsic to the religious life of the Catholic Church. Essential to the rosary is the fact that the sequence of prayers appeal alternately to Father-love (in the form of the "Our Father" with which each set of prayers dedicated to the various "mysteries" begins) and Mother-love (in the form of the ten "Hail Marys" following). In the Eastern-orthodox Church, the veneration of the Mother of God goes so far that in the liturgy the hymn is sung:

> More venerable than the Cherubim,
> Incomparably more glorious than the Seraphim,
> You who have born the God-Word incorruptibly—
> We glorify you the true Bearer of God.

This means that the Mother of God ranks above the highest angelic hierarchy (above the Cherubim and Seraphim), i.e., She belongs to the realm of the Godhead itself, which is beyond the hierarchies. For above the hierarchies of the Cherubim and Seraphim stands the eternal Trinity of God. Here it must be emphasized that this is not a matter of a dogmatically formulated Church teaching. Rather, it is a question of the degree of devotion displayed by believers within the Eastern Church towards Mary as "Holy Mother". In any case, for the hearts of the faithful and in the hearts of the faithful, in Russia (in which land the author was born and raised), Mary is the Queen of Hearts because She is the symbol and archetype of maternal love.

Also Jewish tradition, the Cabbala, answers the question of whether mother-love is essentially divine, having a divine foundation, with a decisive "yes". The Cabbala teaches — corresponding to the verse: "God created the human being in His image and likeness . . . male and female He created them" (*Gen.* 1:26–27) — that God has two aspects, the masculine and the feminine. The Cabbala characterizes them as "countenances": the "great countenance" corresponding to the male aspect and the "lesser countenance" to the female aspect. The "great countenance", the Ancient of Days, is present in the Sephirah Kether (the crown). It is the reflection in this Sephirah of the androgynous Godhead, which is named *Ain Soph* ("unlimited", "boundless"). Proceeding from Kether, polarization begins — into masculine and feminine principles — whereby the right side of the Sephiroth Tree is "male" and the left side is "female". Thus in the world of emanation (*olam ha atziluth*), i.e., in the Sephirah Chokmah (wisdom) and in the Sephirah Binah (understanding, intelligence), Ain Soph (that which is boundless) appears as both the Father of creation and the Mother of creation. In the world of creation (*olam ha briah*), whose center the Sephirah Tiphareth (beauty) represents, the masculine principle is characterized as "king" (*melekh*) or "holy king"; and the female Shekinah ("glory"), which is the divine presence in the beings of creation, is the "queen" (*matrona*).

Just as the king (*melekh*) is compared to the sun, so is *matrona* compared to the moon, as the reflection of ideal beauty. *Matrona* is also called "Eve". For, as the text relates, she is the Mother of all things and everything which exists on earth suckles at her breast and is blessed by her. (*Zohar, Idra Zuta, ad finem.*)

The "king" and "queen", who are also called the "two countenances", constitute a pair whose task it is to impart to the world graces ever anew and, through their alliance, to continue the work of the creation — in other words, to sustain it everlastingly.

According to the *Zohar* the human soul, viewed in its purest essence, has its root in understanding or intelligence (Binah), which is the Supernal Mother. If the soul is to become masculine, it proceeds from Binah on through the principle of grace or expansion (Chesed). If it is a feminine soul, it takes up into itself the principle of justice or contraction (Geburah). Finally, it comes into the world in which we live (Malkuth) through the union of the king and queen, which, as the text relates, is for the generation of the soul that which man and woman for the procreation of the body are. (*Zohar*, 111, 7.)

In the light of the traditional teaching of the Cabbala, also to be found in Hasidism (upon which Martin Buber is an authority), one can summarize the metaphysical-religious foundation for the commandment: "Honor your father and your mother" in the following manner:

Creation, i.e., the world, thanks its existence to the love of the eternal Father and the love of the eternal Mother. Out of their union proceeds — "as Light from Light, God from God" — the Son and the Daughter, designated as the "holy king" and "queen", who together direct the work of creation, leading it to ever further stages of interiorization or spiritualization. However, the dimension of interiorization or spiritualization is not characterized by becoming (coming into existence) and sustaining whatever comes into existence. Rather it stands in the sign of *blessing* which is brought about by the spiritualizing (making holy) of the Holy Spirit, who proceeds from the Father and the Son. Corresponding to the Holy Spirit is the immanent Presence of the spiritualizing blessing — called the "Holy Soul", "the Virgin of Israel", or the "soul of the community of Israel". She is the deeply moving and touching figure, portrayed by Martin Buber, of the weeping virgin who accompanies the chosen people into exile ("exile" meant here not merely in a geographical sense). It is this Presence that underlies the lamentation of human beings at the wailing wall in Jerusalem.

In this respect the tradition teaching of the Cabbala upon the nature of the Godhead and the divine work of creation extends the teaching of the Holy Trinity. It thereby acknowledges that father-love and mother-love are of the same divine origin and worth, as presupposed by the commandment: "Honor your father and your mother".

In the light of this extended teaching, the Three-in-One, the Trinity, becomes a Six-in-One or Hexadity. Nevertheless, the fundamental conception of monotheism is retained and remains just as valid as in the Christian doctrine of the Trinity with its Three in the Unity of One God.

Here, then, to the triangle of Father, Son, and Holy Spirit is added the triangle: Mother, Daughter, and Holy Soul. The two triangles belong inseparably together. Together they represent the six-pointed Star of David or (according to Cabbalistic tradition) the Seal of Solomon.

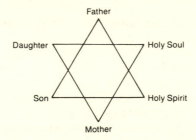

Even though the National Socialists chose this symbol to brand the Jews as inferior, hopefully the above thoughts may stimulate a path of thinking and sympathetic understanding upon which this symbol may again come to be honored in its full depth and holiness. For it is a symbol of faithfulness to the commandment: "Honor your father and your mother — as in heaven so also upon the earth."

2. The law of living tradition ("that your days may be long in the land which the Lord your God gives you")

Natural human reason would not be able to know what to make of the world as it is empirically, if reason were not able to comprehend the world with the help of three basic categories. These are the three ways of looking at and ordering things which are designated as "space", "time", and "causality". The most concrete and simple description of these categories is, for space: that things are next to one another; for time: that things follow one another; for causality: that things exist because of one another. Without these three categories human reason would not only be unable to orient itself; it would also not be capable of asking questions at all. For all questioning presupposes: *where* (where to/where from); *when* (previously/afterwards); *why*, (how/to what purpose) — which is true not only for the empirical outer world, but also for the realm of metaphysics, morality, value, and faith. Correspondingly, the question which the disciples asked Jesus about the man who was born blind — whether his parents or he himself had sinned, resulting in his deserving the destiny of being born blind — was a question that presupposed the law of moral causality. It presupposes it, in fact, in two conceivable forms: either in the sense of the Mosaic commandment of the "sins of the fathers afflicting the children", or in the sense of the own guilt of the man born blind. This latter possibility corresponds to the other conception of moral causality, which exists for the peoples of the East and is called "karma". According to this conception, the person himself has to bear the consequences of his deeds — whether good or evil — and not his children or children's children. Thus the deeper question of the disciples was: Was the fate of the man born blind caused through the guilt of his parents, or was it karma, i.e., his own guilt from a previous existence before birth? The answer that they received is noteworthy: The destiny of the man born blind was neither the consequence of the guilt of his predecessors (in the sense of retribution through heredity), nor was it the penance of his own guilt from the past prior to birth—not moral causality, which works through generations, and not individual karma—but "that the works of God might be made manifest through him" (*Jn.* 9:3). This means that the cause did not lie in the *past* at all, but in the *future*. It was not a question of heredity or karma in the case of the man born blind, but of *providence*.

However, the question of the disciples and the answer of the Master both belong to the realm of the category of causality. For the decrees of providence are also causes that have their effects; it is only that they are future causes and future effects, not consequences of the past. What is most deeply significant about the answer of the Master is that in the case of the man born blind it is a question of causes proceeding not from human subjects (the "guilt" of the parents, or one's own "guilt"), but of a superhuman subject—*God's* providence. However, not just the category of causality alone can be understood in a purely moral sense; the same is true also for the categories of *time* and *space*. When, for example, we pray the opening sentence of the Lord's Prayer: "Our Father, who art in heaven," we do not mean the physical-outer space of planets and stars, but instead moral space. In moral space that which is sublime corresponds to "height" and that which is base denotes "depth".

Correspondingly, the second part of the commandment: "Honor your father and your mother, *that your days may be long in the land which the Lord your God gives you*", does not mean many years of physical life at a certain spatially determined place (such as a field or vineyard), but longevity of that which is for you most important in life—your ideas, ideals, and goals—within the field of activity granted them by God. In other words, in the text referred to it is not a question of the promise of lengthening biological life or that this lengthening will be granted in a certain territorial place. Rather, it is a matter of prolonging continuation of the operational effect of things to which biological life applies—of significance to life's content and worth—and, in fact, in the field of activity that was meant for them. What is meant is the law of the longevity of *tradition*, in the domain peculiar to the tradition.

Tradition is the moral content of time in the same way as just retribution is the moral content of causality. Things following one another conceived of merely as following one another — purely as time — is morally without content and without essence, if they are not bound to one another by the thread of tradition. Tradition is the "moral backbone" of time. It binds that which comes before and that which comes later, whether in progress or regression, in ascension or descension. Culture and civilization are simply alternative designations for tradition.

There is, however, yet another meaning to time endowed upon it by science. This is development in the sense of biological *evolution*. Evolution rests on two factors — on the one hand on preservation by way of the law of heredity, and on the other hand on the appearance of so-called "mutations" in the line of heredity, i.e., new tendencies which burst in from time to time into hereditary succession.

The theory of biological heredity presupposes three things: the principle of preservation through heredity, without which the existence of the species would be inconceivable; secondly, the appearance of mutations, without which there would be no progress and, in fact, no evolution at all; and thirdly, time understood as the all-powerful, sole "master-teacher", guaranteeing through its experience, and by way of chance occurrence, immeasurable opportunity for natural selection, breeding and experimentation. Time is actually evolution — to believe in evolution is, in fact, to believe in time. However, belief in evolution ("belief in time") does not imply a moral conception of time but rather a functional outlook. The doctrine of evolution emphasizes that through the school of trial and error it is *ability* which counts, and this leads to a functional conception in which practicality and usefulness are esteemed. Thus, the evolution of humanity brings forth technicians and engineers, not saints and sages. Human beings with technical ability are able to *accomplish* more in the fight for existence.

In this sense, the official state conception in the Soviet Union of authors as "engineers of the soul life" is nothing more than the incorporation of the role of the author into the general scheme of functionability. He does not have the task of serving truth, goodness, and beauty; instead he must be useful, in that he awakens forces of soul that are useful, indeed indispensable, for the program of growth in production and for the summoning up of all of society's strength towards bringing this program to realization. Communists are believers in evolution and for this reason have no sense for creating truth, goodness, and beauty as ends in themselves. Consequently "truth" is for them, what is useful; "good", what is functional; "beautiful", what functionability allows to appear attractive. Thus, when a new railroad is being built in Siberia, it should not only be built, but also be recognized as an "article of faith" to be artistically represented — to be sung about, to be painted, and to be movingly portrayed in literature — as an additional jewel in the crown of the communist structure.

Time, conceived of as evolution, is amoral. And the fruits of amoral ideas are generally immoral.

One relates to the world in a quite different way when one conceives of time as the bearer of living tradition. Then time becomes transformed. Past, present, and future become a morally connected organic whole in which that which is of the past (i.e., "fathers" and "mothers") is honored, valued, and cherished as inexhaustible sources — sources of fountains of the living water of tradition, which flows into the future. Every moment in the present provides a possibility and an opportunity for reflecting on the *values* of tradition and bringing them to mind, and the future holds the hopeful expectation of the ripening of the fruits of tradition.

Essential to living tradition is its resistance to the powers of forgetting, sleep, and death. For forgetting, sleep, and death are stages of one *single* principle: that of passing away with the course of time.

Now, humanity's general experience teaches that time as such effects a tendency towards forgetting, falling asleep, and death, and that every involvement with time, every reliance on time, and every compromise with time, opens the gates to the path leading inevitably to forgetting, sleep, and death. In the text of the conversation at Caesarea Philippi, the following passage is usually translated: " . . . and the gates of *hell* (Hades) will not overcome it" (*Mt.* 16:18). However *Hades*, which corresponds to the Hebrew *She'ol*, does not mean the place or the condition of the damned, but simply the kingdom of the dead, or also simply death. Therefore it is a matter — with respect to the gates of death — of entrances and exits along the pathways of *time*, all of which lead to death. The promise which lies in Jesus Christ's words, "You are Peter and on this rock I will build my Church, and the gates of hell will not overcome it" contains the mandate, the promise, and the blessing of freedom from *temporality*, i.e., the power to resist the tendencies of death. In other words, on account of this foundation, as long as the Church continues to remain founded upon the See of Peter as a living tradition, it will remain immune to the death-bringing influences of temporality. Such influences will never overcome the Church, and will never attain the upperhand within the Church. The See of St. Peter fulfills Christ's mandate to maintain the living tradition, which is the Church, and by doing so, to protect the Church from passing away.

Every living tradition is based on two forces working together: the sustaining force of memory which is oriented towards the past, and the force of hope which is oriented towards the future. The former preserves the past from being forgotten, while the latter gives shape to the future understood as the path towards perfection. In other words, the motherly principle preserves tradition, and the fatherly principle guides it towards the goal in the future.

The length of the life of tradition — of every tradition — has its basis thus in the commandment: "Honor your father and your mother".

Memory, upon which the life of tradition depends, is not the practice of mere recollection as the ability to recall ideas about the past. Rather, it is the ability of the soul — of the entire life of the soul — to bring the past alive in the present, to *make it present*.

Thus, for example, the practice of devotion to the fourteen stations of Christ's Way of the Cross which, according to tradition, the most holy Virgin Mother herself introduced, is not a mere memory exercise — an impressing into memory of what happened, in the proper order — but the striving to *experience* what is unforgettable about the Way of the Cross in the present.

Also, Christ's last words at the institution of the holy sacrament at the Last Supper: "Do this in memory of me" point towards the sacraments, too, as being a re-enlivening in the present of what happened in the past. In the holy sacrament at the altar, memory becomes an act of the divine magic of transubstantiation, an act relating to the real (not just remembered) presence of the body and blood of the Redeemer. What once took place, takes place now in the present. In the sacrament, memory does not become a journey into the past, but instead a making-present of the past, an evocation that summons something up out of the realm of forgetting, sleep, and death. Memory becomes the bearer of the power which sounded forth in the call of the Master — "Lazarus, come forth!" — a call that proved effective. Memory becomes divine magic, a miracle of great love and faith.

In this sense the words: "Do this in memory of me" actually mean: "Do this, so that I may be *present*". For, one may add, the Son of Man is Lord over time too.

However, tradition would not remain alive for very long just through the sustaining and re-enlivening power of memory alone. It does so also through the *will* which is oriented towards the perfecting of the tradition, the will which shapes the future. Such a will revealed itself in concrete form in figures like St. Augustine and St. Ignatius of Loyola, perhaps too in all *founders of orders*. St. Augustine, with the highest loyalty and devotion, held fast to what the Mother Church treasured in memory. He also held fast to her authority, which he considered to be the highest and most decisive. At the same time, he also depicted the great future goal of the Church and of the spiritual history of mankind in his work *De Civitate Dei* (*The City of God*) — a work which laid a foundation to the history of philosophy. And St. Ignatius founded an order, and a schooling, which educated men towards becoming able fighters for the bringing to realization of Augustine's "City of God". As is well known, the Rules of the Augustinians were taken as the basis for the life and activity of the "Society of Jesus" founded by St. Ignatius.

What do the Rules of an order actually signify? The Rules of a spiritual order are an expression of the will of its founder, the "father" of the order, to whom his "sons" have freely pledged obedience, oriented towards a goal, towards an ideal. By fulfilling the will of their "father", i.e., by making the Rules the content of their own will, they "honor their father". And this is the other side of the secret of the longevity of tradition as expressed in the commandment: "Honor your father and your mother, that your days may be long in the land which the Lord your God gives you".

It is a fact that the religious orders of the Catholic Church (the Eastern-Orthodox Church does not have any orders, only individual monastic communities, which to a greater or lesser extent continue the tradition of the Cenobite communities of the desert fathers) reveal an astonishing lifespan which is surpassed only by the lifespan of the Church itself. What is the secret of this lifespan — the "long life" — of the religious communal orders? It is that they are faithful to the Church as their mother, and that they strive to fulfill the will of their founders — their "fathers" — in accordance with their vows. The secret of their long lifespan lies in their fulfilling the commandment: *Honor your father and your mother.*

VIII

"YOU SHALL NOT KILL"

THE COMMANDMENT AGAINST DESTRUCTION

While the commandment: "Honor your father and your mother", portrays the foundation for the longevity of tradition, it implies also a prohibition against destroying the continuity of life—not just physical life based on heredity, but also the life of tradition understood as the moral-spiritual content of the passage of time. Time is implicitly a process of depreciation, degeneration, sclerosis — and, in a word, dying. In contrast, tradition is the life-sustaining power which counters the "gates of hell", i.e, death. For example, to belong to a long family tradition is something positive only if the "family dynasty" is the bearer of a living moral-spiritual tradition. Otherwise belonging to an "old family" generally means a certain level of physical and spiritual degeneration. This holds true in the case of the descendants of the crusaders, for example, who betrayed their original ideals and duties of Christian knighthood, and became brigands. The reward for the betrayal of tradition is almost inevitably degeneration in the family line of descent, often ending in debilitation and weak-mindedness.

Tradition is "ensouled time". Life is "ensouled corporeality". Killing is "de-souling": the separation of the soul from the body. "You shall not kill" thus forbids not just murder, i.e., the violent separation of the soul of some other human being from his body, but also the violent "de-souling" of tradition, whose life's duration is founded on honoring father and mother. This latter kind of "killing" takes place on a large scale and does not happen less often than the killing of individual human beings. When, for example, Christian missionaries do not convert the so-called "heathens" by allowing the unique moral beauty and spiritual richness of Christianity to speak to them but, instead, by convincing the heathens that their fathers and mothers were in error (e.g. for worshiping the sun, moon, and stars as divine, and for promulgating this worship), then they kill. That is, they "de-soul" a living tradition and, implicitly, they teach: "Do not honor your father and mother". This was, for example, the moral problem that troubled Francis Xavier, concerning which he sought advice by writing to the General of the Jesuit Order, St. Ignatius. In that letter he gave a report concerning the great loyalty of the heathens — whose conversion to Christianity he was occupied with — to the commandment: "Honor your father and your mother". They declared: If the fate of those who were not baptized is the place of damnation and the fate of those who are baptized is the blessedness of heaven, then they would prefer to share the fate of their fathers and mothers in hell, rather than attaining to divine blessedness for themselves without their fathers and mothers. "What can one do or say here?" asked Francis Xavier.

Other missionaries, who were less sensitive than he, supposed that the religion of the natives whom they undertook to convert was the work of the devil, and they acted correspondingly. They sowed doubt and mistrust and — as a result of their disdain towards the "fathers and mothers" — they killed the living tradition in order to make room for a new one. Their attitude can be expressed with the maxim: "Kill to make room for new life". This, however, was not the attitude of the very first missionary, the apostle Paul. In his missionary activity St. Paul established a connection to what was most valuable concerning the living tradition and showed how it finds its perfection and fulfillment in the Christian message. In this sense he was a "Jew with the Jews" and a "Greek with the Greeks". He did not approach the altar in Athens, which was erected to "the unknown God", as an altar dedicated to the devil; and he treated the messianic expectation of the Jews from the point of view that it had its fulfillment in Jesus Christ.

Unfortunately this attitude of the apostle Paul in the missionary activity of the Church was later abandoned. Instead, destruction and compulsion were used — especially in the time when victorious Christianity became the state religion of the Roman empire, approximately from the time of emperor Constantine the Great to the time of emperor Justinian. Initially official practice of the cults of the old religions was forbidden, then temples and other places of such cults were desecrated and closed, and lastly even the private practice of heathen cults was forbidden under punishment of death. Finally emperor Justinian put an end to the teaching of philosophy, by closing the academy in Athens and banishing its teachers from the empire.

Thus the Hellenic religion — its cults, and its philosophy — were killed to make room for the life of the newer tradition. What the ruling paganism as state religion of the Roman empire had tried to do to Christianity as it was coming into existence (namely, to kill it as a living tradition), ruling Christianity as the state religion of the

Roman empire did to the old tradition of the fathers and mothers, i.e., it killed it.

However, the substance of something which lives does not get destroyed. Its soul continues to exist. In becoming free of the body, it simply withdraws itself back into the realm of the unconscious, where it remains active. From there it reveals itself sooner or later in consciousness again. At first it lives as a latent inclination and yearning, in order that one day it may crystallize itself in clear consciousness as an attitude and point of view. Then a "renaissance" takes place — a renaissance of the spirituality which was formerly repressed and seemingly killed. And the old love directed towards the primal ancestral fathers and mothers — seemingly having died away, having been forgotten, having fallen asleep, and having been overcome — returns to life together with the tradition which they represented and for which they lived. The commandment: "You shall not kill" is absolutely true, too, for the reason that in the realm of the spiritual it is impossible to kill something living. In fact, in a deeper sense there is no killing at all. What takes place is simply an inner transformation, an alchemical process of purification and interiorization or spiritualization, but no extinction. In this sense it can be said that all ideals and ideas of the past which were taken seriously — including those that we view as erroneous — do not die. Heresies also do not die. They pop up again and again, even if they are thought to have been overcome long ago. This is true also for pre-Christian paganism, i.e., for belief in the cosmos, belief in the world. Today this takes the form of believing in "all-encompassing evolution". Today belief in evolution dominates educational and cultural life just as in pre-Christian times pagan myths were dominant.

Christianity's suppression in the time of the pagan caesars, who hoped to kill Christianity as a living tradition, led to the domination of Christianity in the Roman world empire. The suppression of paganism, however, in the time of the Christian caesars — who had hoped to kill paganism by persecuting the pagans and thoroughly eradicating it — resulted in paganism's attaining once again to domination in the form of belief in evolution. This is now a fact of life within the entire "world empire" of the western so-called "Christian" civilization.

The lesson of world history is unmistakable. It says: "You shall not kill". For there is no other way of overcoming error than by way of alchemical transformation through interiorization or spiritualization, ennoblement, and contemplation which leads to an inner deepening — along the paths of tolerance, peaceful coexistence, and the open confrontation between error and truth, between what is useful and what is good, between what is impressive and what is nobly beautiful.

However, open confrontation under conditions of tolerance does not mean submersion — leading finally to "drowning" — in the relativism of the Pilate-question: "What is truth?" Rather, it signifies the confrontation between truths and values which are *absolutely* valid — but without wanting to kill. And the tolerance with which we are concerned here ought to be a reflection of God's tolerance in the sense of the following Jewish legend:

As Abraham was on one of his journeys, he wanted to set up his tent for the night to rest. Suddenly a lonely wanderer appeared and requested Abraham's hospitality. Abraham was hospitable towards him and shared his evening meal with him. After the meal, Abraham suggested to the stranger that they pray together. Then it became clear, to Abraham's dismay and indignation, that the stranger was a pagan and, in fact, a fire worshiper. Filled with anger, Abraham wanted to kill him. Then the Lord appeared to Abraham in a vision and commanded him not to do this. The Lord spoke: "Abraham! I have been tolerating this man for fifty years and you do not want to tolerate him even one night?" And Abraham was ashamed and allowed the stranger to spend the night in his tent.

It was not that Abraham acknowledged the "relative truth" of fire worshiping and thus relativized his belief in the one and only God. Rather, he learned that human beings ought to take as their model God's patience when interacting with one other. *Tolerance* is not relativistic indifference, but *patience* which grants to the other the time and opportunity to attain to better insight through interiorization or spiritualization and contemplation leading to an inner deepening. The "rock", the See of St. Peter, is not just a rock of solidity of belief, in the meeting and confrontation with different spiritual streams through the course of time. It is also a rock of patience, which brings with it the certainty of faith.

The combination of an unyielding, unshakable solidity of faith with a patience that can wait hundreds of years makes the "rock" of the See of Peter unconquerable in the confrontation with the streams of time, which are all, indeed, merely temporal winds and waves. For the "demands and needs" of the time are necessarily temporary. Also temporal, therefore, are efforts towards "democratization" of the Church, de-dogmatization of Church teaching through psychological interpretations, and similar endeavors to "modernize" the Church, her teaching, and her rules. They offend against the commandment: "Honor your father and your mother", and they open wide the "gates" of the paths that lead to death ("hell"). May the emulators of such innovations among theologians and the laity consider for once their responsibility in the light of the commandment "You shall not kill".

The life and death of a living tradition is fundamentally similar to the life and death of the individual human being. For the life of the tradition is the "ensouled corpus" transmitted through time, similar to the "ensouled body" of the life of the individual human being. Making "soul-less" — the separation of the soul from the body — is individual death, and the making "soul-less" of the transmitted corpus is the dying of tradition.

What is the mysterious bond which binds the soul and body to one another? What is the power which holds them together? It is more than a mere contract; it is deeper than the mere benefit of mutual dependency. Soul and body yearn for one another; the soul yearns for being enveloped by the blood's warmth, and the body yearns for the stimulation that comes from the soul which permeates it. The power of mutual *love* unites soul and body. Life, which consists of the union of soul and body, is the *marriage* of the soul and body. For this reason the commandment: "You shall not commit adultery" follows the commandment: "You shalt not kill". For adultery is essentially a form of killing — of separating soul and body, whose union is the archetype of marriage.

The notion of marriage as being analogous to the union of soul and body can be traced in unbroken fashion throughout the books of the Old Testament. In all events the Jewish tradition understands the covenant of the community of Israel with YHVH more deeply than a mere contract; it understands the covenant as a marriage covenant. In the Bible, that is to say, in its prophetic books, unfaithfulness towards God, who revealed Himself on Mt. Sinai, is correspondingly conceived of as a "rebellion" against His worship (e.g., in favoring the cult of Baal and Astaroth). It is designated as *adultery* and *fornication*. Amongst all other peoples of the world the people of Israel were chosen as the bride and spouse of the Lord their God, who is a jealous God and does not tolerate other gods before Him. It was not the community of Israel which chose YHVH as its Lord and God; on the contrary, it was chosen by Him. The community of Israel was chosen as the bride of the invisible and unimaginable God YHVH. Thus an eternal covenant arose, one which demanded eternal loyalty: the loyalty of Israel in the form of exclusive reverence and obedience towards the invisible Bridegroom; and the loyalty of God — in the form of an eternal Guide and Presence in the destiny of Israel.

For this reason the Ark of the Covenant, and later Solomon's temple was the place where the meeting with the Omnipresent One could be experienced and where the "splendor" (Shekinah) of God filled the holy of holies. The "splendor", the radiating presence of God was not an idea — even less a theological-poetical conception — but instead a *reality*, which could mean life and death. It was so real that the unauthorized touching of the Ark of the Covenant resulted in death on the spot.

Just how serious and real the covenant between Yahveh and the community of Israel was can be seen, for example, in the book of Job. Job's wife, overcome by the extreme degree of Job's suffering as he was being tried, gave him the advice: "Renounce Yahveh and *die!*" (*Job* 2:9). This advice, desperate as it was, shows that the covenant of the community of Israel with Yahveh was as real and serious as life and death. It was really the same as the bond between the soul and body of the individual human being, where dissolution of this bond means death. In truth, therefore, it was not a mere contract but an indissoluble union of soul and body, where Yahveh was the "soul" and the community of Israel was the "body".

The covenant between Yahveh-Elohim and the community of Israel was also a bond of marriage in the sense that all fathers of the people of Israel created children in the name of Yahveh, out of His impulse and for His future purposes; and in the sense that all mothers of the people of Israel bore their children as a gift and blessing of the God of Israel. They conceived, carried, and bore their children as parts and members of *one* mother, the community of Israel. And as proof that the act of creation is not just an individual, human affair, but that the power of Yahveh plays a part in it, circumcision of the male representatives of the people of Israel was introduced as an obligatory religious practice at Yahveh's behest. For, procreation and reproduction were reserved for Yahveh; in addition, He cared for future generations — for the children and children's children. Yahveh-Elohim was Lord over the destiny of the future generations of the chosen people, *His* people.

Thus the commandment: "You shall not commit adultery" contains a mighty and superhuman justification, just as the Holy One of Israel is loyal to the covenant with the community of Israel, so also ought the community of Israel to be true to its Lord. In the bond of marriage between man and woman is mirrored the marriage covenant of Yahveh with the people of Israel. For this reason adultery was considered to correspond to the people of Israel's violation of loyalty towards their God "before Whom you shall have no other gods".

The commandment: "You shall not kill" also expresses the obligation to the bond that unites the soul to the body, which is, in fact, a marriage between soul and body. Severing this bond is killing; and it is also a form of adultery. Murder and adultery belong together.

The commandments prohibiting adultery, stealing, slandering, and coveting what belongs to one's neighbor, are actually contained in the commandment: "You shall not kill". They are specific manifestations of the prohibition of murder, which is the severing of the bond that holds body and soul together. For the body is the primary, immediate place of action for consciousness. It is the soul's most inherent possession in this world. It is a piece of the outside world that belongs to the soul more than all of the rest of the outside world. This affiliation goes so far, and is so intimate, that the soul's consciousness even identifies itself with the body, and often characterizes and perceives the body as "I". Indeed this identification goes so far that the phrase has been coined: "The human being *has* a soul". Here with "human being" is meant the body. It would be more correct to say that the soul of the human being has a body. For it is the body that the soul *has*. That is, the body is the soul's possession. The human being *is* a soul, and the soul *has* the body as its place of action. If, then, the body is a piece of the outside world which is in the special intimate possession of the soul, so also that portion of the outside world which is called and perceived as "possession" is a kind of extended body, an extension of the field of action of the human soul. In this sense the house, yard, garden, and field of my neighbor is his "extended body". Every human being possesses a body which he has received as his possession, i.e., as the place of development of his consciousness. He also has an "extended body" that is a portion of the external world, which belongs to him as his very own, his property. Just as possession is an "extended body", so is the good reputation, respect, and trust which the human being enjoys with other human beings, an "extended soul". Here it is a matter of the projection of the human being's soul into the life of soul of other human beings and of the manner in which the soul mirrors itself in other human beings. And slander — "false witness against your neighbor" — is a killing of this extended soul life in other human beings, in that the reflection of the soul in the soul life of other human beings is distorted and destroyed. Slander is, therefore, moral murder and robbery. God, however, is the God of life — of joining together, of uniting — and not of death, of separating body and soul, man and woman, possession and possessor.

The last set of commandments, as we have seen, is contained in the commandment: "You shall not kill", which in turn is an extension of the commandment about the longevity of tradition: "Honor your father and your mother". The last set of commandments relates to life, marriage, possession, and honor — honor towards the self of the other ("neighbor"). The life, marriage, possessions, and honor of another human being are just as inviolable as they are for oneself.

The commandment: "Honor your father and your mother" is in turn related to the commandment of keeping holy the sabbath.

"Remember the sabbath day, to keep it holy" refers to the absolute necessity for the soul to have periods of quiet for the sake of interiorization and spiritualization, to keep alive the bond between God and the human self ("I"). This interiorization in peace and quiet makes possible the becoming aware of father-love and mother-love as mirrors of Divine Love.

But what is the relationship of the commandment of keeping holy the sabbath to the preceding commandments of Yahveh? Here we touch upon the union through love of the human being with God. However, this also raises the question as to the identity of Yahveh.

IX

WHO IS YAHVEH?

Now we have to turn to the question: Who is Yahveh? Is the Godhead of the world, i.e., the Creator of the world, the Redeemer of the world, and the Spiritualizer of the world — the eternal Holy Trinity of Father, Son, and Holy Spirit — identical with Yahveh, the Lord of the community of Israel?

The answer is "yes" and "no". This contradiction can be resolved by way of a synthesis, when it is considered that the religion of Israel essentially was, and is, a prophetic religion founded on the revelation of the prophets. Here it is necessary to distinguish between two kinds of prophet: those who proclaimed, such as, for example, Isaiah and Jeremiah; and those who worked actively through deeds, such as, for example, Elijah and Elisha.

The proclaiming prophets did not speak from themselves, but from and in the name of the Divinity transcending the self, to which they offered up their own selves. Thus the proclaiming prophets became "mouthpieces" of God.

In a similar manner the miracle-working prophets became instruments for the works of God's magical power which surrounded and filled them. They emptied themselves of their personal will, so that they could become instruments of divine power.

Moses was both a proclaimer and a miracle worker, while Elijah was above all the bearer of divine-magical power. He was a miracle worker, not a seer.

Now, prophetic missions are not limited, as Scripture shows, to human beings alone. They also extend to beings of spiritual hierarchies who are called "angels" for short.

Thus the first meeting of Moses with God took place when He revealed Himself to him on top of Mt. Horeb in the land of Midian and called to him through the intercession of an angel: "And the angel of the Lord appeared to him in a flame of fire out of the midst of a bush . . . When the Lord saw that he turned aside to see, God called to him out of the bush: 'Moses, Moses!' " (Ex. 3: 2–4).

The "angel of the Lord" was in the burning bush, and through him

God called from the bush: "Moses, Moses!" The "angel of the Lord" who was in the burning bush and called Moses by name did so as the hierarchical bearer and representative of the Lord. It was the same angel through whom God made Himself known as "the God of Abraham, Isaac, and Jacob" and gave Moses the task of leading the people of Israel out of Egypt. In so doing, the angel in the burning bush spoke and acted in a similar manner to the human prophets, who acted and spoke not from themselves, but from the Divine Being of God transcending the self, which Divine Being filled and ruled them.

The idea of the representation of the Most High through human and hierarchical beings is well known to tradition, also to iconography. Thus, for example, the icon Rublev painted, which depicts the three angels welcomed by Abraham, is considered as the "icon of the Holy Trinity". It depicts three angelic beings sitting at a table. However, there is no doubt that it is a matter here not just of angels, but of the Holy Trinity which reveals itself through the three angels. Abraham's meeting with the three angels is understood as his meeting with the *Trinity*, not merely a meeting with three angels.

In this sense — in harmony with Christian tradition — the question of whether the God of Abraham, Isaac, and Jacob, who also revealed Himself to Moses on Mt. Horeb, is the trinitarian God of Christianity, will have to be answered with a "yes". On the other hand, if the role which Holy Scripture grants to prophets and hierarchical beings as representatives of the Divine is considered, it is clear that, for example, "the angel of the Lord" which spoke from the "burning bush" in the name of the God of Abraham, Isaac, and Jacob was just an angel, and not the God of Abraham, Isaac, and Jacob "Himself".

Just as Moses' task to lead the people of Israel out of Egypt was given in the "burning bush" by an angelic being, so too could it happen that the Ten Commandments were proclaimed to Moses out of the dark cloud — amidst flashes of lightning and rolls of thunder — by a representative hierarchical being. And it was this hierarchical being which entered into the special covenant relationship with the community of the people of Israel in the name and on behalf of the Most Holy One. Indeed, Yahveh-Elohim exhibits the individual features of a hierarchical being, just as Elijah, for example, shows individual, human character features. For, a miracle-working prophet as well as a proclaiming prophet — whether a human being or a hierarchical being — retains, in spite of his prophetic mission, his individual character. Thus Moses' smashing of the stone tablets did not fulfill his prophetic mission to proclaim the Ten Commandments, but was an expression of his personal indignation at the rebellion of the people who were worshiping the golden calf at the foot of Mt. Sinai. And the manner in which the Bible depicts Yahveh-Elohim's working (e.g., the punishing decrees of the "jealous God", imposed out of anger and later revoked) shows that Yahveh-Elohim, in fulfilling the task of the eternal Holy Trinity, allowed scope also to his individual manner of being.

Such an individual manner of being, as depicted in the Bible, even indicates which rank of the spiritual hierarchies he belongs to. Yahveh's hierarchical rank is made evident in the Bible in its depiction of his mode of action. Yahveh's characteristic manner of behavior consists in demonstrating his *power*. This began with the transformation of Moses' rod into a snake, which swallowed up the snakes of the Egyptian priests created in the same manner. Next came the ten plagues of Egypt. And then there was the destruction of the Pharaoh's army in the Red Sea. The argument, which should have convinced the Pharaoh and the Egyptians, was that the Israelites had on their side a mighty and invisible ally who had so much power over the elements that it was senseless and hopeless to resist his will.

The traditional teaching about the angelic hierarchies was depicted systematically by Dionysius the Areopagite in his work *Concerning the Heavenly Hierarchy*. The teaching concerning the celestial hierarchies transmitted by Dionysius was later dealt with in an intellectually satisfying way by St. Thomas Aquinas in his tract on the angels and in the *Summa Theologica*. And St. Bonaventure contemplated this teaching as a means on the path of inner enlightenment in his work *Concerning the Three-fold Path*. (*De triplici via*, III [St. Bonaventure, *Opera Omnia*, vol. VIII].) According to this teaching, the heavenly hierarchy has three levels, whereby each of its levels is divided into three orders or ranks. The orders of the lowest hierarchy — the first hierarchy, viewed from humanity's perspective — are the Angels (*Angeloi*), Archangels (*Archangeloi*), and Principalities (*Archai*). The orders of the second hierarchy are Powers (*Exusiai*), Virtues (*Dynameis*), and Dominions (*Kyriotetes*). The orders of the highest hierarchy — the third hierarchy, viewed from humanity's perspective — are Thrones (*Thronoi*), Cherubim (*Cherubim*), and Seraphim (*Seraphim*).

St. Bonaventure elucidates the role which the nine orders of the heavenly hierarchy play in meditatively comprehending truth. He says:

> Take note that in the *first hierarchy* truth is to be called forth by inner sighing and prayer — work of the *Angels*
> is to be perceived and heard through study and reading — work of the *Archangels*

is to be proclaimed by way of example and through preaching—work of the *Principalities*.

In the *second hierarchy truth is to be approached* by taking refuge in it and through devotion to it—work of the
Powers
is to be understood through fervor and emulation—work of the *Virtues*
is to be associated with by way of self-contempt and mortification—work of the *Dominions*.

In the *third hierarchy* truth is to be worshiped through sacrifice and praise—work of the *Thrones*
is to be admired through ecstasy and contemplation—work of the *Cherubim*
is to be embraced in holy kiss and through pious love—work of the *Seraphim*". (*De triplici via*, III, vii, 14, [*Opera Omnia* VIII, 18].)

St. Bonaventure closes this text with the words: "Pay diligent attention to what has been said, for therein is a source of life." (I agree with this advice wholeheartedly, for this text really contains a fountain-head of spiritual life.)

The teaching on the heavenly hierarchies was renewed in the first quarter of this century through the life-work of the great Austrian seer and thinker Rudolf Steiner. The depth and profundity of Rudolf Steiner's contribution to a new understanding of the spiritual hierarchies is such that this theme cannot be seriously taken up today without taking into account his remarkable accomplishment. For his achievement in the domain of the teaching concerning the angelic hierarchies—as far as the wealth of stimulation, the depth and multiplicity of viewpoints, the inner lack of contradictions, the consistency and organic cohesiveness is concerned—cannot be compared with the accomplishment of any seer or thinker of the present, or from the Middle Ages or antiquity. It towers way above them. Rudolf Steiner viewed the spiritual hierarchies as holding sway in all of evolution and world history.

In his writings and lecture cycles—for example, *Occult Science: An Outline* and *The Spiritual beings in the Heavenly Bodies and in the Kingdoms of Nature* (lecture cycles held in Helsingfors, 1912)—he gave a comprehensive description of the nature and the role of the spiritual hierarchies in cosmic evolution and in the cosmic order. Indeed, it can be said that during his entire literary and lecturing activity he constantly had the heavenly hierarchies in view and always made the effort to do justice to their reality. He erected a "cathedral" (on the level of thought) to the celestial hierarchies—and this in the twentieth century, when knowledge concerning the hierarchies has virtually disappeared from humanity's consciousness.

You can take whatever position you want with regard to the various theses and viewpoints of Rudolf Steiner's teaching concerning the hierarchical world-order. Nevertheless, whatever view you take, his decisive service is and remains the fact that the beings and the role of Angels, Archangels, Archai, Exusiai, Dynameis, Kyriotetes, Thones, Cherubim, and Seraphim again became conceivable and comprehensible — renewed and revitalized in the consciousness of human beings. They have been retrieved from the realm of forgetting, sleep, and death — remembered, awakened, and resurrected in and through Rudolf Steiner's life's work. Before anyone tries to explain or "psychologize" away the reality of the spiritual hierarchies, it would be his duty first of all to grapple with the teaching of Rudolf Steiner.

Rudolf Steiner's teaching about the hierarchies is a powerful confirmation of the Church's teaching concerning angelic beings — a teaching which is, for Catholic and Orthodox Christians, an indispensable part of their belief. Should one criticize Rudolf Steiner on account of the fact that his belief in the angelic hierarchies proved to be so fruitful and intellectually enriching? Should he be criticized because his belief became "seeing" (spiritual vision)? If we wanted to criticize him on this account, we would be proclaiming that sterility and poverty in knowledge and the life of thought are the qualities and attributes of belief. At all events, the question as to which rank of the spiritual hierarchies Yahveh-Elohim belongs, obliges us to take account of Rudolf Steiner's teaching concerning the hierarchies.

Rudolf Steiner named the orders of the second hierarchy, i.e., the Powers, Virtues, and Dominions, also as the Spirits of Form, Spirits of Movement, and the Spirits of Wisdom. Further, he named the orders of the highest hierarchy — Thrones, Cherubim, and Seraphim, also as the Spirits of Will, Spirits of Harmony, and Spirits of Love. These designations are just as meaningful as the traditional names which go back to Dionysius the Areopagite.

Now let us return to our question: When Yahveh-Elohim became the special God of the people of the community of Israel and, so to speak, concluded a "matrimonial covenant" with it as a fully empowered representative of the eternal Holy Trinity, when he acted as the Trinity's proclaimer and working hierarchical "prophet", to which of the nine orders of spiritual hierarchies did he belong?

We have already emphasized above the fact that Yahveh's manner of working during the captivity in Egypt as well as during the exodus of the people of Israel out of Egypt is characterized in the Bible by the manifestation of his *power* — power over the elements of nature, too.

The fact that his power extends to the elements of nature indicates that it is a matter not of a being of the lowest hierarchy — the hierarchy of Angels, Archangels, and Archai — for this hierarchy has the *conscience* of human consciousness in particular as its field of activity. In the biblical account, no effect at all on the conscience of the Pharaoh or of the Egyptian people is attributed to Yahveh. Neither enlightenment of conscience nor insight into the right of the people of Israel to leave Egypt made the exodus of the Israelites out of Egypt possible, but the ten plagues and the destruction of the Egyptian army in the Red Sea. In other words, it was simply (and solely) the manifestation of Yahveh's power — his power over the elements of nature — that made the exodus of the people of Israel possible. Now, it is the order of the *Powers* (Greek: *Exusiai*), of the second hierarchy, which rules the elements of nature, and which, when it has authority from above, is capable of influencing natural events. It follows, then, that Yahveh — as the fully empowered hierarchical representative, proclaimer, and miracle-working "prophet" of the Most High — is a being of the *second hierarchy* belonging, in fact, to the order of the Powers (*Exusiai*) or Spirits of Form, (Hebrew: *Elohim*). And it was this being who, as God's representative, entered into the special covenant relationship with the community of Israel and became the special leader and architect of that community's path of destiny.

* * * * * * *

The Ten Commandments are a reflection of the splendor of the world-order. They are an expression of *truth* which, as it were, is "crystallized" in them.

Just as the plurality of the human soul's life of imagination, feeling and will has a focus, a center, around which it orders and orientates itself, so also does the multiplicity of the appearances of the world have *one* center, which orders and holds everything together. Just as the self ("I") of the human being is the centerpoint of the plurality of manifestations of his life of soul, so is the *one* God, transcending the self, the centerpoint of the world. The multiplicity of the appearances of the world may be likened to the "periphery" in contrast to the unity of its center, the self of the world, which holds it together, ordering it, giving the world its meaning and direction. The peripheral multiplicity of the appearances of the world is incapable of having an idea of the God transcending the self and is incapable of proclaiming His name. The unimaginable and unnameable God transcending the self can only be recognized and named in the self's very own language. However, the self's very own language is love. The self of the human being speaks only in and through love, otherwise it remains silent. Love is the self's life element, its substance, and its power of growth. Love is also the source of certainty concerning God's presence in the world. Indeed, love is the bond which unites the human self with God. Love recognizes God, just as the self of the human being is recognized by God.

PART THREE

THY KINGDOM COME

The Three Kingdoms:
Nature, Man, and God

I

THE KINGDOM OF NATURE

The convictions of the educated and semi-educated strata of the civilized world have undergone a radical transformation since the appearance of Charles Darwin's theory of the natural evolution of species. Nature is no longer considered merely to be an arena for the deployment of human activity or an object of research and exploitation, but is also increasingly regarded as a teacher of truth and a source of knowledge concerning life's meaning and goal, and, consequently, also of the principles of morality. What the Holy Scripture — the Bible — meant for Europeans of former days is now supplanted more and more by the significance of Nature or rather *Nature's evolutionary process.*

This evolving Nature, as conceived of in the twentieth century, is no longer that marvelled at by our ancestors as God's creation. For, it was as a "finished work" that Nature appeared to the marvelling, seeking, poetical gaze of human beings. Today, however, Nature is no longer seen as a created work but as a *process*, a becoming. We are witness, so it seems, to the all-encompassing (embracing also we human beings) labor-pains of her unimaginable future. Her glory and perfection lie in the future, not in her origin and past. To be a devout evolutionist — and who isn't one nowadays? — means to believe in the future and to regard as inferior anything whatsoever of the past. It means to believe in a wretched, soul-less, spirit-less past — originating from a blind whirling mass of primeval gas — and in a brilliant future formed and mastered to an inconceivable extent by the faculty of reason.

If it is so that Nature has evolved plants, animals, and mankind — not forgetting the poets and sages — from a vortex of gas, why should we not turn to her (and to her alone) for instruction in the meaning of life and for guidelines of right aspiration, thinking, and behavior? Where better to learn the essentials of the "what", "why", and "how" of life than from Nature, i.e. from life itself? All the more, so as we are nothing other than fragments of Nature become conscious and capable of reflecting upon ourselves!

Untold multitudes of our contemporaries think this way and see it as their most important duty to learn the lessons of Nature in order to apply them as regulating principles for their actions and endeavors.

NATURE'S TEACHING

Contemporary natural science has placed such an exhaustive mass of factual data at our disposal that we are in a position — on the basis of an analysis thereof — to draw certain general conclusions that could be considered as "Nature's doctrines". These doctrines can be inferred from the factual data in the same way as in jurisprudence, for instance, evidence is provided by the acts committed. Nature makes no statements; she does not "teach"; she only acts or "happens". But one cannot deny the value of the acts committed or taking place through the "happenings" of Nature — they express volumes. For example, the fact that the dinosaurs that once ruled the planet we inhabit today disappeared and gave place to the weaker but more adaptable mammals constitutes just such an act committed. From this follows one of Nature's "doctrines": highly specialized creatures — those capable of realizing the highest degree of attainment in some particular direction — are least suited to further development, whereas less specialized creatures — those better equipped to adapt — though weaker, are more talented in a general sense and are better able to survive and to develop further. The one-sided development of a highly specialized creature proves to be an evolutionary dead end leading no further, with no prospect of a step forward. It reaches the highest level of attainment — the "world championship", so to speak — in some particular function but by this same token forfeits the possibility of further development in other directions. Since such a creature has need precisely of such alternative lines of development to survive in ever-changing conditions and to keep step with the onward march of evolution, it perishes. The act committed here — that of the extinction of the dinosaurs — reveals that a "doctrine" of Nature: *specialization is a blind alley and spells ruin; adaptability signifies life and progress.*

Secondly, with regard to the question of the continued existence or the extinction of a species, or that of the preservation or destruction of an individual within a given species, the decisive criterion is: *the fit are worth saving; the weak should perish.* Thus, for example, the warring of stags in the rutting-season establishes which among them are fit (and hence more deserving of begetting progeny) and which are not. And just as the fight for survival determines which individuals within a species will survive and which will be rejected, so do entire species battle for existence in the natural world.

A will to power is at work in Nature, the goal of which is self-assertion for the sake of continued existence. It is as though Nature were dreaming of some mighty creature capable of meeting all challenges and overpowering all opponents, and aims all her activity to the end of producing such a being.

Could this be Man? "Not yet" answered Friedrich Nietzsche. Man only bridges the way and must himself be surmounted in order that Nature's dream—the Superman—might be realized. For if man be Nature arrived at self-consciousness, the Future One—the Superman—will be, not *self-conscious* Nature only, but *self-willed* Nature as well.

The Delphic saying "know thyself" will then be replaced by the will-oracle, "will thyself". For the crown of natural evolution will be, not self-reflection, but self-realization. The Future One will not merely recognize and acknowledge freedom; he will *be* free. His will shall be an inexhaustible fount of creativity, asserting itself as an untrammeled power, conditioned by nothing.

"O Thou my Will, my Necessity, my Law!" Thus resounded Nietzsche's prophetic cry. For he was well-advanced on the way toward the secret of the will that operates in the evolutionary processes of Nature, that slithers upward through the changing forms of her successive kingdoms to arrive at consciousness and freedom, and underlying which there burns the persuasive and compelling promise: "Ye shall be as gods".

NATURE'S OTHER TEACHING

The acts of Nature are not simply the struggle for existence, the survival of the fittest, and natural selection. They comprise a considerable degree of cooperation, association, and social collectivism.

The anthill and termite colony, the wasp's nest and bees' hive, the wolf pack and elephant herd—also each living organism whose cells are not at variance but work together, and, finally, each molecule in a cell and each atom with its system of electrons—all these are instances of cooperation, association, and social collectivism in Nature. Electrons unite in atoms, atoms in molecules, molecules in cells, cells in organisms; and in their turn, such organisms form colonies, communities, herds, tribes, races, nations, governments, confederations.

The late prime minister of South Africa, General Smuts, was so struck by Nature's collective activity that he not only elaborated a philosophy of holism (from the Greek "*holon*" = the totality) but also aligned his country — on "holistic" grounds — with the British Commonwealth. Not only in time of peace, but through both World Wars, South Africa remained a faithful member of the Commonwealth with all the obligations this entailed.

But General Smuts was not alone in being so deeply impressed by a comprehensive overview of the integrative acts of Nature, so impressed as to result in a socio-political theory which became practiced. Over half a century earlier Karl Marx and Friedrich Engels were gripped by the spectacle of the struggle for existence in Nature and the alliance of the weaker into groups and communities, thus gaining in strength. Marx and Engels unleashed upon mankind the impassioned plea: "Workers of the world, unite!"

Their call to those oppressed in the struggle for existence (for this struggle also plays into human society) was a call to unite and to take action together against the oppressors in the higher echelons, to shake off their rule and to replace competition and rivalry with a new worldwide social order based on cooperation. In such a communist society there ought to be as few exploiters and exploited as, for instance, in an anthill, where no one exploits or enslaves another, but rather each serves as a part in the whole, and none claims a position of power or special prerogatives over the others. What is realized by way of instinct, in the case of an anthill, ought to be able to be effected by reasoned conviction in a communist society. For reason is nothing other than instinct become conscious, and instinct in its turn is only the categorical expression of the essential nature of matter of which everything is made up. But matter is inhabited by a primal instinct that will one day arise resplendently as the great, all-embracing knowledge known to the evolved reasoning faculty. This is the primal instinct of progress — progress not for the few or the elect only, but for all. This promise smolders in the depths of the "instinct for progress" which is evolution: "Ye shall be as gods". (Note, however, that it is not: "You or he shall be as a god".) "Being as gods" is the concern of humanity as a whole; it represents its collective goal.

THE CUNNING OF THE SERPENT

Taken as a whole, the conception of evolution presented by modern scientific research can be regarded as an "intelligent happening". It points to the indefatigable endeavor of a motivating force at work in the depths of all becoming, adopting then discarding myriad forms, ever striving to mount from the darkness of instinct to the clear light of reason. Evolution is synonymous with instinct seeking to become reason.

However, this process does not proceed in a straightforward way. Rather, it takes place according to the principle of trial and error. Testing and experimenting, from time to time it takes byways or even finds itself in a blind alley, and then searches for a way out, only to leave this behind upon returning to its primary direction again. Evolution follows a winding path with bends and curves similar to those traced out by a serpent creeping in darkness. Nonetheless it indicates a general direction in which the movement takes place, one proceeding toward organic formations capable of reason.

It is instructive to note the peculiar role attributed to the serpent by primitive — and not so primitive — peoples. Several years ago a British television network broadcast the first (and perhaps only) film documentary of the rites of the Australian aborigines. It was produced and commentated by David Attenborough, a depth-psychologist with a special interest in the "mysteries" of so-called primitive peoples. The aborigines made an exception in the case of this congenial and sympathetic young man and accorded him the high and well-deserved honor of attending their mystery rites. He did not misuse this trust, for the documentary he produced offered profound insights into the aboriginal mystery rites and could not do otherwise than to awaken in the viewer respect for the childlike seriousness with which this small group of our fellow men, poor and naked though they may be, enacted in deepest reverence that which to them is most holy. The main rite comprised a presentation in dramatic form of their central tradition — evoking the primordial memory subsisting in their subconscious — regarding the origin and evolution of consciousness. A man, evidently in a trance in which he had identified himself with a serpent, crept out through a cleft in a rock and, swaying rhythmically, slowly approached a group of men before him. When he reached them, he snapped out of the trance and collapsed. Then he came to and stood up as a man among men.

In the grotto behind was a slab of wood inscribed with symbols depicting the serpent's journey from the dark depths of matter up to man. This "book" was then clearly shown.

In her major opus, *The Secret Doctrine*, H.P. Blavatsky assembled and presented many of the Indian and Tibetan traditions concerning the serpent and the "sons of the serpent". They illustrate that the serpent was regarded in those regions as the originator and teacher of civilization of the arts and sciences, invention, and use of tools. The message of these traditions is that the "Nagas" or "sons of the serpent" were mankind's first teachers, the serpent being the principle of material and intellectual progress.

The gnostic sects of the Naasenes (from naas or *nahash* = serpent) and the Ophites (from *ophis* = serpent in Greek) worshipped the serpent as the cosmic principle of progress. They took as their symbol the serpent swallowing its own tail, the same chosen by the Theosophical Society as its seal and standard.

The Bible, however, does not ascribe to the serpent the role of man's benefactor, but that of his tempter and malefactor. For the serpent effected the most radical alteration possible in the conditions of man's existence, and in the destiny of the whole of humanity. This was the fall from the condition of being, the realm of divine archetypes (the Garden of Eden, planted by God), into that of evolution, a world that is directed by the serpent and seeks by means of toil, suffering, and death to attain its stated end: "Thou shalt be as gods". Friedrich Weinreb writes in his important work *The Bible and Creation*: "The serpent does indeed have something to offer mankind, for one could say that it is the 'material Messiah'. It offers the kingdom of this world, the kingdom of never-ending evolution." This means a kingdom evolving toward totally automatic (and hence godless) consciousness — a consciousness "like God and, consequently, in no need of Him". This and the following quotations have been translated from the German edition; Friedrich Weinreb, *Der Gottliche Bauplan der Welt* (Zurich: Origo, 1969), p. 86.

> It may be observed that the Hebrew word for serpent, *nahash*, has a numerical value of 358: nun = 50, heth = 8 and shin = 300. The letters of the Hebrew for Messiah, *masiah*, give the same sum: 40–300–10–8 (mem, shin, yod, heth). The serpent is the redeemer "from the other side" which presents its own path of redemption by proposing that one sets to work oneself and takes evolution in hand oneself. The serpent's cunning strategy is to present itself as the Redeemer.

Through the Bible and the people of Israel, an inestimable service was performed — that of exposing evolution as the work of the serpent, unmasking the serpent as the teacher of a path leading further and further away from God and from Man's true home. The serpent is venerated everywhere — whether expressly or not — in the sense that evolution is acknowledged as the guiding power of the world and all take part in it, whilst the Bible stands alone in the world warning of the serpent's path and recalling the supra-evolutionary homeland and destiny of Man.

Continuing on from the Old Testament, the Gospels speak of the "sons of this world" and the "sons of light" (*Luke* 16: 8). The former are the "peoples" (*gentes*, usually translated "heathen"); the latter are those who want to serve God and not the "Lord of this world" who is the serpent, the guiding being of evolution. For the sons of light, evolution is the path of the serpent, the way "leading astray".

> The Hebrew for "lose" or "go astray" is abed, assigned 1-2-4 (aleph, beth, daleth). Consequently its very structure points to the development from "one" to "two"; but no return to "one" follows; rather it progresses further to its highest perfection, to "four" . . . Now, this development of creation from "one" to "two" and further to multiplicity (shown by the principle of "four") signifies essentially that all is lost or gone astray.

It is written in the Gospels that the "sons of this world" are wiser after their fashion than the "sons of light" (*Luke* 16: 8). Here a comparison is drawn between the wisdom of the divine light and the serpent's cunning. For this cunning, taken as the sum total of experience offered by evolution and perfect earthly realism undoubtedly exists and holds with respect to the evolutionary realm. Therefore the gospels do not deny it, but acknowledge it as valid in its own domain.

> Be ye wise as serpents and innocent as doves (*Matthew* 10: 16)

was the Master's counsel to his disciples. Correspondingly, there is the divine decree from the Old Testament concerning the serpent: "On thy belly shalt thou creep and dust shalt thou eat all thy days", (*Genesis* 3: 14). To this divine decree corresponds the serpent's cunning, that of earthly realism moving horizontally in time from one experience to the next, never raising itself up, but "creeping on its belly" and nourishing itself on "dust", that is, on the increasing division and analytic splintering of the totality of the world of appearances into ever smaller pieces, e.g. atoms, electrons, particles, etc. "Knowledge" to earth-bound intellectual realism signifies dissecting everything to the end of ascertaining how it is joined together in the larger whole. This is nothing other than "eating dust". The essence of the serpent's cunning is most clearly and comprehensively revealed in empirical, materialistic science, which is where the cunning of the serpent has blossomed. And the collectivism that utilizes the results of this science — where science "becomes flesh" — represents the unfolding of the *morality* of the serpent, a morality that is rooted in the promise, "Ye shall be as gods". It aspires to unbounded collective progress in the conquest, utilization, and control of the world by means of a collectively organized rationality. The essence of the morality of the serpent — the morality of evolution — is the collective will to power, and this is directly continued in the natural evolution of mankind.

THE OTHER SIDE OF NATURE

Nature in the process of evolution, as discovered and investigated by modern science, does not represent the whole of Nature, however. Admittedly, it is the greater part, yet it remains only a cross section of the totality. Part of Nature is not caught up in evolution. This part is usually overlooked because it does not fit in with the evolutionary view, and so is of no interest. That evolution, as currently understood, does not encompass Nature in its entirety is clear from this simple question: If it be true that the mineral kingdom evolved into the organic (vegetable) kingdom, the vegetable kingdom into that of the animals, and the animal kingdom into the human kingdom, why does the mineral kingdom still remain alongside the vegetable kingdom, the vegetable kingdom alongside the animal kingdom, and the animal kingdom alongside the human kingdom? One cannot in all seriousness speak of "advanced" and "retarded" stones or "advanced" or "retarded" plants. How is it that though situated in the selfsame terrestrial conditions the greater part of Nature has been unable to progress?

It is of no avail here looking to some analogy with the human organism for help. For, in doing so we do not find first a mineral-like skeletal system that then gradually develops through stages to evolve tendons, muscles, veins, arteries, etc., finally to evolve the cerebral-nervous system — such as one would expect to be the case if, in fact, there were an actual correspondence with the evolutionary scheme. On the contrary, from a single reproductive cell there arises by way of cell-division not only brain and nerve cells but also those of the tendons, muscles, veins, arteries, and bones as well. From the original cell there is a differentiation into all the various "kingdoms" within the organism, a process corresponding far more to the biblical principle of "each according to its kind" than to that of progressive evolution — that is, the development of the mineral into the organic and the organic in its turn into a nervous system able to be a vehicle for the psyche (soul). If it is the case that ontogenesis is an accelerated recapitulation of phylogenesis, the conclusion to be drawn is that the macrocosm, by analogy with the microcosm represented by the human organism, is not only the outcome of an evolutionary process, but also primarily the product of a process of differentiation. Thus, from a single substance (whether in the form of a primeval gas or not is immaterial here) not only the mineral, but also the vegetable and animal kingdoms, entered into manifestation simultaneously, corresponding to the biblical axiom of "each according to its kind".

Nature has two sides. On one hand, she is the field of action wherein the principles or archetypes of the various species are manifested, according to the biblical (and Platonic) maxim, "each according to its kind". On the other hand, she is the battlefield of evolution — with its struggle for existence, its survival of the fittest, and its natural selection.

The "first" Nature — Nature as a reflection and incarnation of the archetypes — is primary, whereas the other Nature, that of evolution, is secondary. The solar system with its sun and orbiting planets; the atom with its nucleus and cloud of electrons; the living cell with its cellular nucleus surrounded by a moving plasma of molecules: these are not arenas for the struggle for existence, and still less for evolution, which is valid only for part of Nature as this manifests itself upon the earth's surface. No, these three — solar system, atom, and living cell — are structural forms representing the outward expression of an archetype of primal phenomenon (*Urphaenomen*). And if the most all-encompassing among them (the solar system) as well as the smallest (atom and cell) manifest one and the same structural archetype (*Urphaenomen*), why should there not be manifestations — within these limits — of still other structural archetypes? Was Goethe mistaken in describing the *Urphaenomen* or structural archetype of plants, that is, the prototype underlying all the various species of plants, constituting the "theme" of which all plant species are only variations?

A general (non-specific) view of the world shows us an edifice whose pillars are the archetypes; evolution snakes its way through this edifice adapting, re-adapting, and varying the archetypes in diverse ways in conformity with the end that it — and not the world — has in view.

Evolution proper actually made a later appearance, at a time when the process of differentiation had already formed the world into a cosmic organism that can supply the so-called "natural evolution" with a field of action. Evolution does not represent what is primary and primordial but something secondary and superimposed. It begins its work in the organic realm — at first in a limited way in the vegetable kingdom — in order to determine in ever-increasing measure the fate of the animal kingdom and mankind. In other words, within the biblical (Platonic) creation, there arose an evolutionary process signifying what might be called the growth of another "world" within the world of creation, a "world" for itself which — like a parasite — took root and spread throughout the organism of the world.

There is, therefore, a "virgin" Nature as well as a "fallen" Nature. The first is that of the divine archetypes — Nature bearing Paradise within her. The second is Nature which has "fallen" into the process of evolution that re-shapes and modifies these archetypes according to its own designs.

That Nature was at first archetypal, i.e. paradisiacal, and only subsequently fell into the realm of "serpent-guided evolution" is also evident from the fact that the predatory characteristics of many animals only appear or break through after a "paradisiacal" infancy. It is a case here of ontogeny in a way recapitulating phylogeny. For instance, lion cubs begin as merry and friendly creatures no less tame or trusting than lambs, only to undergo a somewhat abrupt change later into predatory lions. The same could be said of many other beasts of prey. However, this does not apply in the case of reptiles. Young snakes and crocodiles are as though already fully mature right from the beginning. One cannot avoid the impression that such creatures originated on "this side" of the threshold of evolution, i.e. that the history of these species cannot be divided into distinct "pre-evolutionary" and "evolutionary" periods. They are pure products of evolution. The "serpent" is their creator. Similar remarks could be made regarding many species of insects.

How does Man stand in all this?

II

THE KINGDOM OF MAN

From an evolutionary point of view, Man is at the culmination, at least for the time being. For, if it be evolution's purpose to raise its underlying instinct — that is, the serpent's guile — to self-consciousness, it is no doubt true that Man is that creature in whom this purpose takes place. Man is, in fact, the least instinctive and most intelligent being yet to appear on the stage of evolution; and it was by virtue of his skill with tools and his intelligence that he wrested dominion over the earth from the great saurians of the past. In Man the will to power — the moving force behind all evolutionary processes — has attained its highest level yet. His sovereignty is undisputed; no rivals remain. In the use of tools, through which his dominion over Nature has been made possible, he has advanced from the stone ax to the interplanetary rocket, from the hand spear to the hydrogen bomb. Yet all these represent nothing but steps along the way leading to the conquest and control of Nature by sense-bound reason. These steps on the path of progress all have in common that they are achievements of intelligence applied to the acquisition of power by means of perfecting the design and use of tools. All such attainments lie on the same plane, namely that of the struggle for existence and the will to power. They are simply an intellectual extension of the instinctual behavior of animals. No essential moral distinction is to be made between the behavior of an ape hurling a coconut at the head of someone passing by and that of the pilot who dropped the atomic bomb on Hiroshima. The difference consists merely in the technology employed. The sum total of all technological development, along with the scientific research in mathematics, chemistry, and physics upon which it rests, is simply "natural evolution" extended by mankind, the only difference being that its guide is now reason, not instinct.

If Man were nothing other than a product of natural evolution he would abide exclusively on the plane of the will to power and would persist in the application of all his faculties to this end. He would be completely submerged in the horizontally advancing evolution of the serpent, with whom he would have identified himself for all eternity.

But there occurred a miracle in human history: whilst swimming with the tide of progress, imbued with empirical and materialistic realism, Man arose and raised himself above the plane of natural evolution, the plane of this very realism. A non-empirical idealism lit up within him. This took place long before the historical appearance of Platonism and Stoicism, or of the Vedanta and Buddhism. In principle, it occurred in the far-distant past when someone first erected an altar of unhewn stone. All else — the great religions, as well as the totality of mankind's idealistic philosophies — followed upon the erection of that altar, an act that was to have far-reaching consequences. It was an action "vertically" opposed to evolutionary processes, lying neither on a level with, nor in the direction of, empirical-materialistic realism.

To what does this miracle of idealism, appearing like a comet in the world of evolution, attest? First and foremost it points to the nobility of the human being. It bears witness that in his deeper being Man is not a mere product of natural evolution; it is a testimony to his true nature and true spiritual home.

The first stone altar, which was neither a weapon in the struggle for survival nor a sheltering haven from storm or foe, offers proof, beyond any shadow of doubt, that Man professed his allegiance to a cosmic order other than that of natural evolution. Kant's two sources of wonder — the starry heaven above and the moral law within — give conscious expression to that which the first altar-builder had intimated in a non-verbal way through the "act committed", that of erecting an altar. For the starry heaven is an image of the divine-archetypal Nature that is not under the sway of natural evolution; and the moral law inscribed in the human soul — Kant's categorical imperative — signifies the reality of the presence in the human being of what the Bible calls the "image and likeness of God", that is, the principal archetype of Man.

The miracle of Man's raising himself up, over and against natural evolution — and this is what is especially wonderful about idealism — is that he does not merely postulate a world-order and a morality other than those of the serpent. Rather, over and above this, he employs the very faculties whose development he owes to the serpent — reason and its attendant senses — in a direction counter to the purposes and ends of this evolution itself.

Applied to the utilization of tools and the exercise of control over Nature, reason — with its capacity to calculate, to establish causality, and to achieve the greatest yield with the least effort — this reason, we say, has been raised by Man to the level of pure contemplation. Man's true nature wrenched it away from natural evolution—like a kind of booty—insofar as it was capable of being directed to pure contemplation. Contemplation is the condition of the mind concentrated upon transcendental concepts, ideas, and ideals, and not upon utility and advantage in the field of materialistic realism. Thereby it sets itself in harmony with man's divine-archetypal nature and becomes a creative fountainhead of things which, as regards natural evolution, are not only unnecessary or of no utility, but downright troublesome. We have to thank contemplation for the origin of such philosophies as Sankhya, Vedanta, Buddhism, Pythagoreanism, Platonism, Stoicism, and Kantianism. All these idealistic philosophies are "strangers to the world", understanding here the "world" as that of natural evolution. Mankind does not owe any inventions or new tools to these philosophies—at best perhaps a few musical instruments. But music does not signify technological progress.

We have referred to idealistic philosophies here and not to religions, because they are not only purely human but also they have applied the faculty of reason stemming from natural evolution to raise it up to the level of contemplation. In contrast, religions cannot be regarded as purely human expressions or creations. Their provenance transcends the purely human; they spring from the fount of divine supra-human revelation. For this reason it is in idealism— which is not divine revelation—that the purely human manifests itself. Here it is that Man expresses his innermost being. Idealism is the "voice of one crying in the wilderness" that lies between the domains of natural evolution and divine revelation. Only in this place can the voice of Man, and Man alone, be heard. Not the voice of those mastered and bullied by natural evolution—the "children of this world"—nor that of the illuminated and inspired prophets and seers, but the voice of those crying out from the loneliness of their own true being. For the true being of Man is not revealed in technological progress, which is really only an extension of natural evolution, but in an idealism that represents the capacity for contemplation with no practical end in view.

With idealism Man, in the true sense of the word, begins to be Man. Whatever in him is pre-idealistic is at the same time pre-human, and belongs to the realm of natural evolution—the realm of the serpent. The morality of those who adhere to this latter—the empirico-materialist realists—is rooted in the principle of utility and expediency, no matter whether on an individual or on a collective basis. In contrast, idealists—those human beings capable of contemplation—have a morality which is rooted not in shrewd intelligence but in knowledge of the nobility of Man's true nature. Their fundamental rule is that of self-mastery, that is, control by the higher Man of the natural Man in whom he dwells. What is at issue here is the mastery of the contemplative mind over the human being's impulsive and passionate drives.

Thus it was so that Plato regarded intellectual discernment, which he called *wisdom*, as the root and source of all the virtues. The others, namely *courage*, *prudence*, and *justice*, result from the penetration of the whole human being by the ever-intensifying light of wisdom. Plato conceived of justice as the ultimate fruit of the process of this penetration by the light of wisdom — this being none other than self-mastery. Thus, justice represents the crown of Man's moral development — what might be called "wisdom become flesh".

The Indian sage, Sankaracharya, also describes four fundamental virtues in connection with the way of realization. The first, which constitutes the root-principle of the others, is discernment (*viveka*) between the essential and the non-essential. From this follows equanimity (*vairagya*). Equanimity makes possible the development of the so-called "six jewels", that is, the moral habits that together enable and guarantee prudent conduct in every circumstance. The fourth and last virtue or quality is the aspiration to liberation from the shackles of Nature (Nature is the process of natural evolution).

For Sankaracharya, as for Plato, it is a matter of establishing the sovereignty of the contemplative mind over all other aspects of human nature. Just as Plato regarded wisdom as the basis for moral growth, Sankaracharya pointed to discernment between the essential and the non-essential, a faculty very similar of course to Plato's wisdom. Sankaracharya's equanimity corresponds to the courage of Plato, and the "six jewels" are none other than Plato's prudence. The sole divergence appears in the final crowning and integrating virtue which, for Plato, is justice, and for Sankaracharya, the aspiration to freedom or liberation.

The morality of Buddhism presented in the "Noble eightfold path", oriented as it is toward "right meditation", i.e. toward contemplation, is likewise essentially nothing other than a development leading to a full unfolding of the contemplative mind. The same can be said of the Stoics. Their morality is that of the sovereignty of the contemplative mind — Man's self-mastery through reason.

Such is the kingdom of Man, situated between the kingdoms of Nature and of God. Sovereignty of the contemplative mind, along with the morality this gives rise to, represents the pure humanism that stands between Nature and God.

III

THE KINGDOM OF GOD

SALVATION IN HUMAN HISTORY

If we regard human history as a phase in the evolution of the world, there expands before our eyes a range of events leading beyond the region of natural evolution (including its extension in the human realm as technological evolution), and beyond that of divine-archetypal virgin Nature (including its human extension through idealism and pure humanism). This further realm is that of the interventions of the supra-natural and supra-human in the affairs of the kingdom of Nature and the kingdom of Man. Taken together, these supra-natural and supra-human interventions, representing a working in from the kingdom of God on the course of evolution and the history of mankind, constitute the history of revelation and the work of salvation.

Evolution as a whole consists of: "natural evolution"; purely human or "humanistic" cultural history; and the history of revelation and the work of salvation. Natural evolution, together with its extension in human history as technological progress, stands under the motto "ye shall be as gods". It is an unending development distancing itself further and further from God as the Creator of archetypal Nature and archetypal Man. From the standpoint of spirituality and morality it represents the "way of eternal damnation". "Damnation" here signifies enclosure in the closed circle of the serpent biting its own tail. It means the final imprisonment of consciousness in the closed circle of the serpent which is natural evolution — an imprisonment from which there is no escape. In the context of world history, "hell" is the world of the "eternal return": a world without "miracles", a world harboring no hope of escape from the mechanism of causality. Damnation means "being as gods" — without God.

On the other hand the work of salvation (and its historical manifestations) breaches the circle of "damnation" or "natural evolution", thus providing the possibility of entrance to and exit from the circle. Salvation is the helping hand offered to idealistically minded human beings who, though no longer identifying themselves with natural evolution, still lack sufficient strength of themselves to alter its course. That is, they are unable by themselves to alter "the way of the world", just as they are also unable themselves to ascend to a higher sphere (as did the famous Baron Muenchhausen who reputedly extricated himself from a swamp by tugging on his own pigtail). The idealist can indeed raise himself up to his own true being and on this basis postulate another world order, but this remains merely a postulation. At best it represents only his acknowledgement that he has a "true nature". But there comes a helping hand in the course of world history and this is the work of salvation. Revelation from the sphere lying beyond that of natural evolution begins to flow in to those human beings who yearn after the "beyond". The work of salvation is thus the history of religion as revelation. It is in truth the "hand of God" stretched down from on high to human beings mired in evolution's stream so that they may be raised up and helped to return to the divine archetypal world. It is the answer to the call best expressed in this Psalm of David:

> Save me, O God!
> For the waters have come
>   up to my neck.
> I sink in deep mire,
>   where there is no foothold;
> I have come into deep waters,
>   and the flood sweeps over me.
>   (*Psalms* 60: 1–21)

The answer to this plaintive cry came in the form of successive stages of revelation, descending like tumbling cascades of a waterfall, awakening the consciousness of mankind to its divine archetype. This process of revelation took place through seers and prophets and was subsequently recorded and preserved in holy scriptures. Thus, for instance, the revelation vouchsafed to the seven Holy Rishis forms the basis of the Vedas — the Holy Writ of India. The *Zend-Avest* of ancient Iran records the revelation communicated to Zarathustra when, on a high mountain fastness, he confronted the God of Light — Ahura Mazda — face to face. The Bible tells of the revelation received by Moses on Mount Sinai, where he encountered, also face to face, the God who bore the ineffable name of YHWH.

The primordial revelation of India announces the "good news" (*evangelium*) that the divine-archetypal Man, the true self of mankind, is not the empirical self, and likewise that the world — the real world that is, the divine-archetypal world — is not the empirical world of natural evolution. The "good news" of Zarathustra was that the world and Man represented an admixture of two distinct world orders — that of the principle of light and that of the principle of darkness, or the divine-archetypal world order and that of natural evolution — and that the latter would in the end be vanquished by Soshyans "who through will overcomes death", to be followed by the resurrection of the dead. Finally, the "good news" revealed to Moses and the prophets proclaims that mankind, having fallen into the serpent's domain through the Fall, can yet be redeemed, for the very essence and epitome of the divine-archetypal world order Himself was to become Man so that mankind might thereby triumph over the domain of the serpent and the dead might resurrect.

Such, in essence, are the messages of the revelations represented by the great pre-Christian religions. Buddhism, rooted as it is in Brahmanism, was not a religious revelation proper but the culmination of pure humanism. Confucianism is not a religion either but represents a socially and ethically oriented practical philosophy. The post-Christian religions — Mithraism, Manicheanism, and Islam — are essentially "renaissances" of Zoroastrianism or Mazdeism (Mithraism), of Buddhism (Manicheanism), and of the monotheism of Moses (Islam).

Each of these religions or stages of revelation crystallized into a Law, i.e. a system of precepts or injunctions and prohibitions adapted to regulate the life of the faithful in accordance with the content of the particular revelation or divine promise. The moralities of the various religions have in common with that of idealism a preoccupation with self-control and discipline, but with the difference that the injunctions and prohibitions comprised in the morality of humanistic idealism pertain to the contemplative mind, whereas those of the religions are rooted not in the human intellect but in divine revelation. The convincing power of this latter lies not in intellectual insight, as is the case with humanistic idealism, but in the authority of the revelatory source. It was belief in this divine source that disposed believers to comply with the injunctions and prohibitions derived therefrom.

THE BEATITUDES

"Blessed are the poor in spirit"

Now it happened that during the history of the work of salvation — that is, the history of religion — a voice was raised on earth, a voice that not only countered natural evolution through the archetypal nature of Man, and not only pointed to the divine-archetypal world order as opposed to that of the serpent, but beyond this proclaimed that the kingdom of God had come into the realm of the destiny of mankind. The Sermon on the Mount is not concerned merely with Man preserving his true nature in the face of natural evolution, nor even with him simply obeying the divinely revealed law, but that, in accordance with his archetype — "the image and likeness of God" — he becomes as God. "Be ye perfect therefore even as thy Father in heaven is perfect." This central statement from the Sermon on the Mount is a call to ascend from the kingdoms of Nature and Man to the kingdom of God. It summarizes the essence of the Sermon on the Mount and at the same time signifies the motto of the *New Evolution*. The motto of the "old" natural evolution is "ye shall be as gods" — but without God. To this the Sermon on the Mount opposes its own motto and reveals the path leading to the very summit of the promise, "ye shall be as God, in God".

The Sermon on the Mount is the event in mankind's spiritual history which is the counterpart to the temptation by the serpent in paradise. It promises freedom in God just as the temptation in paradise promised freedom without God. It stands in complete contrast to the "natural evolution" of the serpent. The serpent promised a state of self-sufficiency obviating any need for a God on high, implying that the knowledge and power of Man in such a state will suffice completely — he will be "rich". In contrast to this the first Beatitude of the Sermon on the Mount proclaims: "Blessed are the poor in spirit for theirs is the kingdom of heaven", i.e. blessed are those who regard as poor any knowledge of power without God — that is, any knowledge or power not of God himself — for they shall participate in the divine archetypal creative work of God.

"Blessed are they that mourn"

Another of the promises of "natural evolution" is the happiness that will accompany the conquest of suffering, sickness, and death. To this the second Beatitude replies: "Blessed are they that mourn, for they shall be comforted". They that mourn or bear sorrow neither strive after a pain-free existence nor turn away from pain, but *bear* it with acceptance. For the fullness of existence, life's true richness, does not consist solely in health and happiness but in an ever-expanding range of joy and sorrow; and the broader the range, the richer life becomes. Goethe expressed it thus:

All do the gods give, the infinite ones,
  To their loved ones all,
All joys, never ending,
All sorrows, yea infinitely, all
(*Alles geben die Gotter, die unendlkichen*
Ihren Lieblingen ganze,
All Freuden, die unendlichen,
Alle Schmerzen, die unendlichen, ganz.)

And this richness, this extended range in the capacity for joy and sorrow, reaching upward to the divine, is precisely blessedness (*beatitudeo*).

"Blessed are the meek"

Natural evolution rests on the principle that dominion over the kingdom of Nature — over the earth — belongs to those with the greatest will to power. It is predestined for the tough and the toughest. For example, the Romans did not acquire their rulership over the Mediterranean region — from Britannia to Mesopotamia and from Germania to Egypt — by making friends with and winning over these peoples to their side, but by subduing them through the conquering military prowess of its legions. And what holds true for political history holds true also for the expansion of mankind's power over the kingdoms of Nature: animal, vegetable, and mineral — this latter being the kingdom of the elements, with its molecules, atoms, and electrons. To all this the new, divinely directed evolution announced through the Sermon on the Mount opposes the principle: "Blessed are the meek, for they shall inherit the earth".

Not the tough but the meek shall rule earth's natural kingdoms. The power that St. Francis of Assisi, for instance, wielded over birds and fish and wild wolves was not of a kind that any natural scientist, fisherman, forester, or hunter has ever possessed. The same is true of the obedience rendered toward St. Anthony by the hyenas in the Egyptian desert, as well as of many other instances of deference from the side of so-called dumb nature toward truly meek men. Political life also is not wanting in examples where meekness proves stronger than force. That Christianity prevailed in ancient times despite its persecution is an instance on a global scale — one that cannot simply be explained away — where meekness took possession of the "earthly kingdom" (*orbis terrarum*) of that time. Our own time also provides us with a convincing example: this is India's liberation from British rule by the non-violent — hence "meek" — movement of Mahatma

Gandhi, inspired by the Sermon on the Mount. This triumph of meekness cannot be simply explained away by referring to "native Indian passivity" and such things.

"Blessed are they that hunger and thirst after righteousness"

The objection customarily raised against the renunciation of force is that such renunciation is tantamount to a renunciation of righteousness. For, whether one permits an injustice against oneself or against another to go unrequited, in either case free rein has been granted to unrighteousness. But righteousness is not merely Man's primary legal right, it is also the deep-rooted foundation of his moral life. In fact, the need for righteousness is something that lives in Man with an elementary force, to be compared only with hunger and thirst. There is nothing to which children are more sensitive than injustice, and nothing wounds them more deeply and lastingly than occurrences that violate their sense of righteousness. This is known to all who can recall their own childhood or who have had any part in educating children. This sense of righteousness is also especially pronounced among so-called primitive peoples. The North American Indians did not so much hold the occupation of their lands against the white men as they did the repeatedly broken promises, and it was this that led to the majority of the bitter Indian Wars. A tribe that is ceremoniously assured that the portion of their lands presently being taken from them will be the last, and that the remainder will be guaranteed to them forever only to discover some years later that this remainder is also to be annexed by white settlers — such a tribe cannot but suffer a suffocating indignation at this mockery of elementary righteousness. "As is well-known, the natives count for nothing", remarked an embittered Immanuel Kant. And indeed they did not for the "discoverers" of their lands, something with which the natives themselves could never come to terms. Their sense of righteousness bristled at the fact that the promises made were not treated as binding, and that their homeland was regarded as a no-man's land open to settlement by outsiders.

This selfsame sense of righteousness however, is also the main target of state and party propaganda in so-called civilized societies. It may be likened to a fire-belching volcano as far as all revolutions, insurrections, and mass movements are concerned. But none of these has ever yet been able to satisfy the hunger and thirst for righteousness. Neither communist nor capitalist social forms have been — or are now — able to satisfy the sense for righteousness, and this for the reason that both merely represent variations of the same evil, namely an industrialism which enslaves and degrades the human personality. It is industrialism — self-created by human beings, like Frankenstein's monster — that has degraded individuals to units of production, at best mere regulating appendages of machines, it being a matter of indifference whether these machines belong to the state or to private individuals. And just as no social form can bestow freedom on the individual, neither can it grant equality. For the worker, the engineer, the factory manager, the soldier, the officer, and the general are not equal — and this is irrespective of whether they belong to a communist or capitalist society. Industrialism brings in its train its own forms of constraint and inequality, even as feudalism did in its time. And how would it be possible to banish industrialism from the world at this time of a population explosion?

Righteousness — that is, freedom and equality — remains an illusion when sought within the realm of natural evolution with its extension in human history. It is simply not to be found there — and never can be — because the "struggle for survival", translated from natural evolution to the arena of human history, has nothing to do with righteousness. Righteousness must be looked for elsewhere, in another dimension.

This dimension is perpendicular to the horizontal stream of natural evolution (together with its extension in human history). Perfect equality and freedom can actually be experienced, e.g. when people from all stations of life — rich and poor, young and old — kneel at holy communion during the Mass and pray together that formula of human self-knowledge and faith in divine mercy: "Lord, I am not worthy to receive you, but only say the word and I shall be healed". They all are equal in the divine presence and in the knowledge of their own imperfections and in their profession of the divine perfection. Righteousness holds sway, and the hunger and thirst for righteousness is stilled. What is of earth alone, within the stream of natural evolution, cannot still this hunger and thirst, for righteousness is a state wherein the soul experiences the presence of the supra-earthly, the heavenly. "Blessed are they that hunger and thirst for righteousness, for they shall be filled" proclaims the Sermon on the Mount. What is meant here is not an unrealizable terrestrial equality and freedom but the equality and freedom of that state of consciousness designated as the "kingdom of Heaven" in the Sermon on the Mount. The "stilling" of this hunger and thirst for righteousness does not entail terrestrial compensation but participation in an existential state wherein there is no *unrighteousness*. The Sermon on the Mount expresses it thus: "Blessed are they that are persecuted for righteousness' sake for theirs is the kingdom of heaven". The fact of their persecution for righteousness' sake is manifestly something unrighteous that befalls them in earthly life, but the share in the kingdom of heaven they attain thereby reduces such unrighteousness to naught.

"Blessed are they that are persecuted for my sake"

This is expressed with even greater precision and significance in the last Beatitude: "Blessed are you when men hate you, and when they exclude you and revile you, and cast out your name as evil, on account of the Son of man! Rejoice in that day, and leap for joy, for behold, your reward is great in heaven" (*Luke* 6: 22–23). One could wish for no clearer statement than this, indicating that the compensatory balance lies in the vertical earth-heaven axis and not along the horizontal axis of terrestrial events. It is the "reward in heaven" that illumines from above the unrighteousness endured in the current of evolution, driving it away like a shadow before the light. This compensatory balance, in the sense of vertical or divine righteousness, consists in the "reward in heaven", that is, in the enrichment of Man's being and not in the punishment of the perpetrator of unrighteousness in accordance with the principle of horizontal justice: "An eye for an eye, a tooth for a tooth" (*Exodus* 21: 26).

The righteousness of the "kingdom of God" differs from that expressed in the law of karma — as understood both in the Orient and in Western occultism. For the righteousness of karma likewise signifies a compensatory balance taking place at sometime within the course of terrestrial events; and consequently it corresponds to this same principle: "An eye for an eye, a tooth for a tooth". However, this latter form of compensatory balance implies atonement rather than punishment, because the idea of karma is essentially humanistic in that it is conscience-oriented. Thus, for example, the one who commits an unjust act against another searches out an opportunity — which he will assuredly find, be it even in another earthly life — to atone for and make good his offense. The human conscience "hungers and thirsts" for just such a law, one of atonement rather than punishment. It is essentially this law of conscience that operates in destiny. Karmic determinism is to be distinguished both from astrological determinism (the movements of the stars as the determining factors of destiny) and from biological determinism (heredity as the determining factor in destiny) in that factors pertaining to conscience (i.e. prenatal factors) preside over the choice both of heredity and the birth horoscope. For this reason the concept, the idea, and the ideal of karma belong to a loftier moral plane than the legal concept of righteousness as retribution on the part of an external power. And the same holds true to an even greater degree with regard to the concepts, ideas, and ideals that underly not only the deterministic principles of astrology and biology, but those of certain religions as well (predestination in Islam and Calvinism).

However, just as the law of karma morally surpasses both determinism and retributive justice, so it in turn is surpassed by the law of righteousness of the "kingdom of God" as expressed in the Sermon on the Mount. For the latter is operative in the highest and most essential region of all. It heals the wounds of the heart suffered at the hand of injustice and transforms the pain of unjustly inflicted suffering into everlasting bliss. At the same time, without inflicting punishment, it leaves the offender to the tribunal of his own conscience — that is, to his karma. Thus, does the righteousness of the kingdom of God transcend both righteousness of retribution and that of atonement (karma) in that it is a bountiful and merciful righteousness. It bestows gifts of eternal value in whose light the shadows cast through suffering injustice disappear.

"Blessed are the merciful"

All those who desire — that is, actually make the effort — to practice a morality transcending retribution and atonement will have their place in the kingdom of God and his righteousness. Hence, "Blessed are the merciful, for they shall obtain mercy".

That the actual application of the will — its concrete engagement — in the practice of merciful righteousness is a necessary pre-condition of partaking of the benefaction of this righteousness is evident not only from the Beatitude cited, but also from the words that follow immediately on the Lord's Prayer, which provide a kind of commentary on its fifth petition, "And forgive us our debts as we also have forgiven our debtors". We refer to the words: "For if you forgive men their debts, your heavenly Father also will forgive you; but if you do not forgive men their debts, neither will your Father forgive your debts" (*Matthew* 6: 14–15). It is thus not the will for the good favor and benefaction of merciful righteousness that makes one a partaker thereof, but the will for the kingdom of God and his righteousness in itself — will that is put into actual practice. "Seek first the kingdom of God and his righteousness and all else shall be added unto you" (*Matthew* 6: 33).

"Blessed are the pure in heart"

It is just those who "seek first the kingdom of God and his righteousness" who, in the Beatitude "Blessed are the pure in heart, for they shall see God," are to be understood as the "pure in heart". A "pure heart" in the sense of the Sermon on the Mount is a heart turned away from the realm of natural evolution and the promises it offers—a heart devoted entirely to the kingdom of God and his righteousness. It may be granted to such a heart not to discern God in his works only, but, beyond this, to rise to the vision of him as he is in himself.

> Were the eye not sunlike,
>   How could we behold the light?
> If God's own might were not in us,
>   How could we find joy in things divine?

> *Wär' nicht das Auge sonnenhaft,*
>   *Wie könnten wir das Lichterblicken?*
> *Lebt' nicht in uns des Gottes eig'ne Kraft,*
>   *Wie könnt' uns Göttliches entzücken?*

This verse by Goethe is entirely in conformity with the moral logic underlying the Sermon on the Mount, which promises the vision of God to the pure in heart. The fruit of this vision, however, is an active cooperation in bringing to realization the kingdom of God within the terrestrial domain, i.e. in the transformation of natural evolution into a new evolution, an evolution willed and directed by the Divine.

"Blessed are the peacemakers"

This transformation, entailing the conversation of natural evolution to the good, leads above all to the replacement of its guiding principle—the struggle for survival—by that of peace as the basis of the new evolution. For this reason it is said in the Sermon on the Mount that the peacemakers are called "sons of God", i.e. not only do they behold God but also take up his work, just as sons take up and continue the work of their fathers.

The Sermon on the Mount, considered a historical event of universal significance, marked a turning point of evolution after which the principle of peace is gradually coming to replace the principle of war. The path of transformed evolution, in the case of individual human beings and of humanity as a whole, begins with a *purification* of the impulses, instincts, habits, and customs attached to natural evolution. Then it leads on to *illumination*, i.e. to intuition of the truth, beauty, and goodness of divine evolution — the kingdom of God and his righteousness. Finally it culminates in the *union* of will, feeling, and thought with the Will, Feeling, and Thought that underlie divine evolution or the *work of salvation*. St. Bonaventure characterized this path of purification (*purgatio*), illumination (*illuminatio*), and perfection (*perfectio*) in the simplest and clearest possible way (De triplici via, Prologus, 1):

> Purification leads to peace,
> Illumination to truth,
> Perfection to love.
> *Purgatio autem ad pacem ducit,*
> *illuminatio ad veritatem,*
> *perfectio ad caritatem.*

As is evident from the foregoing exposition, the destiny — or history — of mankind is played out simultaneously in three realms or "kingdoms", namely, those of natural evolution, Man, and God. On the one hand Man is a warrior and hunter; on the other hand he is a being gifted with reason and conscience; and at the same time he is also a seeker of God — endowed with the capacity for love. He is a conquerer of Nature (*homo faber*), a thinker and knower (*homo sapiens*), and a praying worshipper (*homo pius*). For these reasons human history is essentially tripartite, comprising a history of *civilization*, a history of humanistic culture, and a history of *religion*. The culmination of civilization is to be found in technology, that of humanistic culture in the treasures of philosophy and that of religion in sanctification — that is, in the bringing to realization of the "kingdom of God" as the "kingdom of love".

Now these three realms are all intimately interconnected, with links extending from one realm to the other. For example, surveyors and architects who in their practice of measuring and planning arrived at arithmetic and geometry were able to apply this practical knowledge to contemplation, that is, to relate the purely quantitative to the qualitative. For them numbers became principles and geometric figures became symbols. Pythagoreanism offers an example of the transformation of the civilizational into the cultural, or the technical into the philosophical. In a similar way there have always been (and still are) transitions from the philosophical to the religious realm. Thus, the concern of philosophy — that is, the application of human reason to truth as such — could not do otherwise than to become occupied with the fact and the problem of death.

The fact that life ends in death formed the moral "center of gravity" for all serious philosophy that did not permit distraction from reality by all manner of secondary problems and research minutiae. Indeed, the problem of death was of such importance for the ancient philosophies that to be a philosopher came to mean "one preparing for death". Not only Socrates and the Platonists but the Stoics, Neoplatonists, and the Neo-Pythagoreans were human beings who lived with the *"memento mori"* ("remember that you must die") ever before them. The same holds true — if not in even greater measure — of the Indian and Buddhist philosophers who crowned death in the world of natural evolution with the ideal of extinction, or *nirvana*.

This earnest consideration of the problem of death was bound to lead in turn to a search for practical experience that could provide at first hand some knowledge and, consequently, certainty regarding the human being's fate beyond the portal of death. It was precisely this search for practical knowledge and then the actual experience of this knowledge that constituted the meaning and purpose of the ancient mysteries; they represented the transition from the philosophical to the religious life. Through the mysteries — the Orphic, the Eleusinian and, in Egypt, those of Osiris and Isis — human beings participated in and acquired experience of the religious realm just as, by turning their minds from practical concerns to contemplation, they participated in pure humanism. The knowledge aimed at in the mysteries which, according to the testimony of the ancients, was really communicated, consisted in the experience of a state similar to death (along with its subsequent conditions of consciousness). This was designated as "resurrection". Jean Marques-Riviere writes:

> We find here again the mysteries of Isis and Osiris, and the initiatic value of the *Book of the Dead*. The holy verses, the rules of conduct, and the practical instruction contained in this Egyptian book, a book treating of the way of the dead and also — as we have established previously — the way of the "living", are precisely what we rediscover in the temple of Elusis. We find them yet again in the rituals of the Orphic initiation, which contain in fact a burial rite of the same type found in the Egyptian *Book of the Dead*: it was with this rite that the Orphics had themselves interred. However, the essentials of the esoteric doctrine are the same for Egypt, Eleusis and the Orphics: what is revealed and experienced are the mysteries of the beyond, beyond the portal of death. It is the post-mortem state that the adept experiences. (Jean Marques-Rivière, *Histoire des doctrines ésoteriques*, p. 71)

Victor Magnien assembled a collection of ancient testimonies concerning the Eleusinian mysteries in his book *The Mysteries of Eleusis*, among which we find the following:

Blessed are they that while yet on earth have seen these things! They that have not known nor had their part in the holy "orgies" will suffer a destiny unlike that of those that have, when death bears them to the *Land of shades*. (*Homeric Hymn to Demeter*, p. 27)

Or:

Blessed is he that hath seen these things ere he descendeth into the caves of the underworld. He knoweth life's end and he knoweth life's beginning — yea, even the gift of Zeus! (Pindar, quoted by Clement of Alexandria, *Stromatis* III, 3)

Or again:

Thrice-blessed are those mortals who, after beholding these mysteries, enter Hades. They alone can thrive therein: for the others all will be suffering. (Sophocles, *Fragment* p. 348)

Victor Magnien himself conceived the nature of initiation as follows:

In point of fact initiation is similar to death. It is the human being's return to his origin. To be initiated means learning how to die, i.e. how to reascend to the light. Or, put another way, it means to die a symbolic death by virtue of which all imperfections are left behind. On its journey to life in the material realm, the soul descends through several levels. To return to its origin it must reascend through these various stages. . . . It is for this reason that initiation comprises a sequence of steps. (Victor Magnien, *Les mystères d'Eleusis*, p. 98)

And let us add that these steps can ultimately be traced back to three fundamental states of the soul: purification (*purgatio*), illumination (*illuminatio*), and perfection (*perfectio*); or, the *laying aside* of the habits, customs, and instincts attached to natural evolution, the *awakening* to the reality of the divine world of archetypes, and the *entry* into this latter world.

The stages of purification, illumination, and perfection described by St. Bonaventure are the same as those of the ancient mysteries insofar as in each case it is generally a question of progress through these stages. They differ, however, in content. For the way of Christian mysticism described and taught by St. Bonaventure does not consist in learning to die — utilizing for this purpose the magic of initiatic rites and symbolic acts — but in learning to live and to love, that is, in entering the "kingdom of God" even during terrestrial life, living in and for this kingdom.

The mystery-initiate underwent a unique, extraordinary, and dramatic experience of the beyond. The Christian mystic learns to live into the coming of the kingdom of God from "this side". His aim is not a single experience of the beyond in order subsequently, through the memory thereof, to live in the fervent hope of leading a "philosophic" life. Rather, his goal is to live his daily life in perpetual union with the divine and with the spiritual in the world. A distinction is to be made between the perfection of the mystics and that of the mystery-initiates. That of the former — the mystical union (*unio mystica*) — is a *condition*, a state of life; that of the latter is a unique and dramatic experience undergone through initiation into the mysteries, whereby the aspirant is raised to the rank of initiate or *epopt* ("eyewitness" or "he that hath seen"). The epopt lives on in the after-effect of what he once experienced; the mystic who has attained the state of perfection lives in perpetual communication, union and, finally, unity with God.

Should mankind choose the way of return to God in preference to indefinitely distancing itself from Him by being washed away in the flood of natural evolution, it must tread the path of purification, illumination, and perfection (or union): and it is precisely this that will constitute its real and true history, for such is its final destiny. The historian of the future, if he has discerned the difference between the way, the truth, and the life on the one hand and the stream of natural evolution on the other, will not compose a history of civilization — that is, the story of technological progress and socio-political struggles — but will trace the path of mankind through the stages of purification and illumination to its ultimate attainment of perfection. His narrative will detail mankind's temptations and their vanquishment, the standards set by particular individuals and groups, and the progressive lighting-up of new insights and the awakening of spiritual faculties among human beings. In short, it will in some sense continue the Bible — taking the concerns of the Bible as its own. It will attempt to portray the history of mankind at the same level and along the same lines as is found in the Bible. Only then will the full purport of the dogma of the inspiration of the Holy Scriptures be fully understood. Then, also, answers and solutions will be found to theological controversies over such questions as to whether the Scriptures are inspired according to the "letter" or according to the "spirit"; whether, in addition to what is inspired, there are also to be found "uninspired" (that is, purely human) sayings; whether there exist "levels of inspiration", ranging from passages where God himself speaks to those of simple eyewitness accounts of external historical events; whether the Holy Scriptures are essentially symbolic or realistic; whether external objects and events are depicted as symbols of spiritual realities; etc. All of these difficult questions regarding the inspiration of the Holy Scriptures will be resolved and laid to rest when a sufficient number of people with the required vocation and sense of responsibility will have taken upon themselves what was also the concern of the Bible, i.e. to hold ever firmly in view mankind's true path as the essence of history — as distinct from the way of natural evolution, to which it forms the antipode. Such historians will recount, for example, how "in the wilderness" mankind was thrice tempted: with power ("I will give thee dominion over all the kingdoms of the world and their glory"), with materialism ("command these stones to become loaves of bread"), and with the experimental method ("throw thyself down from the pinnacle of the temple", to put God to the test). And they will recognize and portray as various manifestations of these same three "temptations in the wilderness" many great ideological and socio-political movements as well as many epoch-making scientific discoveries and technological accomplishments. That is, they will portray them as so many vital events along the way of purification. Then they will trace how the deepening insights garnered by mankind in consequence of overcoming these temptations first shone forth, and they will describe the manifold forms that the latter then assumed; and this for the purpose of depicting mankind's way of illumination. Then, finally, these historians — scribes of the spiritual history of mankind — will tell of individuals and of particular groups who have pointed the way to perfection; that is, whose qualities and capacities have borne witness that the "kingdom of man" can unite and be fused with the "kingdom of God".

PART FOUR

THE BREATH OF LIFE

A Fragment

INTRODUCTION

Even the most perfect and complicated structures in the organic world may be traced back to a single cell, a seed. Similarly, the result of growth in the realm of spiritual life can also be followed back to a certain "seed" experience or "seed" thought. And the author of this fragment is no exception here. It is thanks to a kind of "seed" that he owes his growth to the heights, breadths, and depths of the many-branched tree of knowledge of God. From this seed, growth has taken place throughout the several decades of his life, enabling him to feel and think his way into all forms of mankind's religious life from different countries and at different times in history. In this it was neither a matter of an analytical study of research into the comparison of religions nor a case of building up a syncretistic philosophical system. Rather, the author's endeavor was purely and simply to inwardly sense and experience whatever is able to contribute to a deepening, to an elevation, and to an expansion of the fundamental "seed" thought and "seed" experience, which became conceived and arose in the author as follows:

One day, sixty-eight years ago, when the author was four years old, he was playing with some building blocks whilst sitting on a colored carpet on the floor. The window was wide open, through which a cloudless blue sky could be seen. Close by, the child's mother was sitting in a chair watching the child playing. Suddenly the child looked up and, gazing at the blue heavens, asked his mother, without any prompting, the question: "Where is God? Is he in heaven? Does he float there? Or is he sitting there? Where?"

The child's mother sat up straight and gave the following answer, which remained valid and meaningful to the child for decades: "God is present everywhere: where the air is invisible and penetrates everything. Just as we live and breathe in the air, and it is thanks to the air that we live and breathe, so our souls live and breathe God and it is thanks to him that we live."

This answer was so clear and convincing that, like a breath of fresh air, it blew away all conceptual problems and left behind certainty concerning God's invisible presence everywhere. This "seed" thought later grew into the heights and depths and breadths, representing the primal seed from which there grew a many-branched tree of insight and faith during the subsequent decades of the author's life.

I

THE MYSTERY OF BREATH

If one is searching for the sense and meaning of the mysteries of
breath, one cannot do otherwise than to make the deeply significant
biblical text of *Genesis* 2:7 the center and starting point of one's
meditation:

> And YAHVEH ELOHIM formed man of dust from the ground (*adamah*),
> and breathed into his nostrils the breath of life (*neshamah hachayim*), and
> man became a living being (*nephesh chayah*).

A meditative contemplation of the deeper meaning of this text has to
be preceded by attaining an understanding of the concepts and ideas
comprising it. The sequence of the text makes it clear that the creation
of man consisted of two divine acts: the forming of man's corporeal
nature and the breathing of the breath of life into it. Yahveh Elohim
formed (*yetzer*) man from the dust (*aphar*) of the earth (*min
ha-adamah*). St. Jerome, who translated the Bible into Latin,
translated this as follows: "*Formavit Dominus Deus (Yahveh Elohim)
hominem de limo terrae*". Here *limus* does not mean dry dust, but
rather moist mud or slime. This is more in accordance with the
biblical context, since in the same chapter, verse 6, we read: "But a
mist went up from the earth and watered the whole face of the
ground". Thus, it is quite natural to picture the substance from which
man's corporeal nature is formed not as dust, which presupposes
dryness and drought, but as a result of the working of mist surrounding and penetrating everything, i.e., as mud or slime.

Luther's translation was still more radical and concrete: "The Lord
God made man from a clump of earth". This certainly presupposes
and emphasizes the presence of some moisture. But also the translation "from the dust of the earth" found in the Septuagint is not without
foundation. For, what is "dust of the earth"? For many centuries dust
was thought to consist of minute elementary particles ("atoms" of
dust). In the sixteenth century St. John of the Cross wrote in his work
The Night of the Spirit and the Night of the Senses that light as such
is invisible. It becomes visible by virtue of the many particles and

larger and smaller objects which offer resistance to light on its path. Thus we see the sun's rays because the sun's light falls upon the "atoms" of dust and illumines them. The same holds true for the light of the spirit. As such it is dark, but when it falls upon something — such as the problems and riddles of existence — it becomes visible and illumines them by effecting insight and understanding.

For St. John of the Cross the dust permeating the atmosphere is made up of "atoms". Could it not be that the same conception underlies the biblical dust (*aphar*)? In this case one would be justified in reading that the human being was formed from the smallest particles or "atoms" of earth (*adamah*). And what does the expression *adamah* mean?

According to the Jewish esoteric tradition (Cabbala), there are seven regions or types of earth: *eretz, adamah, geah, nesiah, tziah, arkoah*, and *thebel* (*Zohar* I, 40a). *Eretz* is used in the sense of "land", whereas *adamah*, in biblical language, means "ground" or "soil". Thus the expression *adamah* indicates the nature of the substance of the earth. It points to the qualitative aspect of the earth. Correspondingly, "dust (or slime) of the earth" can be interpreted as signifying the atoms or smallest particles of earth which have the latent tendency and propensity to become human corporeality. For *adam* means "man" and *adamah* signifies something like "latent humanity". Consequently, the designation "dust of the earth" (*aphar ha-adamah*) implicitly contains the philosophical principle that the elementary particles of soil (the "atoms" of the earth) tend, according to their natural propensity, to become constituent parts of the human body. *Adamah* is the tendency of the earth toward taking on human form. Therefore, it was not any kind of compulsion acting upon the atoms of *adamah* as they were summoned by Yahveh Elohim from the "four corners of the world" (*Zohar* I, 205b) to form the human being. The summons was a fulfillment of their own desire toward humankind (*adamah*). The word *adamah* points to the mystery of formation (*yetzirah*) of the human being from the atoms of earthly substance, which quivered in ecstasy as the "breath of life" penetrated the human form and reached them.

The work of formation of the human body was followed by its becoming "enlivened" by the breath of life and its becoming "ensouled", where the human being became a "living soul" (*nephesh chayah*). Here, another source of the coming into being of man is indicated: from God, rather than from the substance of the earth. The human form, shaped from earthly matter, was filled with content of divine origin, with the living breath of God. Thus, there arose at that

time — just as it is so now (and will be for all future time) — the human
being as a living soul. The Jewish tradition of the Cabbala says
concerning the nature of the human being:

> Observe that when the Holy One, blessed be He, created Adam, He
> gathered his earthly matter from the four corners of the world and
> fashioned him therefrom on the site of the Temple here below and drew
> to him a soul of life out of the Temple on high. Now the soul is a com-
> pound of three grades, and hence it was three names, to wit, *nephesh*
> (vital principle), *ruach* (spirit), and *neshamah* (soul proper). *Nephesh* is
> the lowest of the three, *ruach* is a grade higher, whilst *neshamah* is the
> highest of all and dominates the others. These three grades are har-
> moniously combined in those men who have the good fortune to render
> service to their Master. For at first man possesses *nephesh*, which is a holy
> preparative for a higher stage. After he has achieved purity in the grade
> of *nephesh* he becomes fit to be crowned by the holy grade that rests upon
> it, namely *ruach*. When he has thus attained to the indwelling of *nephesh*
> and *ruach*, and qualified himself for the worship of his Master in the
> requisite manner, the *neshamah*, the holy superior grade that dominates
> all the others, takes up its abode with him and crowns him, so that he
> becomes complete and perfected on all sides. . . . Observe that *nephesh*,
> *ruach* and *neshamah* are an ascending series of grades. The lowest of
> them, *nephesh*, has its source in the perennial celestial stream, but it can-
> not exist permanently save with the help of *ruach*, which abides between
> fire and water. *Ruach*, in its turn, is sustained by *neshamah*, that higher
> grade above it, which is thus the source of both *nephesh* and *ruach*. When
> *ruach* receives its sustenance from *neshamah*, then *nephesh* receives it in
> turn through *ruach*, so that the three form a unity. (*Zohar* I, 205b–206a).
> (The translation of the *Zohar* used here and in the following is that of
> M. Simon and H. Sperling [Soncino Press: London-Jerusalem-New York,
> 1970].)

This teaching concerning the being of man is expressed still more
clearly in another passage from the *Zohar*, where Rabbi Simeon com-
municates the following to his son, Rabbi Eleazar, and his comrades
Rabbi Abba and Rabbi Judah:

> "I marvel how indifferent men are to the words of the Torah and the pro-
> blem of their own existence!" He proceeded to discourse on the text: *With
> my soul have I desired thee in the night, yea, with my spirit within me
> will I seek thee early* (Isaiah 26: 9). He said: "The inner meaning of this
> verse is as follows. When a man lies down in bed, his vital spirit (*nephesh*)
> leaves him and begins to mount on high, leaving with the body only the
> impression of a receptacle which contains the heartbeat. The rest of it tries
> to soar from grade to grade, and in doing so it encounters certain bright
> but unclean essences. If it is pure and has not defiled itself by day, it rises

above them, but if not, it becomes defiled among them and cleaves to them and does not rise any further. There they show her certain things which are going to happen in the near future; and sometimes they delude her and show her false things. Thus she goes about the whole night until the man wakes up, when she returns to her place. Happy are the righteous to whom God reveals His secrets in dreams, so that they may be on their guard against sin! Woe to the sinners who defile their bodies and their souls! As for those who have not defiled themselves during the day, when they fall asleep at night their souls begin to ascend, and first enter these grades which we have mentioned, but they do not cleave to them and continue to mount further. The soul which is privileged thus to rise finally appears before the gate of the celestial palace, and yearns with all its might to behold the beauty of the King and to visit His sanctuary. This is the man who ever hath a portion in the world to come, and this is the soul whose yearning when she ascends is for the Holy One, blessed be He, and who does not cleave to those other bright essences, but seeks out the holy essence in the place from which she originally issued. Therefore, it is written, 'With my soul have I desired thee in the night,' to pursue after thee and not to be enticed away after false powers. Again, the words 'With my soul have I desired thee in the night' refer to the soul (*nephesh*) which has sway by night, while the words 'with my spirit within will I seek thee early' refer to the spirit (*ruach*) which has sway by day. 'Soul' (*nephesh*) and 'spirit' (*ruach*) are not two separate grades, but one grade with two aspects. There is still a third aspect which should dominate these two and cleave to them as they to it, and which is called 'higher spirit' (*neshamah*). . . . This spirit enters into them and they cleave to it, and when it dominates, such a man is called holy, perfect, wholly devoted to God. 'Soul' (*nephesh*) is the lowest stirring, it supports and feeds the body and is closely connected with it. When it sufficiently qualifies itself, it becomes the throne on which rests the lower spirit (*ruach*), as it is written, 'until the spirit be poured on us from on high' (*Isaiah* 32: 15). When both have prepared themselves sufficiently, they are qualified to receive the higher spirit (*neshamah*), to which the lower spirit (*ruach*) becomes a throne, and which is undiscoverable, supreme over all. Thus there is throne resting on throne, and a throne for the highest. . . . For *nephesh* is the lowest stirring to which the body cleaves, like the dark light at the bottom of the candle-flame which clings to the wick and exists only through it. When fully kindled it becomes a throne for the white light above it. When both are fully kindled, the white light becomes a throne for a light which cannot be fully discerned, an unknown something resting on that white light, and so there is formed a complete light." (*Zohar* I, 83a–83b)

A short, clear summary of the thoughts and ideas which lived (and live on) in the Jewish mystical tradition concerning *nephesh*, *ruach*, and *neshamah* is given in the following discourse of Rabbi Isaac:

Happy are the righteous in this world and in the next, because they are altogether holy. Their body (*kuph*) is holy, their soul (*nephesh*) is holy, their spirit (*ruach*) is holy, their super-soul (*neshamah*) is holy of holies. These are three grades indissolubly united. If a man does well with his soul (*nephesh*), there descends upon him a certain crown called spirit (*ruach*), which stirs him to a deeper contemplation of the laws of the Holy King. If he does well with this spirit (*ruach*), he is invested with a noble holy crown called super-soul (*neshamah*), which can contemplate all. (*Zohar V, 70b*)

Returning now to the main theme — the mystery of breath — it should be remembered that the breath of life (*spiraculum vitae* in the translation of St. Jerome; *neshamah hachayim* in the Hebrew text of *Genesis* 2: 7) is the highest being of man; it proceeds from God and is the actual kernel of the human being. As may be seen from the original biblical text (*Genesis* 2: 7), and also from the *Zohar* commentaries quoted above, it is the source, the foundation and the cause of human life — of the soul-physical, the spiritual, and the divine-spiritual life. Breath and heartbeat, thought and idea, prayer and meditation — all are expressions (on different levels) of one single life, that of the breath of life (*neshamah hachayim*).

In other words, just as breathing and the beating of the heart are an expression of the breath of life in the waking and sleeping conditions of the body, so may conscious thinking and conceptualizing be compared to the breath and heartbeat of the spirit. Similarly, prayer and meditation are the breath and heartbeat of the breath of life in the human being's higher self (*atma* is Hindu philosophy), above and beyond which God himself exists as its source and origin.

Now, the being or substance of the true self of man, the breath of life, which is "breathed out" by God, is the breath of love, of God's love, which is the origin — and also the very being itself — of the life of the soul. If this breath descends to the spirit (*ruach*), it becomes the striving for truth which is active and alive at the basis of the thinking, conceptual life. If it reaches the soul-physical organization (*nephesh*) of the human being, it becomes a fountain of health, bringing about a harmonious working together of the soul and the physical-organic life-functions. Nowadays one would say that it brings about "psycho-physical parallelism" (signifying *nephesh*). Thus the sequence or grades *nephesh*, *ruach*, *neshamah* signify health, truth, and the reality of love. Here the breath of life (*neshamah*) is the foundation and primal impulse of the religious life; the spirit (*ruach*) is the basis and cause of the striving after knowledge; and the principle of ensoul-ing the bodily functions (the bringing down of soul activity and the

various "states of soul" into corporeality) — the principle of *nephesh* —
is the essential basis of the life of human beings incarnated on earth.
Love, wisdom, and health thus arise through the activity of a single
life-stream, whose source is love. It is essentially the breath of life,
breathed out by God, which constitutes the human being's life as a
living soul.

From the very beginning, man was created as a bearer of love. He
is not simply *homo sapiens*, but over and above this he is potentially
homo amans. In this sense the biblical account concerning the coming
into being of man as a living soul through the breath of life from God
can be translated into the language of the apostle John, as summarized
in the sentence: "God is love, and he who abides in love abides in God,
and God abides in him" (I *John* 4: 16).

Life is breath, and there are two kinds of breathing: the breathing
of air, which maintains the bodily penetration of the blood with
oxygen, ozone, and the life element (*prana*, as it is designated in San-
skrit), all of which are necessary for life, and the inner breathing of
the soul, which "breathes in" God through prayer and meditation, just
as the body takes in air. The one kind of breathing is that of health,
the other is that of religion. And just as the human being needs the
air to breathe for his physical life, so he also has need of breathing in
God — through religious prayer and meditation — for his soul life. The
primal religion of humanity (*religio naturalis*) is grounded and rooted
in the breath of life spoken of in the Bible (*Genesis* 2: 7). The breath
of life never ceases and will never cease; it lasts eternally. The German
theologian and philosopher, Friedrich Schleiermacher, held that
religion results from the feeling man has that he is absolutely dependent. This feeling of dependency is actually the feeling of being
breathed out from God. It is the primal human experience — and the
most universal one — of the reality of God, and it is the main "proof"
of God for the human soul.

Originally, breathing was different from what it has become now.
In a certain sense it was *total*. It was both vertical (comprising prayer
and meditation) and horizontal, i.e., the breathing in and out of air
containing the "vitamins" of life force (*prana*). It was at one and the
same time reverence for and worship of the Divine, union with God,
understanding of and insight into the Eternal — human feeling, willing, and thinking. The memory of the original total breathing of
humanity still lives on in the Hindu practice of yoga, and also in the
practice of the "Jesus prayer" in Eastern Christianity. The words of
this prayer are: "Lord Jesus Christ, Son of God, have mercy on me,
a sinner." These words are repeated over and over again until they

take on a life of their own in connection with breathing and the beating of the heart. They become prayed with the breath and heartbeat, continuously day and night. In this way the injunction of the apostle Paul to "pray without ceasing" (I *Thessalonians* 5: 17) can be fulfilled.

The primal, total breathing of humanity corresponded to the original, universal language of mankind. For, speech is the formation of the breath into sound. The loss of the single universal human language after the building of the tower of Babel, reported in the Bible (*Genesis* 11: 9), actually signified the disappearance of the primal, total breathing, which became individual and arbitrary. And the Whitsun miracle, where the apostles spoke a single language, which was understood by human beings from different lands as if it were their own, was a resurrection of the primal breathing and the original language of humanity.

The original language spoken prior to the building of the tower of Babel was also *total*. It was more than a mere communication of information. Rather, it was a kind of thought transmission (telepathy), which had the effect of awakening insight, instead of simply informing. It served to awaken insight and understanding, rather than explaining things. It communicated an intimation of things. Not that the intimations were indefinite, having multiple meanings which had to be explained. No, they were like rays or bolts of lightning bearing light and clarity within them. Both the speaker and the listener partook of this light, which came from the depths of the heart and penetrated into the depths of the heart — a kind of "heart magic". This was also so with the speaking of the apostles at Whitsun, which was experienced by all those from different countries as their mother tongue. For what could be closer to each human being than the language of the heart?

*   *   *   *   *   *   *

The gift of feeling one's way into things and penetrating them with insight presupposes the ability to concentrate. This ability is often described and presented as the result of a kind of mental gymnastics involving arbitrary exercises. The thoughts and concepts of normal, associative thinking are of an arbitrary nature and arise "by themselves" in such a way as to divert and scatter attention. One exercise is to practice forcefully to lead one's thoughts again and again to concentrate upon a chosen object. In this exercise limits are imposed upon the automatic arising — by way of mental association — of thoughts and concepts. Ultimately, thinking is brought to rest.

"*Yoga citta vritti nirodha*" — yoga is the suppression of the automatic movement of the thought substance. This is the opening sentence of Patanjali's *Yoga Sutras*, the classic work on yoga. This precept is translated into practice by European pupils through bringing to a halt the free play of memory, fantasy, and associative thinking. The course of associative thinking is reversed by leading it back to its starting point each time it is noticed that an arbitrary thought creeps in. In this way the suppression of associative thinking is practiced. At the same time the endeavor is made to focus attention upon a specially chosen object, to hold it (and nothing else) in consciousness without attention being diverted. This exercise is often done in an unnaturally forced way. What, however, is the ability to concentrate in its true sense?

It is not a result of forcing the focusing of attention upon a single object. Nor is it a tortured battle against the arising of associative thoughts. Rather, it is solely a product of the inner peace and stillness of a breathing "living into" a single object. It is an expression of the *condition* of inner peace, of the stillness or becoming still of the life of the soul, taking effect even upon the breath. Breathing becomes as deep and peaceful as the soul concentrated in a state of inner stillness and calmness. Thus true concentration is not a condition of tense concentration, but one of relaxation, which expresses itself in breathing that is deep and peaceful. The psycho-physical key to the gift of concentration is the breath; ultimately it is a matter of breathing.

However, it would be a mistake to believe that exercises to control and master breathing should precede concentration. For, such exercises which consist of breathing the air in for a certain number of seconds, holding the breath for a certain number of seconds, breathing the air out from the lungs for a certain number of seconds, and then holding the lungs empty of air for a certain number of seconds, often have a negative result. Exercises of this kind, which are frequently recommended in yoga books, often result in the loss of the automatic, (and natural) regular breathing on account of the consciously directed breathing regulated by the mind. Consequently, the practitioner of such exercises may experience during the night, whilst asleep, unpleasant (or even dangerous) attacks of asphyxiation. For the development of the faculty of concentration, it is not a matter of arbitrarily controlling and regulating the breath by way of the conscious mind, but rather that breathing mirrors the peace and quiet of the soul's condition in a pure way, without any conscious arbitrary interference. Breathing becomes as regular and natural during concentration as it is during the sleeping state. Then it is just as free and automatic as in sleep, the only difference being that the human being is not asleep but is experiencing the heightened waking condition of concentration.

A pure conscience and love of nature and of one's fellow man contribute more toward the attainment of concentration than any breathing exercises of an artificial nature such as those mentioned above. However, breathing is not limited to the role of mirroring the soul in its various states. It can be spiritualized and raised up to mirror the human spirit (*ruach*) transcending the soul, or even to mirror the true and immortal human Self, the "breath of life" (*neshamah* according to the *Zohar*). In this case the breath becomes an organ for harmonizing with or participation in the divine breath — the breathing of the breath of life, which is the kernel of the human being, eternally coming into being from God. For, God is eternal Being. And the true Self of man is eternally coming into being as the breath of life from eternal Being. The Self of man rests in the breath of the Godhead — the breath which bestows being. In spiritualizing and raising up breathing to the highest level, man experiences his true Self as a star in the heaven of God's eternal Being. And he also experiences the breath of God, bestowing being, which brings with it certainty concerning God and immortality. For, faith is not simply a matter of holding something to be true but of experiencing the breath of eternal God, bestowing being. It is the experience of the breath of eternity, felt in the depths of the life of soul, which is the source and origin of religion — of every religion of mankind. Belief in God and immortality is more than holding these things to be true, since holding them to be true is essentially the recognition and acknowledgement of an experience undergone in the depths of the soul.

This view concerning the origin of religion and belief in God has virtually no chance of being recognized in the world of today, with the possible exceptions of the Jungian school of depth psychology and the Platonic school of philosophy. Research of the Jungians has arrived at the conclusion that in the depths of his soul man is a religious being. Moreover, it is only Platonic philosophy that is in a position to do justice to the fact that certainty concerning God and immortality (certainty not acquired empirically, but by way of "vertical memory" recollected in normal consciousness by the empirical ego) is based upon experience of the higher Self.

Now, there are three basic phenomena that may be experienced by everyone which convey something of the breath of eternity. These phenomena recall the breathing experience of the higher Self in the heaven of the eternal Being of the Trinity and bring it to consciousness. The phenomena of sunset, night, and sunrise, experienced in connection with the mystery of breath (the path of inner transformation of breathing), impregnate man's soul-life, when it has become quiet and still, with the reality of the Trinity; and this takes place in a natural (but at the same time supernatural) way.

II

NATURAL-SUPERNATURAL IMAGES OF THE HOLY TRINITY

The starry heaven at night impregnates the soul that has become quiet and still. It speaks to the soul of the silent majesty of God and bears witness to the kingdom of eternal Being — beyond birth and death, beyond evolution and involution. The solemn majesty of the starry heaven proclaims the presence — the all-pervading presence — of the holy Being underlying the universe. It is as if the world of evolution and involution were caught up in an all-encompassing embrace, pressed to the bosom of eternal Being. Eternal Being draws so near, so close to existence, to the pulse of evolution and involution, that one is astonished that one had not noticed during the brightness of day the reality of the presence of the great peace and stillness of eternal Being underlying existence in all its multiplicity. One is astonished that the starry heaven at night was necessary for one to become conscious of the reality of the all-pervading presence of eternal Being within temporal existence. The presence of the eternal in the temporal, spoken of by the starry heaven at night, is sensed as an all-embracing, all-permeating *holiness*. For, holiness is a perception of the presence of eternal Being within the temporal world. And the soul which senses such holiness cannot do otherwise than to be certain that what it is feeling is experienced far more intensely by the blessed incorporeal spirits of the universe the heavenly hierarchies: Angels, Archangels, Principalities, Powers, Virtues, Dominions, Thrones, Cherubim, and Seraphim. This "breathing experience" of the starry heaven at night is expressed perfectly in the closing acclamation of the prefatory of the mass:

> . . . the Cherubim and Seraphim who day and night never cease to sing: "Holy, holy, holy Lord, God of power and might, heaven and earth are full of your glory.
>   Hosanna in the highest.
> Blessed is he who comes in the name of the Lord.
>   Hosanna in the highest."

Here the threefold use of "holy" does not portray an evaluation or judgment. Rather, it signifies that through the world of temporal existence there streams the breath of the presence of eternal Being. In other words, it is a perception of the presence of eternal Being on the part of the heavenly hierarchies who have a share in eternal Being. "God of power and might" is the God of the heavenly hierarchies, who is recognised and acknowledged as the source and origin of all selfhood of all beings who are selves, in that all sing in unison:

> Holy, holy, holy Lord, God of power and might, heaven and earth are full of your glory.
> Hosanna in the highest.

Is it conceivable that a being who experiences his true Self as belonging to the eternal hierarchies — whether a human being, an Angel, or some other hierarchical being — would not join in this heavenly chorus? For, this chorus signifies acknowledgement of the highest good, the loftiest gift that there is and that could be thought of in the whole universe, namely, the bestowal of being, with its endless possibilities for unfolding — given by the Bestower of being, God the Father.

Thus speaks the starry heaven at night — of the reality of the Father God — to the soul that, breathing the depths, has become inwardly still.

THE MESSAGE OF THE SETTING SUN

Just as the starry heaven at night impregnates the breathing soul with the all-pervading presence of eternal Being and with the holiness of the Bestower of being, so the experience of the setting Sun proclaims the descent of the Son from the heaven of eternal Being into the realm of existence, the domain of birth and death. The glorious colors of sunset are not experienced merely aesthetically. For, over and above this aesthetic experience, they are a natural-supernatural likeness and symbol for the unspeakable beauty of the Son's sacrifice of love. The setting Sun tells us of the Son's departure from the kingdom of eternal Being in order to descend into the world of temporal existence, the realm of birth and death. In the words of the Creed:

> He came down from heaven: by the power of the Holy Spirit he became incarnate from the Virgin Mary and was made man (*descendit de coelo et incarnatus est de Spiritu sancto ex Maria virgine et homo factus est*).

Furthermore, the setting Sun also mirrors the unspeakable beauty of Jesus Christ's sacrifice of love when he took leave of his disciples to undergo the sacrificial death on Golgotha. On the one hand, it proclaims the heavenly event of the Son's taking leave, prior to the Incarnation, from the kingdom of the Father in heaven; and on the other hand it mirrors the earthly event of Jesus Christ's taking leave of his disciples at the Last Supper. In other words, the "breathing immersion" of oneself into the setting Sun enables a melody to sound forth — the same melody of departure as that which is evoked through meditation on Christ's farewell discourses from the Gospel of St. John (*John* 14–17). With the setting of the Sun, the soul undergoes an experience similar to that evoked by the farewell discourses of St. John's Gospel, and likewise experiences anew the heavenly mystery of sunset when these passages from the Gospel of St. John are read. Is it not this twofold experience of departure, which the Mexican-Indian peasants and cowboys daily behold ("eavesdropping") each evening when they silently experience the setting Sun, which for them is a necessity of life? Every farmer and ranch owner in Mexico knows that the Indian peasant-labourers have to have the time of sunset free in order to be able to contemplate the beauty of the setting Sun ("beauty" meant here in more than a merely aesthetic sense). Is it not the same beauty of the sacrifice of love of the Son of God which can be experienced not only in Jesus' farewell discourses from St. John's Gospel but also in the setting Sun? Is it not a longing for *absolute* beauty which takes hold of those simple Indian souls and which is a necessity of life for them?

One cannot help thinking of the saying of St. Augustine that the natural constitution of the human soul is Christian (*anima humana naturaliter christiana*). It is only in the light of this saying that the need of every Mexican-Indian farm worker to experience and contemplate the setting Sun can be understood. It is the unspeakable beauty of the Son of God, who left the heaven of eternal Being for incarnation into the realm of birth and death, and who, as the God-Man Jesus Christ, took leave of human life to go to the death of sacrifice. Neither in heaven nor on earth can anything so beautiful and moving be found as the descent of the Son of God from the heaven of eternal Being and the farewell of the God-Man prior to his passion and death on the cross. It is this beauty which takes hold of the souls of the poor Mexican-Indians and which is inwardly experienced by them. For, a soul that is really a soul cannot do otherwise than be deeply moved by the beauty of the Son of God, seeing as "the natural constitution of the human soul is Christian". If this were not so, how would it have been possible for the apostles to have been given the mandate to "go and make disciples of all nations, baptizing them in the name of the Father and of the Son and of the Holy

Spirit" (*Matthew* 28: 19)? Bread and water presuppose hunger and thirst, and the working of grace and revelation presuppose questions and longing. The Mexican-Indian villagers seem to fulfill these conditions in view of their need to experience the setting Sun in the stillness of the deeply moved soul.

It would not be right, however, to simply conclude from this fact of life concerning the Mexican-Indians that European Christians must surely also be endowed with such sensitively gifted souls. The fact that Mexican-Indian farm laborers are capable of sensing the mystery of the setting Sun speaking to the human heart does not mean that this necessarily applies elsewhere; generally speaking, it doesn't. For, there have been (and still are) times in Europe and elsewhere during which for whole nations the life of the soul as such has been (and still is) in grave danger, having been smothered and reduced to a minimum. This holds not only with respect to the tidal wave of materialism that has flooded across the world in this century, but also for the outpouring of "intellectual enlightenment" during the age of rationalism in the eighteenth century which paved the way for materialism. At that time the danger facing the human soul was so great that, in order to avert it, a special intervention from heaven proved necessary as a preventive measure. This took place during the second half of the seventeenth century. It was then that the revelation of the most sacred heart of Jesus occurred. This led to the cult of devotion to the most sacred heart of Jesus which spread rapidly in Catholic countries and took root there. Devotion to the sacred heart of Jesus was to save the soul of humanity. For, with the intellectual enlightenment the danger threatening to break in upon human beings was that of the *centaur*. Human beings would have been turned into a kind of centaur — a being consisting of head and limbs (intellect and will), but without heart — that is, a "clever beast". Devotion to the sacred heart of Jesus had the task of rekindling the heart. Thereby the light, warmth, and life, streaming from the heart of Jesus, was to counteract the will-to-power and the intellect serving this will.

Be that as it may, the soul — understood as the most refined and deepest life of the heart — is by no means certain of survival, not even within Christian, civilized mankind. All kinds of dangers threaten, and destruction is an ever-present danger. The life of the soul has to be cultivated and stimulated, as took place (and is still taking place) with the help of devotion to the sacred heart of Jesus. What deeply moving moral deepness and beauty can be seen and experienced through devotion to the sacred heart of Jesus! It is this which is seen and experienced by the Mexican-Indian farm workers through their beholding and meditative contemplation of the setting Sun. For, the deepest essence of the experience of the setting Sun is the being of the most sacred heart of Jesus. This is the Sun of all hearts, as the *Litany of the Sacred Heart* says:

> Heart of Jesus, King and center of all hearts
> (*Cor Jesu, Rex et centrum omnium cordium*).

THE MESSAGE OF THE BIRTH OF THE NEW DAY

Dawn, as the birth of the new day, is a magnificent event of awakening — the awakening of the many beings who were immersed during the night in sleep and in the state of forgetting. What is awakening? It is the lighting up anew of the memory of the past and a renewed arising of hope in the future. The essence of the force which brings about awakening, overcoming sleep, and the state of forgetting, is *hope*. Considered as an awakening, the dawn of a new day is an event — a flood of the force of hope — which pours through the beings of nature and human beings. The chorus of birds which greets the birth of a new day with song points to the fact that it is hope which is experienced by the beings of nature upon awakening.

(End of the manuscript. The author died on February 24, 1973.)